Here's some dynamite from
John McKay's book:

The cruelty of liberals - "No one has the right to take one penny you've earned without your approval. Yet welfare-state liberals presume the right to steal up to 50% of your money in taxes . . . It's liberals who are cruel and vicious. They have no mercy for the middle class, no mercy for those who work and struggle to pay for liberals' alleged compassion. *It's so easy to be noble with other peoples' money.*"

The arrogance of liberals - "Liberals don't *ask* you to pay for entitlement programs. Instead, they point a tax gun at you and say, 'your money or your life.'"

Safety net - "If we dismantled the Welfare State, we could still have a safety net. A free economy can give us unemployment insurance, low-cost health insurance, and a nest egg for our retirement. It would also create millions of new jobs and opportunity for everyone."

Entitlements - "Welfare, food stamps, farm subsidies, corporate subsidies, and thousands of other entitlements aren't rights. They're handouts that liberals give to some people by robbing others. So an economic 'right' is not a right at all. Instead, it's simply a license to steal."

Compassion - "Liberals turn our natural compassion into a moral and political duty—they turn compassion into compulsion."

Progressive income tax - "The progressive income tax is morally obscene because it's a tax on virtue. The more you earn, the more you pay. The harder you work, the more government confiscates from you. Your ability determines your punishment."

Environmental regulations - "From the Revolutionary War to Desert Storm, hundreds of thousands of brave Americans have died fighting to defend our freedom. Yet today, with little protest, we throw our liberty into the gutter for the sake of rats, owls, and wetlands swamps."

The Welfare State:
No Mercy For The Middle Class

John McKay

LIBERTY BOOKS
Los Angeles, CA

THE WELFARE STATE: NO MERCY FOR THE MIDDLE CLASS
Liberty Books/September 1995

Liberty Books
Los Angeles

Printed in the United States of America
First Liberty Books hardcover printing September 1995

10 9 8 7 6 5 4 3 2 1

Library of Congress Catalog Card Number: 95-76043

ISBN: 0-9645693-0-2

CONTENTS

ACKNOWLEDGMENTS

Writing a book is a difficult but exciting struggle. You have to fight your own limits and test your endurance. But when you finally complete the work, you know the struggle was worth it.

Also, in writing a non-fiction book, you have to do a great deal of research. As a result, you need other people's guidance and support. So it was with writing this book. Without the authors, publishing companies, and other sources for my research material, this book would not have been possible.

In particular, I would like to thank the following:

The New York Times was an endless source of timely articles on many of the issues I discussed in my book. Thanks to the New York Times for their permission to quote from some of these articles.

I would like to thank the Heartland Institute, Westview Press, Random House, Regnery Gateway, Inc., and Reader's Digest for publishing books or articles I used in my research. Thanks to Robert Poole of the Reason Foundation for writing some of the books I used as research for my chapter on Regulations.

Special thanks goes to the Cato Institute, whose books were invaluable in my research. Thanks to David Boaz of the Cato Institute for allowing me to quote material from these books. Also, we should all thank the Cato Institute for the continuing work it does to defend our liberty.

I would also like to thank a wonderful San Francisco bookstore, Laissez-Faire Books. For many years it has been my best source for books on politics, health care, history, economics, education, regulations, philosophy, and psychology. Most of the books in their catalogue address one central theme: they explain, defend, or give the history of individual liberty, the free-market, and limited government. I recommend their books to all my readers who want to learn more about the issues I discuss in my book.

Writing this book was a challenge for me. I had to explain complex moral, political, and economic issues in a way that my readers would understand and enjoy. I'd like to thank my editor, Joyce Brody, for showing me how to make my writing simpler, stronger, and more to the point. She helped me on that difficult road called editing.

Lastly, I would like to thank the late Ayn Rand. Her books, ideas, and moral passion greatly influenced my life.

This book is dedicated to the
best within all of us

"Of all tyrannies, a tyranny sincerely exercised for the good of its victims may be the most oppressive . . . those who torment us for our own good will torment us without end, for they do so with the approval of their own conscience."

C.S. Lewis

INTRODUCTION

In a frightening *New York Times* article in February, 1992, the author asked average Americans around the country how they felt about their lives and the future of America. Brian Williams, employed by a printing company, replied,

> Given all the trouble we're having governing this country and keeping the economy going, I'm not sure the great American dream will come true for my children the way it did for me. It seems to me that for the first time in American history, there is a real possibility that the next generation may have less opportunity than the current generation.[1]

B. Drummond Ayers, the author of the article, found a deep and growing pessimism throughout America. He said,

> In dozens of interviews conducted during a 1500-mile journey across the country, pessimism emerged again and again as the dominant mood within the electorate . . .What remains is a nagging doubt about the strength and viability of American capitalism and,

for that matter, the viability of the whole American system of government.[2]

Rick Anderson, a 40-year-old coal miner who had just been laid off, told Mr. Ayers,

People are mighty angry out here, and I'm one of them. We're fed up with the way things are going in this country. Something's not right. I'm not scared of automation and new technology and all that kind of stuff we've had to deal with in the mines for years. And I'm sure as hell not scared of hard work. So why don't I have work? I want an answer. What's gone wrong?[3]

My book is about why Brian Williams, Rick Anderson, and millions of hardworking, taxpaying Americans are suffering. It's about why liberals have endless compassion for those seeking handouts and unearned subsidies, but have no mercy for you, the middle class who pays for the Welfare State. My book is a moral defense of the middle class. It defends those who work hard, take responsibility for their lives, and ask nothing from government but to leave them alone to pursue their dreams.

The middle class *is* America. You make this country, you support it, and you defend it. Yet there's a moral obscenity taking place in our country. Welfare-state liberals have turned you into a beast of burden, into a sacrificial animal whose only purpose in life is to pay for an endless parade of handouts, subsidies, and entitlements.

Worse, liberals tax us into poverty and then call us immoral if we oppose their legal theft. They say it's our duty to support other people, and if we refuse this duty they call us cruel and mean-spirited. They say we have no right to our lives, our paychecks, or our profits while others are in "need." Liberals claim that other peoples' financial problems are a mortgage on our lives, a mortgage never to be paid off.

My book asks these questions: Why do we accept this burden and this guilt? By what right does our own government turn us into sacrificial animals? How do we throw off our yoke and end the Welfare State, once and for all?

I love America so much. This country was once the shining hope for the world, a place where people came to find freedom and their dreams. Now I'm afraid we're losing that freedom and those dreams. I wanted to find out what's threatening us, and how we can turn things around. I believe I've found a surprising answer to these questions.

America is a democracy. Liberals couldn't enslave us *unless we let them.* So why do we let them? Because we've accepted a moral code that's destroying us, a moral code that liberals use as a weapon against us. We've accepted the deadly belief that helping others is a moral and political duty, instead of a personal choice.

We've also accepted the idea that government's job is to make us all equal. How do liberals make everyone equal? They rob you, the hardworking middle-class taxpayer, and then "redistribute" your money to entitlement beneficiaries. Where else could liberals get the money? An entitlement beneficiary is a person or special-interest group who didn't earn your money, but demands the right to take your money because they *want* it.

Most of us go along with this. We let our government steal from us. Why? Again, because we believe it's our political duty to help others. We believe that government has the right to force us to help others, regardless of how this hurts us or our families—that we have no right to our lives, paychecks, or property while other people are in "need."

Throughout history, many societies were founded on these ideas and called by various names: fascist, socialist, communist, welfare state, theocracy, or benevolent monarchy. But the rulers of these societies always had a major problem—they ran up against the brick wall of human nature. They couldn't convince people to be unselfish and live for the sake of others. They couldn't convince their subjects to sacrifice themselves voluntarily. So in the end, they resorted to force. They turned to the one institution that had the legal right to use force against its own citizens—government.

But rulers know that force is never enough to gain lasting power—they have to convince their captive subjects to go along with them. For the past sixty years, welfare-state liberals have persuaded us that government should act as our safety net. They claim that government should protect us from the pain and setbacks of life. This doctrine gave birth to the Welfare

State—the monster that now devours us.

Politically, liberals achieve this goal by creating economic rights. An economic right is an alleged right to basic human needs like housing, health care, and education, whether or not we can pay for them. Government secures these rights by forcing us to pay heavy income taxes that support thousands of entitlement programs. Welfare, food stamps, Medicare, farm subsidies, subsidized housing, corporate subsidies, public education, and Social Security are a few examples of these programs.

You may ask, so what? Why is this important to me and my family? It's important because the Welfare State now threatens your life, your country, and your children's future.

Do you have less income to spend from your dwindling paycheck? Are you struggling just to pay your bills? Is it hard to save money to buy a house you can't afford anymore? Are you afraid to send your children to the local government-run public school? Are you afraid of losing your job, like the tens of thousands of workers already laid off across the country? Do your real estate and other taxes keep going up? Is health insurance getting so expensive that you can't afford it anymore—and does the thought of getting seriously ill terrify you? The Welfare State, and the philosophy that justifies it, is causing your problems.

Do you own a business? Government uses the welfare-state philosophy to justify regulations that now strangle you and add thousands of dollars to your cost of doing business. Regulations control every aspect of your business. And local, state, and federal business taxes loot your profits and leave you struggling. Worse, the moral doctrine behind the Welfare State has infiltrated our belief systems so thoroughly that we automatically turn to government to correct the mess that government first caused. We keep voting for politicians who promise to solve our problems by creating yet more regulations and entitlement programs. We keep asking for more poison to cure the poison we've already swallowed.

The Welfare State will eventually ruin our lives and destroy our country. Yet most of us agree with the notion that someone should guarantee our safety and sustenance; someone should guarantee that we have food, clothing, shelter, education, and health care. That someone has become government. The moral doctrine behind the Welfare State is turning us into a nation of dependents.

Sixty years of socialist propaganda have taken their toll. We've lost the understanding that each of us should be responsible for our own lives. Instead of asking what we can do for ourselves, we now ask what government can do for us. But depending on government just doesn't work. To paraphrase Benjamin Franklin: those who sacrifice liberty for a little security, soon find they have neither liberty nor security.

That's exactly what's happening to us. The deadly result of accepting these ideas is all around us. Millions of people around the world live under socialist, fascist, communist, formerly communist, or welfare-state governments. The results are usually the same—people in these countries who surrendered their liberty for economic security are poor wretches living under the thumb of bureaucrats.

America was the only country in history that was founded on the idea that we have an inviolate right to our lives. Our greatest tragedy is that Americans have forgotten the moral and political ideals our country was founded on. Even worse, we've gradually accepted the ancient doctrine that government has the right to control our lives.

My book examines the one, crucial idea on which the Welfare State depends: that helping others is a moral and political duty, instead of a personal choice. I examine why this idea is immoral, how it's used to justify the Welfare State, and why it's the root cause of our unemployment, health care crisis, and declining standard of living. We'll see why welfare-state liberals have no mercy for the middle class. We'll also see why their compulsive need to solve everyones' problems blinds them to the devastation they wreak on our lives.

But understanding the problem is not enough—we have to do something about it. Half measures won't work anymore. In the final chapter, "The Last Amendment," I describe a new amendment to the Constitution that would end the Welfare State, once and for all.

CHAPTER 1

ENTITLEMENTS: COMPASSION OR COMPULSION?

Imagine America in a state of anarchy: Poor people are looting the homes of the rich and middle class. Middle-class workers with skyrocketing taxes are attacking people on welfare. Workers are looting factories because they've lost their jobs and want them back. Minorities are bombing local banks who refuse to lend them mortgage money. Young workers paying 30 percent social security payroll taxes are gunning down old people. Single people are bombing public schools so they don't have to pay taxes for educating other peoples' children. New Yorkers paying heavy taxes for federal farm subsidies are burning farmers' crops in Kansas. Patients going bankrupt are attacking hospitals that are bankrupting them. Sick people paying outrageous drug prices are blowing up pharmaceutical company factories. Healthy people with skyrocketing insurance premiums are attacking poor, sick people without health insurance.

Fear, murder, and bloody conflicts are everywhere. America has become an armed camp of millions of murderous, economic pressure groups. Everyone has joined a gang for self-protection or to loot or gain power over others. Each gang claims the right to steal from everyone else. Each claims it's the most important economic group in the country.

Does this imaginary picture scare you? Well it should because, in essence, that's the state of America today. The fighting hasn't reached open, armed conflict yet. Instead, the warfare is "civilized" and waged in the halls of Congress. America has become a land of economic warfare, where each gang demands the right to handouts or subsidies from everyone else. The gangs are called lobbyists and special-interest groups. The name for this economic war is the *Welfare State.*

Every society lives by a code of morality that creates ground rules for that society. Throughout history, most civilizations accepted the idea that the state should have supreme power over its "subjects," and that the individual has no importance. America was the first country founded on the principle that each of us has inalienable rights, and that government's job is to protect those rights. Individual rights gave birth to our freedom, and the destruction of those rights now threatens our freedom.

What are rights? Where do they come from? Why are they so important to us? What's the difference between political and economic rights? Why do economic rights polarize us, and lead to so many conflicts? These aren't just meaningless philosophical questions—they affect every part of your life. They determine your ability to afford a house, whether the company you work for stays in business, and your children's future. To understand why, let's look at these precious things called rights.

WHERE DO RIGHTS COME FROM?

A living creature's highest value is its life. Without life, nothing else is possible. Everything a plant, animal, or human does is ultimately for one purpose—to stay alive. Also, every living thing is an end in itself, including human beings. Each of us is a unique, precious, one-of-a-kind living miracle.

But to live, we have to live for our own sake. Since life is a constant struggle, our own life has to be our first and highest priority. We can't sacrifice ourselves to other people or ask other

7

people to sacrifice themselves to us, because that would threaten our lives. No living species is suicidal, and we aren't exempt from that fact of nature.

So helping others is not our primary moral duty. That doesn't mean we're cruel, self-sufficient beasts. On the contrary, we're the most social animals on Earth. Our social "instincts" help us survive and prosper. We group together for comfort, protection, companionship, mutual help, and to share our labor and knowledge.

We naturally value other people because they're like us. They're our friends, neighbors, family, business associates, and fellow travelers on this difficult road called life. Helping others also makes it likely that others will help us in our time of need. But helping others is an *option*, not a moral duty. If the help we give others threatens our life or most important values, then we should withhold this help. We first have to secure our own life. After doing this, then we can help others if we want to. This attitude toward our life is what it means to be selfish in the highest and most moral sense.

Because we have only one chance at life, our life's purpose should be to fulfill our highest potential and be as happy as we can. That doesn't mean we should be indifferent to other peoples' problems. But it does mean that relieving those problems can't be our primary concern. The help we give others must come from the heart, not be forced on us at the point of a legislative gun. Otherwise, it ceases to be genuine compassion.

BY THE SWEAT OF OUR BROW

Living creatures have a fixed nature, and their nature determines the special way they survive. Bees build hives. Lions hunt antelope. Giraffes eat leaves off trees. Plants face toward the sun. Birds fly to escape from predators.

An animal's knowledge is automatic and instinctual. Most animals can't change their behavior or their environment. They act on instinct, and their ability to learn anything new is limited. Human beings are different. We don't have instincts that tell us what to do. And we're physically puny—we don't have the turtle's shell, the eagle's wings, the antelope's speed, the polar bear's fur, or the lion's claws and strength. Compared to most other animals, we are miserable creatures that should have died out long ago.

But nature gave us a unique, powerful weapon to compensate for our physical weakness—our ability to reason. With our reason, humans can think conceptually. We can invent tools, clothes, weapons, and agriculture. Our unique minds made us rulers of the Earth.

Because we can reason, we're not limited by our environment. We can understand the forces of nature. We can adapt to many different environments, change our environment to suit our needs, and live almost anywhere on Earth under the most varied conditions. We can feed ourselves by planting corn, defeat animal predators with our weapons, and overcome natural calamities like floods, drought, and disease by inventing dikes, storage tanks, and medicine.

Yet there's one unique aspect of our minds that makes us vulnerable: we have no instinct that forces us to think. Reasoning is not automatic. In any given instant, even when our life is at stake, we can choose not to think. We can choose to evade knowledge or let our emotions overrule our reason. Thinking is something we have to do by choice.

And even if we reason to the best of our abilities, there's no guarantee that we'll be right. We're not computers. Even under the most favorable conditions, we can and do make mistakes, and mistakes are often our best means of learning.

After we make mistakes, we then have to enlist our emotions. We have to call on our courage and perseverance to try again and correct ourselves. This process can be difficult. It can threaten our self-esteem and bring emotional pain.

Like all living creatures, we have to learn how to use what nature gave us. As birds have to learn how to fly, we have to learn how to use our minds. But we have no instincts to guide us. We don't automatically know what's true or false, good or bad, or what values to choose to help us survive. We have to learn these values.

To decide, we need a standard of value to choose by. That standard has to be our life, our highest value. And because we're living creatures with a specific nature, the values we choose have to agree with our nature.

For example, being able to fly would give us added survival benefits, but we can't fly. So, it would be stupid for someone to imitate Superman and jump off a roof. Nature would prove he made a bad decision when he hit the pavement. It's the same with the values we choose.

To judge the best values to pursue, we have to understand our nature. We can define human beings as animals who have the ability to reason (though we're irrational at times). And nature gives us nothing automatically—we have no instincts. So we have to invent everything we need to survive. Our values and actions should take that into account.

Anything we do that agrees with these facts is good because it helps us survive. Anything that restricts our freedom to think or blocks our ability to invent the tools we need to live is bad. A value, action, or social system that doesn't recognize our life as our highest value is wrong.

Nature gives us nothing on a silver platter. We live on the food, clothing, and shelter we create for ourselves. If we spend our precious time and effort to produce these things, we obviously need the right to keep what we make.

We support our lives with the sweat of our brow. If we have a job, we earn our paycheck. If we own a business, we risk our hard-earned savings to start the enterprise, then struggle to make it succeed. Making money requires the best in us. It takes courage, intelligence, and perseverance to succeed, no matter what business or profession you choose. The income we make is our property because we *earn* it. We can invest the money, buy a house with it, or put it in the bank. But whatever we decide to do, the money remains ours by right. *Our right to keep what we earn is simply an extension of our right to hold our life as our highest value.*

Property rights is the idea that embodies our right to keep what we earn. Property is anything you own or earn. It's your paycheck, the profits from your business, or the car, house, or clothes you buy. Your property is yours by right *because* you worked for it. This may sound like obvious common sense, but too many Americans have forgotten what it means to say, "This

10

is mine, I earned it."

Property is also the assets and profits of businesses and public corporations. Millions of people invest their money in the common stock of corporations. Banks also lend money to corporations, and get their capital from their depositors' savings accounts. Any business, from the smallest two-man office to General Motors, uses the savings or property of average people.

Property *rights* simply mean that you have the right to use or dispose of your property as you see fit, as long as you respect everyone else's similar rights in the process. It means that no one has a right to your property without your consent. Property rights recognize your inviolate right to keep what you earn.

Because we support ourselves with our profits or paychecks, property rights protect our lives. Think what your life would be like if government confiscated all your money—you would end up begging in the streets with a tin cup. You would have no life.

Property rights also protect our cherished political rights. If government could impose heavy taxes on "uncooperative" newspapers, our right to a free press would vanish. All newspapers might end up like Pravda, in the former Soviet Union—owned and operated by the government. If government imposed heavy occupancy taxes on the assembly halls of political parties they didn't approve of, these parties would have no place to meet. Our right to free assembly would end because government taxed all meeting places out of existence.

Anytime government controls your property, it controls your life. Does anyone have the right to one penny that you earned or one minute of your life without your approval? Yet welfare-state liberals presume they have the right to up to 50 percent of what you earn in taxes. The Welfare State is immoral and illegitimate because of its utter contempt for and systematic violation of your property rights. It's immoral because it presumes to own up to 50 percent of your *life*.

WHY THE WELFARE STATE IS IMMORAL

Human beings are social animals. Being social helps us survive but sometimes gets us into trouble. This is especially true when we create social or political organizations that have good intentions but end up hurting us.

The Welfare State is such an organization. We created it because most of us have a natural desire to help people less fortunate than us. We want to cure the sick, feed the hungry, and shelter the homeless.

But the Welfare State turns our natural compassion into a moral and political duty—it turns compassion into compulsion. The Welfare State makes compassion a political duty rather than a personal choice. It claims that our highest moral duty in life is to help others. It holds that we should consider other peoples' lives more important than our own. Liberals create the Welfare State to enforce this moral code at the point of a legislative gun.

Liberals don't *ask* you to pay for entitlement programs. Instead, they point a tax gun at you and say, "Your money or your life." They confiscate up to 50 percent of your earnings in taxes. If you refuse to pay, you go to jail. If you defend yourself against the robbers, you get shot.

The progressive income tax loots our hard-earned money, then gives this money to special interest groups we wouldn't give to if we had the choice. Liberals justify this looting with the usual argument. They say that the groups who get our money allegedly need it more than we do, and it's therefore our moral duty to support them.

The Welfare State depends on the idea that the collective good, or the good of others, is more important than your life and rights. It holds that the misfortune of some people is a mortgage on your life. Welfare-state liberals then claim that if you don't volunteer to do your moral duty, they have the right to force this duty down your throat.

Many school districts around the country now require high school students to do community service *as a condition for graduating.* Local school officials now blackmail students with this outrageous choice: either do your moral duty, or don't get your diploma.

In 1990, the Steirer and Moralis families challenged mandatory community service in a Bethlehem, Pennsylvania court. Lynn Steirer, a senior at Liberty High School in Bethlehem, refused on principle to go along with the school's mandatory service program. Because her family lost their court case, she didn't graduate with her class.[1]

Local liberals held Lynn Steirer's future hostage because they saw nothing wrong with involuntary servitude and believed they had the right to turn high school students into sacrificial animals. This is a typical but vicious example of liberals' contempt for personal liberty and individual rights.

Liberals believe there's a mythical entity called society and that society has rights that supersede our individual rights. Yet society is exactly that—a myth. It doesn't exist. Only individual men, women, and children exist. America is just you and I and over 250 million other precious, individual human beings who live together under a set of mutually accepted rules of conduct.

Only human beings have rights. Because society is only a voluntary association of individuals, it can't claim rights that individuals don't have. In a lawful, civilized society, no one has the right to use force against others. Therefore, no group can claim such a right, either. We can't delegate to a group or to a government a right we don't have as individuals.

Yet the Welfare State says that we can. It claims that the end justifies the means, and that a group can violate the rights of its members to help others. Welfare-state liberals don't respect individual rights. To liberals, collective rights are more important. That's why they create entitlement programs.

As we discussed earlier, we have to value our own life above anything else. Welfare-state collectivists believe the opposite. They claim that anything you do for yourself is evil or selfish, while anything you do for others is good. If you keep what you earn and spend it on yourself or your children's education, you're immoral. If you give away up to 50 percent of your paycheck to strangers, then you're moral.

Most liberals don't care about the means they use to reach their ends, or about the misery they inflict on real people. They see nothing wrong in taxing us into poverty to pay for entitlement programs. Liberals also ignore results and evade the fact that their programs end up hurting the people they say they want to help. They evade the fact that socialist schemes never work and bring only misery and poverty to millions of people.

What's important to radical liberals is that they "care" about people. They see themselves as saviors of the poor, oppressed, and downtrodden, as white knights to the helpless. *That's what feeds their ego and makes them feel important.*

Liberal politicians are like mules who wear blinders by choice. They *have* to evade facts and the consequences of their actions. Otherwise, they can't keep feeling good about "helping" people. Liberals need the Welfare State to feel morally superior and to give meaning to their lives. As a result, they don't care about the means they use to keep the Welfare State alive.

This end-justifies-the-means reasoning is what produced the Hitlers and Stalins of this world. Such men *only* wanted to help others. They wanted to do good for the German or Soviet peoples. Their purpose was "noble," so in their minds it didn't matter what means they used or what devastation they caused. It didn't matter that they killed six million Jews or thirty million kulak peasants. Vicious means, even for an allegedly noble purpose, lead to vicious or destructive results.

This attitude also produces the civilized versions of these dictators—welfare-state liberals. Liberals act on the same moral premises as "benevolent" dictators. They believe that selfishness is immoral, self-sacrifice for others is good, and the end justifies the means. They have no mercy for the middle class who they use as a means to their ends, and few regrets about the havoc they wreak on our lives. If they act selflessly to help others, in their minds that's all that matters.

Liberals live to help others—that's the meaning and purpose of their lives and the basis of their self-value. With each new entitlement program, they congratulate themselves on how wonderful they are because they've helped other people. They conveniently forget that they did nothing but loot our hard-earned money to pay for their compassion and good deeds. They evade the fact that their self-congratulations are built on the backs of hardworking Americans who pay the taxes to support entitlement programs. *It's easy to be noble with other peoples' money.*

POLITICAL RIGHTS

Unfortunately, human nature has a dark side. Throughout history, there were always vicious, violent, and irrational misfits who robbed and murdered their fellow man. These misfits sometimes gain control of governments. They then use the power of government to wreak havoc on the rest of us.

This dark side of human nature is why political rights are so important. Political rights protect us from power-hungry misfits who use government for their own benefit. We give government a monopoly on the use of force to keep social order and to protect us from criminals. But we also have to control government to prevent that monopoly from backfiring on us. To do this, we write laws that recognize and protect our individual rights. That's the purpose of the Constitution and Bill of Rights.

For example, we need free speech to survive as civilized human beings. We have to be free to say what's on our minds and to express our thoughts to others, without fear of being punished. Sometimes other people don't like what we say and threaten us with violence to keep us quiet. And governments sometimes try to silence us when we criticize them. To protect free speech, we wrote it into the Bill of Rights.

Political rights like free speech recognize our inalienable rights as free, living, human beings. In a free society, these rights can't be violated by government and are outside the jurisdiction of government action. But other people can violate our freedom with violence. So a right requires that we be protected from physical coercion or interference by others. Government's most important job is to protect our rights.

A right defines and approves your freedom to act in a social situation. The Declaration of Independence said that we have the right to "life, liberty, and the pursuit of happiness." Notice it didn't say we have the right to happiness, only to its *pursuit*. It didn't guarantee happiness, because nothing in life is guaranteed. The Declaration of Independence guaranteed our freedom to work for our happiness. But it didn't guarantee that we succeed or that we have a right to something we didn't earn.

For example, we have the right to earn money to buy food, a house, clothing, education, or health insurance. But we don't have a right to these things if we can't pay for them. We have a right to freedom of assembly but we don't have a right to own the assembly hall. We have a right to freedom of speech but we don't have the right to own a newspaper.

ECONOMIC RIGHTS

In contrast, liberals claim that we have the right to happiness, not just it's pursuit, and to economic security, whether or not we earned it. They say we have a right to housing, health care, and education, even if we can't pay for them. These economic "rights" spawned the entitlement programs of the Welfare State.

A right has to apply to all of us or it can't be a right. If it applies to some people but not to others, it stops being a right. Instead, it becomes a special privilege enforced by government. Medicare, farm subsides, food stamps, bank bailouts, and thousands of other entitlement programs aren't rights. They are special benefits given to some people at the expense of others.

If an alleged right violates someone else's rights, it's not legitimate. Any alleged right that takes money from you by force to give unearned benefits to others, can't be a right. So an economic "right" is not a right at all. Instead, it's simply a license to steal.

Food, houses, and education don't grow free in nature. Millions of hardworking Americans create these things. Farmers work from sunrise to sundown to grow our food. Construction workers build our houses. Taxpayers work hard to pay for school buildings and teachers' salaries.

Millions of people also create health care with their labor and dedication. Doctors train for more than ten years and spend thousands of dollars for tuition. Entrepreneurs risk millions of dollars to build hospitals. Masons, plumbers, and electricians work for years to build the hospitals. Pharmaceutical companies risk years of work and millions of dollars to create and test new drugs.

When we claim the right to health care, we claim the right to these peoples' time and labor. If we don't have money to pay for health insurance, the right to health care also means claiming the right to *force* others to pay for us (such as with Medicare).

Ask yourself these questions: If you wanted to buy a house but couldn't afford one, do you have the right to rob a bank to get the money? If you needed money for your daughter's college education, do you have the right to point a gun at the college's dean of admissions and force him to educate your child? If you needed money to buy extra clothes for yourself, do you have the right to mug someone on the street and take his money?

You probably answered no to these questions. You know it's wrong to steal from others. You know that you have to work for what you want, just like everyone else, and that your hardships don't give you the right to hurt others. But if you claim the right to education or health care, you're demanding the right to rob others. The only difference is that government does the robbing for you.

A person who demands an economic right usually can't pay for, or doesn't want to pay for, something he needs. But to satisfy that alleged right, *someone* has to pay for it. That someone is you—working Americans who government taxes to pay for other peoples' unearned food, housing, health care, education, farm subsidies, or Social Security. In effect, welfare-state liberals turn you into a sacrificial animal. You do double work because you pay for your own food, housing, or health care and then pay again for other people. Other peoples' problems or laziness become a permanent yoke around your neck. Ask yourself this question—by what right?

No one has a right to someone else's life and income. If you claim that right, you're simply claiming the right to steal. *You're also giving others the right to steal from you.* It's a two-edged sword: you can't steal from your neighbors without giving your neighbors the right to rob you in return.

Some people have died trying to stop a mugger from stealing $50 in their wallet. They felt outraged by someone trying to steal their money. Yet when government takes our money indirectly through taxes, we think it's moral and acceptable. But theft is theft. It makes no difference whether a mugger robs us on the street or a special-interest group robs us by lobbying Congress for a new subsidy or entitlement.

One person's need for something can't be a mortgage on someone else's life. We all have unlimited needs. If everyone had a right to anything they needed, then we would be slaves to each other's needs. There can't be such a right. The idea is mad and leads to eternal warfare between competing economic pressure groups—it leads to the Welfare State.

Once government forces you to help someone because that person needs it, then it's open season on everything you own or earn. Looters who claim the right to your paycheck will be on your doorstep with one hand out and a shotgun in the other. Once other peoples' needs dictate who gets your money, then your rights go out the window.

In the end, force becomes the only way we deal with each other. Instead of respecting each other's rights, we become mortal enemies. Each special-interest group tries to force others to satisfy its needs at everyone else's expense. That's what an army of lobbyists does in the halls of Congress.

America is stumbling down the path to economic anarchy. Other countries before us, like India, the Soviet Union, and even ancient Rome tried variations of socialism. They all failed. Like them, our Welfare State will eventually disintegrate into economic chaos and bloody conflict between special-interest groups who demand economic rights.

There are only two political alternatives in a society: either everyone has an inalienable right to their life and property, or no one does (eventually). Either we're free or we're slaves. You can't be half-pregnant. The Welfare State is a mixed society where government respects some of our rights but violates others. A system like this is like a house built on quicksand. Human nature and the internal logic of the system will eventually drive it into the abyss of poverty or anarchy.

If government violates only *one* person's rights in one instance, then we've accepted the principle that we don't have an inalienable right to our life and property. Then it's only a matter of time until government violates all our rights and wrecks our lives. Government has no right to control your life, confiscate your salary, or violate the same rights of business people. As someone's hardship is not a claim on your life, so your hardship is not a claim on a business person's life, profits, or property.

If you agree that government has the right to control the wage an employer pays you, the rent an apartment house owner charges you, or the price of your prescription drugs, you're accepting its right to violate a business person's rights. Yet these

18

are the same rights you insist on for yourself.

No one has the right to use force (taxes and regulations) to confiscate another person's property to satisfy his needs. No one has the right to what someone else earned, whether that someone is you, your neighbor, or Mobil Oil Corporation.

Liberals sometimes relent a little and admit that too many taxes and regulations are bad for us. But in the next breath they claim we should keep a few regulations and entitlement programs as a safety net. By doing that, however, they still claim it's morally acceptable to force some people to give unearned benefits to others. Their actions grant legitimacy to the idea and open the door to more regulations and entitlement programs.

When you agree that your life and property are yours by right, then you agree it's the same for everyone else. *You can't violate the rights of one person or company without giving others the same right to violate yours.*

Life has risks and suffering. Some people get sick, all of us get old, and some of us fail in business or our personal lives. That's just life and human nature and you can't tax or regulate all the risks out of existence. Yet that's exactly what liberals try to do. In their well-intentioned but futile attempts to end all suffering in life, liberals create a Welfare State that threatens our liberty, our economic security, and our future. In the end, liberals hurt far more people than they first wanted to help.

ENTITLEMENTS: MONSTERS OUT OF CONTROL

The notion of economic rights gives birth to entitlement programs and then justifies these programs after they've become out-of-control monsters. Every entitlement program is spawned by some group's alleged right to an unearned income or special subsidy.

Liberals justified Social Security by claiming that we have a right to financial support in old age. They justified Medicare by claiming that elderly people have a right to health care. They justified farm subsidies by claiming that farmers have a right to stay in business, regardless of market conditions or their business competence. Liberals justify every entitlement program by claiming a similar right for the particular group getting the subsidy.

Government creates entitlement programs out of a sincere humanitarian desire to help people. The federal government created Social Security in the 1930s to help destitute older people. Congress created Medicare in 1965 to protect retirees from the devastating costs of a catastrophic illness.

Medicare and Social Security started small but grew into massive, out-of-control income-transfer machines. When Medicare began, the program cost about $500 million. It now costs about $177 *billion* a year.[2] Social Security expenditures were $10 million in 1938 and are now $335 *billion* a year and growing.[3]

It's no accident that entitlement programs grow out of control; this result is inevitable from the start. Once we give a group the right to an unearned subsidy, human nature takes over. Unfortunately, many of us are weak, lazy, or greedy. If government tells us that we have a right to money we didn't earn, we readily agree. Who wants to work and struggle when we can get free money? Of course, we know in the back of our minds that something is wrong, but we evade that unpleasant thought. We feel a little guilty for taking the government check at first, but that soon passes.

It passes because liberals tell us we have a right to this money. It passes because millions of other people also get subsidy checks from the government, so we believe it's all right. We join the parade for our fair share of the loot. Once we're hooked, we keep demanding ever more subsidies. We ask for cost-of-living increases to keep up with inflation. We demand higher payments to keep up with the higher payments other groups have wrangled from Congress.

A vicious cycle is created. We soon depend on these government checks rather than on our own initiative. Many Americans don't save enough for their retirement because they think Social Security will support them. They don't save for retirement medical expenses because Medicare will pay their bills. This attitude makes sense. Why save for something when government will take care of you?

Once they depend on government checks, entitlement-program

beneficiaries defend their program with ferocity. They join special-interest groups who lobby Congress to protect their program. They put political pressure on Congress to make sure their benefits don't change. Entitlement programs then become entrenched and almost impossible to reverse. This process has been going on and accelerating for over forty years and we're coming to the end of our rope.

Liberals say that helping others is our political duty, and that government should force this duty on us through regulations and entitlement programs. This idea is threatening our lives and our future. Later we'll see in more detail how the Welfare State, and the philosophy that justifies it, is wrecking health care and other areas of our lives.

CHAPTER 2

LEGAL THEFT—TAXES AND THE WELFARE STATE

In 1979, the people of California finally had enough. Their property taxes were so high that they wouldn't tolerate it anymore. In a statewide referendum, they voted to slash these taxes. In 1991, New Jersey voters sent a similar message to Governor Florio. They threw out most of the Democratic legislature and elected Republicans who promised to cut taxes.

Americans are angry over high taxes. That's why the Democrats lost control of Congress in the November 1994 elections. Tax levels in this country have reached painful heights. The average family now pays almost 40 percent of its earnings in sales, income, property, Social Security, and other taxes to city, state, and federal governments.

The Tax Foundation, a private research group that educates the public on the fiscal aspects of government, said that May 3 is the current Tax Freedom Day. That means that the average American worked the first 123 days of the year just to pay all federal, state, and local taxes.[1]

In 1993 the top federal tax bracket jumped from 31 percent to

36 percent for a family earning over $140,000 per year. An additional 10 percent surcharge on incomes over $250,000 raised the top rate to 39.6 percent.[2] Americans who make over $250,000 a year now pay almost 40 percent of their income in federal taxes alone. Their Tax Freedom Day extends into June. In short, we now have to work from four to six months a year to pay our taxes.

The tax revolt is long overdue, but it's a tragically typical example of the modern American approach to solving deep-rooted economic and political problems. The tax revolt is a short-term, short-sighted patch job designed to solve a problem we've found no solution for.

Why are taxes so high? They're high because government has become a devouring monster called the Welfare State. We have a welfare state because liberals have brainwashed us into thinking that government's job is to protect everyone with regulations and entitlement programs. Taxes are only revenues that government needs to pay for these programs. Big government means high taxes. It's that simple.

In effect, we tax ourselves, so we have no right to blame government for our heavy tax load. If we want government to give us welfare, health care, Medicare, farm subsidies, Social Security, and hundreds of other entitlements, we can't blame it for taxing us to pay for these programs. Americans are not immune to the laws of nature—you can't have your cake and eat it too.

If we want a sharp and permanent reduction in our taxes, we need to ask the question: What's the proper function of government in a free society? To find an answer, let's ask our Founding Fathers.

When we look back at history, we see people living in squalor, hunger, and disease for thousands of years. If you see how people live today in places like China, India, and Africa, you realize how much America achieved in the brief span of two hundred years. Yet our greatest achievement is something simpler and more profound than a high standard of living, a thing that made all the rest possible—an idea.

The idea has two parts: first, that a single human life is the most precious thing on Earth; second, that we have natural, inalienable rights that no group, majority, or government has the right to violate. It was the idea that government is simply a political organization we create to protect our rights—that government is our servant, not our master.

This idea was revolutionary in 1776. Before then, people considered the collective—the tribe, state, church, society, or majority—to be more important than a single human being. Average citizens were low on the totem pole and treated like unimportant servants whose primary reason for living was to serve the state or society. People had no inalienable rights. They only had temporary privileges that the current ruler could grant or withdraw at whim. In most clashes between the individual's life, liberty, or happiness and the interests of the state, the individual was sacrificed.

The rulers and aristocracy of these countries taxed and regulated their subjects into poverty to build palaces for themselves. Poverty went hand in hand with tyranny, as it usually does. In these societies, your social status was fixed and you had little freedom to improve your life.

The American revolution changed that. Human liberty didn't start in America, but our Founding Fathers were the first men to create a nation on that idea. Through the Bill of Rights and Constitution, they created a political structure designed to guarantee our individual rights and protect us from our eternal, deadliest enemy—unlimited government.

Once this political structure was in place, it was as if a great breath was released. The dead weight of tyranny fell away and now human beings could soar. Americans were now free to think, to create, and to pursue their dreams, secure in the knowledge that government no longer had the right to steal what they earned.

Now what someone achieved was limited only by his goals, ambition, and perseverance. The crucial link between effort and reward had been reestablished. The dazzling explosion of energy, production, and achievement that followed over the next two hundred years was the inevitable result.

Our Founding Fathers based their government on the philosophy of the Enlightenment, born in England and transported to its real home in America. Philosophers like John Locke and Jean Jacques Rousseau proclaimed the Rights of Man. They developed the revolutionary idea that life and liberty are ours by right, and that government is just a necessary evil we create to keep order and protect our rights.

Unfortunately, in every society there are always vicious and immoral people who don't respect other peoples' rights. They rob and murder to get what they want. If a society is to survive, criminal behavior has to be stopped. But if everyone took the law into their own hands for self-defense we would have anarchy like in the Wild West.

Government's job is to create a political structure that lets us live together in peace. To do this, we give it the exclusive legal and moral right to use force. But government is allowed to use force only in retaliation against someone who uses force against others, and only when it has evidence to prove this. Police can arrest a person only if they suspect he's deliberately hurt someone. A judge can send someone to prison only after a jury finds that person guilty in a court of law.

But once government has an exclusive right to use force, it's easy to abuse this power. And here is the crucial political problem that wrecked most societies before America. How do you control government once you give it this frightening power? How do you stop those who control government from threatening their own people? For five thousand years most rulers used government to gain absolute power and loot their own people. Europeans fled to America to escape from such tyrannical governments.

Our Founding Fathers created the Constitution to overcome this problem. The Constitution and Bill of Rights placed strict limits on government power. Government became an agent for the people, limited to the role of policeman and guardian of our rights. Ordinary people could now pursue their dreams and ambitions free from the threat of force by others, or as important, by government itself.

Our Founding Fathers knew that unlimited government is our most dangerous enemy. They created the Constitution and Bill of Rights *to protect us from our own government.* That's why America prospered—because the Constitution restricted government power and protected its citizens' lives, liberty, and property.

Government protects us in three ways. First, it creates laws that punish criminals. Second, it establishes police and court systems to carry out the laws and settle commercial disputes. Third, it raises armies to protect us from foreign countries that threaten us. The Constitution gave these basic functions to the federal government. As a result, government didn't need much money to operate, and taxes were low.

At the end of the nineteenth century, federal taxes only absorbed about 3 percent of the national income ($6.64 per person), and state and municipal taxes added another 6 percent ($13.28 per person). There was *no income tax*, except a temporary one during the Civil War, until the 16th Amendment to the Constitution established this tax in 1913. The bulk of federal revenues came almost entirely from tariffs, excise taxes, and customs duties. The federal debt was small and steadily contracting. There were minor outlays for social services, and the Treasury often had a *surplus*.

Low taxes meant that workers or business owners kept most of their wages or profits to spend on themselves or their businesses. At the end of the nineteenth century, Americans had the right to keep what they earned. The combination of a free economy, political liberty, strict protection of property rights, and a small federal government was the spark plug that turned America into the most productive nation on Earth.

The Founding Fathers created a brilliant political structure, but they also made some serious mistakes; there were holes in the dam right from the start. Unfortunately, the Constitution gave the federal government the right to coin money, regulate commerce, and promote the general welfare of the nation. At the time, these phrases were strictly interpreted and government interference in the economy was minor.

But gradually those general phrases took on an ominous new meaning as the country's moral-political philosophy took a sharp turn to the left. Over the years, like a spreading malignant cancer, government's right to regulate commerce and protect the general welfare turned into government's right to create the Welfare State.

The dominant political doctrine ruling America today is socialism. Socialism rests on the idea that compassion is a moral and political duty, not a personal choice. Under the socialist Welfare State, government forces us to help others, whether we like it or not.

As a result, the guiding principles of our Founding Fathers have been all but forgotten. Limited government and the scrupulous protection of property rights are just a fading memory. In their place, government is again telling us that society is more important than you and I. Liberals tell us that the public good and the economic rights of the needy are more important than our liberty.

Need, not individual rights, has become the ruling principle of our time. Government uses regulations and entitlement programs to allegedly protect the common good and create a safety net for everyone. Our government now forces us to live by the political dogma of socialism and communism: "From each according to his ability, to each according to his need."

That's what a welfare state is all about. And when I say welfare I don't mean simply for the poor, *but for everyone*. Most government subsidy, insurance, and entitlement programs are a form of welfare. Government taxes us to pay for food stamps, Medicare, bank bailouts, rent subsidies, farm subsidies, Social Security, unemployment insurance, and handouts to corporations. There's an endless list of programs that benefit every conceivable pressure group.

Three entitlement programs are the powder keg behind exploding federal deficits: Medicare, Social Security, and federal pensions. In 1993, they accounted for 75.3 percent of all federal entitlements.[3] These programs' millions of beneficiaries are not welfare recipients; they are middle-class retirees. Almost 75 percent of federal benefits are paid with no regard to a person's financial status, and only about 17 percent of these benefits help Americans get out of poverty.[4]

If we add up all the taxes we pay, including sales taxes, property taxes, Social Security taxes, city, state, and federal income taxes, and hundreds of business taxes passed on to consumers, we'll find that government takes anywhere from 35 percent to 50 percent of our income. In the Middle Ages, feudal lords took about 25 percent of their serfs' crops to pay for the lords' protection. The medieval serfs of Europe were taxed less than the new middle-class serfs of America.

It doesn't matter that we voted ourselves into serfdom. If government confiscates 40 percent of your salary or profits, it doesn't matter if your ruler is a dictator, a medieval lord, or the will of the majority. Our Founding Fathers didn't base our government on unlimited majority rule. Instead, they designed a political structure *to protect us against majority rule.* Freedom of speech and religion protects us against a majority mob that may not like what we say or who we pray to. That's the purpose of the Bill of Rights and Constitution.

Majority rule doesn't sanction or guarantee personal liberty. Instead, it often violates personal liberty. A majority of the German people voted the Nazi party into office and approved most of its policies. Our own government has become dangerous precisely because it uses majority rule to justify violating our individual rights.

THE SLAVE TAX

To understand the real meaning of compassion as a moral duty, look at the tax that embodies this idea and pays for the Welfare State—the progressive income tax.

Before Congress passed the 16th Amendment in 1913, the Supreme Court had stopped previous attempts to create a federal income tax (except for a temporary income tax during the Civil War). Americans hated the income tax because it violated their property rights and confiscated their property for social purposes.

Unfortunately, socialist ideas from Europe gradually influenced American intellectuals and political leaders. Karl Marx's Communist Manifesto of 1848 bluntly proposed "a heavy progressive or graduated income tax." In Marx's socialist paradise "the proletariat (today's poor, my insertion) will use the political supremacy to wrest, by degrees, all capital from the bourgeois (today's middle class, my insertion), to centralize all instruments of production in the hands of the State," and to make "despotic inroads on the right of property, and on the conditions of bourgeois production (today's regulations, my insertion)."

With a few adjustments, this describes the political philosophy of America's welfare-state liberals.

These ideas gradually filtered into the American political psyche. Congress passed an income tax during the Civil War, but soon repealed it because it was unpopular. The second try came in 1894 after the bloody labor movement riots the year before. The Populist party and the progressives of the Republican and Democratic parties lobbied for the tax and were successful. But in 1895, the Supreme Court declared the law unconstitutional. After 1895, socialist pressure groups kept pushing for the income tax, which Congress finally created with the 16th Amendment.

The progressive income tax embodies a radically different philosophy about property rights and the function of government. It implies that your property is not yours by right, that there's a higher value than property rights—the collective good. Other peoples' financial problems are your responsibility, and your duty is to share your property with those less fortunate than you. It turns government into a morality cop who forces you to help others.

The income tax, designed to redistribute property to achieve this radical new goal, ended the strict protection of property rights in America and created a new revolution through taxation. This revolution reversed the political principles America was founded on.

James Madison, one of the architects of the Constitution, expressly denied that society has higher rights than individuals. He and the other Founding Fathers considered our natural rights (property and individual rights) to be the highest rights under the law.

We fought the American Revolution to defend our property rights against the dictatorial power of the English monarchy. John Locke, the English political philosopher and intellectual father of the American revolution, stated: "The great and chief end, therefore, of men's uniting into commonwealths, and putting themselves under government, is the preservation of their property."[5]

Without property rights, government has us by the throat. It doesn't have to violate our political rights of free speech, freedom of worship, and so on. Bureaucrats can enslave us with a web of regulations. Government can control us by dictating how much money we're "allowed" to keep, and by turning us into dependents who live off entitlement programs. Through taxes, government can force us to work four to six months of the year to support farmers, retirees, welfare mothers, savings and loan depositors, or anyone else bureaucrats choose to make the lucky winners of our labor.

The progressive income tax is a tax on virtue. In a free society, where we're not allowed to use force to settle disputes, we earn wealth only by trading or creating economic values. Creating goods or services that other people value isn't easy. It requires the best in us: ambition, integrity, intelligence, perseverance, creativity, and the courage to take risks.

Anyone who's ever been in business and succeeded understands that. Anyone who has ever struggled to become a nurse, artist, doctor, electrician, or other professional knows what I mean. Anyone who works for a company and is competent and conscientious also has these qualities. In a free society, if you're rich or successful, you've usually earned it.

The progressive income tax confiscates your income for the crime of virtue. Under this tax, the more profit or salary you make, the more taxes you pay; the more wealth you earn, the more government takes from you; the more honest, creative, ambitious, courageous, productive, and intelligent you are, the more government punishes you. Your ability determines your punishment: those who offer the greatest economic values to others are punished the most.

Conversely, the less a person earns, the more he's rewarded. The more lazy, dishonest, or incompetent the person is, the fewer taxes he pays and the more unearned income he gets from subsidies or entitlement programs. His faults determine his reward: those who offer the least economic values to others, gain the most benefits.

Therefore, in the Welfare State, an obscene moral reversal takes place. Human virtue is punished while human faults are rewarded. Success is punished and failure is rewarded. Government's role is no longer limited to policeman and arbitrator. Government becomes an equalizer, a redistributer of our income. Even more insidious, it becomes a redistributer and destroyer of virtue. In effect, the Welfare State says there's no moral difference between hardworking people who earn their money, and looters who make their money by stealing from others.

If helping others is a duty, it follows that no one has the right to be rich or middle class while others are poor. We have a moral obligation to support those less fortunate than us. If people "lucky" enough to be better off than others won't voluntarily accept this moral and financial duty, then society must force them.

Liberal politicians do this by creating entitlement programs, and then taxing us to pay for these programs. Witness the 1993 fiscal-year tax increases passed by President Clinton and the Democratic Congress. They raised the top income tax rates from 31 percent to 36 percent and then added a punitive 10 percent surtax. The surtax and high tax rates force higher-income taxpayers to pay their "fair share."

The idea of forcing someone to pay his fair share of taxes applies only to a society of cannibals. It applies to a society where the majority has the right to devour those people who earn more than others. Paying your fair share implies that all of us have a responsibility to support the Welfare State, but some of us have more responsibility than others. It implies that the more money you earn, the larger your fair share should be, simply because you have more to give. In other words, fair share means Karl Marx's "from each according to his ability, to each according to his need."

This is the philosophy of socialist looters who are consumed by envy. This policy simply justifies stealing from those people who earn more than others. And since there's always someone richer or poorer than you, the policy turns into universal looting. Everyone steals from the next victim above him on the economic ladder. Paying our "fair share" appeals to looters or parasites who have no idea how wealth is created or why it's wrong to steal.

To see what fair share really means, imagine the following. You have $10,000 saved in your local bank. You worked for ten years to save this money. The bank then gets a new "progres-

sive" manager. The manager finds that most of the bank's customers have less than $500 in deposits, which he thinks is
grossly unfair. So he makes new rules for the bank. He sends
you a letter telling you that he is going to redistribute your
$10,000 to all his poor depositors so that everyone has their fair
share. Do you think the bank manager should be arrested or
sent to the loony bin? What if the government passes a law that
lets him get away with this theft? You know that the bank manager has no right to "redistribute" your money. Does the government? Yet progressive income taxes and entitlement programs
do exactly the same thing the bank manager did.

In a free society, the taxes a person pays should depend on the
services he gets from government, his agent. We should only
pay for services that we use. We could devise a system where
each of us paid taxes for government services we bought—a voluntary trade between a citizen and his agent. But this system
would be possible only if America had a limited government.

This goal is entirely possible. In 1914, the federal government's
budget was $725 million. The 1995 fiscal-year budget is close to
$1.5 *trillion*, a 2000-percent increase from 1914. Why the in-
credible difference? The income tax revolutionized the role of
government from limited agent to safety-net builder. It gave
government the income-raising tool it needed to create the Welfare State.

We could have a contractual tax system if we reduced government to its size in 1914. A contractual system would be easy
then, because the budget would be so small. Imagine that the
annual federal budget is $750 million because we phased out
regulations and entitlement programs. To be more realistic, let's
increase the budget to $75 billion (one hundred times the
amount in 1914) to account for inflation, defense costs, and the
general increase in population.

The United States today has a population of about 250 million
people. If we had a simple flat tax calculated by dividing the
total budget of $75 billion by the population of 250 million, the
tax per person would be $300 a year. Do you think you could
afford $300? This figure also excludes money the federal govern-
ment collects from other taxes, such as excise, tariffs, and user
fees, which were its primary taxes before 1913. These extra

taxes would further reduce the income taxes needed and give government more funds to work with.

Most of us would be so happy about our low tax bill that we wouldn't want to bother with a complicated contractual tax system. We would be happy to pay the $300 and be done with it. Except for this small tax, you could keep everything you earned. Add up all the taxes you now pay and then subtract $300. *Everything else would be yours.*

But low taxes are possible only if we totally reject the philosophy behind the Welfare State. We pay heavy taxes only because we have thousands of regulations and entitlement programs and millions of government bureaucrats. The Welfare State and unlimited government can be swept away only when we reject the idea that helping others is a moral and political duty.

Until then, the Welfare State forces us to help others at the point of a legislative gun. Our paychecks and savings accounts are no longer private property to be scrupulously protected and used for our own benefit. Instead, liberals assume that your salary, profits, and property are collectively owned. They assume that your income is a national resource they can give away to anyone who needs it. They assume that the only person who has no right to your money is you, the person who earned it.

Are they right? Should you let them get away with that? Does your hard-earned money belong to you, or to any looting moocher who wants to steal it from you? The next time you go into a voting booth, ask yourself these questions. Every liberal, most Democrats, and too many Republicans believe in the welfare-state philosophy. Vote only for those who don't believe this.

LOOK OVER YOUR SHOULDER

If it's true that helping others is a duty rather than a personal choice, then it's reasonable to loot the rich. They have more money and therefore should give their money to people who have less. But progressive income taxes hurt the middle class more than the rich. The middle class is the bulk of our population, and they pay most of the taxes.

To balance the budget on the backs of the top-earning 1 percent of Americans, we would have to tax 100 percent of the income of everyone who made over $175,000 a year. If this outright expropriation is too extreme even for liberals, we would have to double the income taxes of households earning over $50,000 a year.[6]

Stealing from the rich won't support the exploding Welfare State. But it does satisfy our secret desire to punish people who are rich. It helps satisfy that green monster in us called envy. Looting the rich lets us believe we have a moral and legal right to steal money from those who earn more than us. The progressive income tax rears it's ugly head from this common but destructive side of human nature. It appeals to the worst in us.

Middle-income taxpayers might think the progressive income tax gets them something for nothing. But looting the rich only sets them up for slaughter by the same scheme. Why? Because everyone below the middle class on the economic totem pole *will be looting them*.

To poor people, the middle class seems rich, though the middle class is struggling to keep its head above water. Since only about 6 percent of taxpayers make over $130,000 a year (my arbitrary definition of rich),[7] entitlement beneficiaries have to knock on the middle class's door for their benefits. After the rich, the middle class is next in line for the guillotine because it pays almost 80 percent of the taxes that support the Welfare State. If you're middle class and support higher income taxes for the rich, *look over your shoulder*. Someone poorer than you is breathing down your neck. If you support government's right to loot the rich, you support government's right to loot you. You can't have your cake and eat it too: either we respect each other's rights and property, or government loots us all in the end. Once government loots one person's property with progressive income taxes, then we're all in danger.

You may think looting the rich is moral because we have a duty to help others less fortunate than us. But if you believe this, you become vulnerable to the liberals' propaganda. Your conscience shames you into helping others. If you were consistent, you would feel morally obligated to give all your surplus income to the poor. Too bad that your kids can't go to college now. You would feel immoral spending money on your children's future while people are starving in Appalachia.

But compassion can't stop there. Many poor people in America are rich by comparison to the poor in underdeveloped countries. Mexican illegal aliens who sneak across the Rio Grande at night to work for minimum wages in the fields of California know this. If helping others is a moral duty, it would be immoral to stop at America's borders. Our altruism would have to take in the whole world. We would have to tax America's poor to feed the starving masses of Africa and the rest of the world.

So there's no end to it. If compassion is our moral and political duty, then no one has a right to one penny of extra income or savings while another human being is worse off than we are. Each of us would be morally and financially responsible for human suffering everywhere.

But if you believe that your life and paycheck are not other peoples' property, then the progressive income tax is a moral obscenity. The progressive income tax becomes a burden and a punishment you don't deserve and shouldn't tolerate.

To reject the Welfare State, ask yourself these questions: *Why* is helping others a moral and political duty, instead of a personal choice? Why should government rob you for the sake of others? Why is their life more important than yours? Does government have the right to punish you because you work hard and are successful? Does government have the right to turn you into a sacrificial animal?

A BETTER TAX SYSTEM

If we accept the idea that government is our agent and not a redistributer of our income, then we should radically alter our tax system. Taxes should not be progressive. Instead, they should be regressive: tax rates should go *down* as a person's income goes up.

If government is our agent, then anyone who gets the same services from this agent should pay the same taxes. A rich person and a poor person both pay the same for a loaf of bread in a grocery store. That's only fair. If both receive the same loaf of bread, why should the rich person pay more? It's unjust and goes against common sense.

The same applies to the loaves of bread we get from government. Assume that a rich person and poor person receive the same police protection or use of the court system from government. Why should one pay more for this service than the other? Again, that wouldn't be fair. But to make sure that the rich and poor person paid the same, we'd have to have a regressive tax system.

For example, lets say the rich person makes $100,000 a year, while the poor person makes $10,000. Under a progressive tax system, if the rich person's tax rate is 40 percent and the poor person's rate is 20 percent, the rich person pays $40,000 in taxes while the poor person pays $2000. Yet both get the same government services! In a flat tax system, if government taxed everyone at a 25 percent rate, then the rich person pays $25,000 in taxes while the poor person pays $2500. This is still grossly unfair.

Therefore, the only way to have both pay the same is to create a regressive tax system. If the person who earned $100,000 pays a 5 percent rate while the person who earned $10,000 pays a 50 percent rate, then both would pay $5000 in taxes.

Of course, liberals would scream that a regressive tax system is cruel and vicious. But cruel and vicious to whom? Is it cruel and vicious for a rich and poor person to pay the same $8 to see a movie, or the same $20 for a T-shirt? Why should a rich person pay twenty times more for the same government services as a poor person?

Of course, liberals will protest that government's function is not simply to give us police protection and a court system. They claim that government's most important job is to redistribute income to achieve "social justice." Well, I submit that social justice is simply another word for theft, plain and simple, and nothing justifies theft.

Isn't it cruel and vicious to loot middle-class families of their hard-earned money to give handouts to others? Isn't stealing cruel and vicious? Does one person's financial problems justify stealing from others? Does theft become moral if government does it? It's welfare-state liberals who are cruel and vicious.

They have no mercy for the middle class, no mercy for those who work, struggle, and pay for the Welfare State.

Worse, we have no defense against this theft. When a mugger robs us on the street, we can try to defend ourselves. If the police catch the mugger, he goes to jail. With the progressive income tax, government is the mugger. If we refuse to pay, *we* go to jail.

Don't be fooled into accepting government's right to steal from you because we elected our politicians by majority vote. No king, dictator, or duly-elected representative has the right to rob us. When we don't have the right to keep what we earn, when our salary or profits are considered public property, then we're slaves in our own country.

Most of us, given a choice, would not voluntarily sacrifice ourselves or our family for society, the majority, or the government. If someone asked you to give away 35 percent to 50 percent of your paycheck or profits to support total strangers, would you? Of course not. *That's why you have to be forced.*

When government confiscates our hard-earned money with ever-increasing progressive income taxes, one result is inevitable—a socialist America where the economy and our lives are ruined. To confirm this, look at the former Soviet Union—the former Soviet *socialist* republics are now destitute.

America is heading for the same fate, I'm afraid to say. We're like a healthy young boy with malignant cancer, and only moral and political surgery can save us. We can slash our taxes and breathe free again when we understand that helping others is a personal choice, not a political duty.

CHAPTER 3

DISCRIMINATION AND THE AMERICAN DREAM

Imagine the following. Suppose you want to sell your house. It's too small for your growing family, so you need a larger one. You place an ad in a local newspaper and after several people respond, one young couple offers a price that's satisfactory to you.

You're relieved that someone offered you a price you could accept. Now, knowing that your house is sold, you make an offer on a new house that you and your wife love. You offer more than market price because you want this house very much. You feel secure knowing that the money you'll get from the sale of your old house will pay for the new one.

The owners of the new house accept your offer and you pay a $10,000 deposit on signing the contract. Your lawyer tells you that if, for any reason, you can't complete the purchase of the new house at closing time, ninety days from now, you'll lose your $10,000. But you don't worry because you're closing on your old house within thirty days.

A week after you sign the contract for your new house, you receive a visit from a man representing the local office of the

Equal Housing Opportunity Administration (EHOA). You've never heard of this agency and you don't understand why he's here. As he explains the purpose of his visit, you become shocked and horrified.

He says you've committed a crime. You sold your house too quickly and to a white couple. You're guilty of denying equal housing opportunity to minorities. He tells you that EHOA regulations require that a community must have a minimum number of minority residents. Otherwise, this is evidence of collective discrimination. In such a case, the community must submit an affirmative action program within ninety days to correct the situation. If it doesn't, the EHOA will enforce the following regulations:

1. All individuals wishing to sell their homes must advertise in at least two newspapers in minority neighborhoods.

2. The seller must submit, in triplicate, a complete record of all letters and telephone conversations with potential buyers who visited or made an offer on the house.

3. No acceptance of any offer shall be made for a period of four months from the time the house is first placed on the market, to give enough time to notify all minorities that the house is for sale.

4. No sale shall be made until at least two minority individuals have made an offer on the house.

5. The owner must sell his house to the minority buyer who offers the highest price, even if this offer is far below the price offered by nonminority buyers.

6. If the seller doesn't comply with the above regulations and enters into a contract for sale with a nonminority buyer, that contract will be null and void.

Then this man says you violated the law, your present contract is void, and you must now comply with the law. Failure to comply would result in a fine or imprisonment.

You must now put your house back on the market. It will probably sell for a price far below the price the young couple offered, and you'll never find another buyer within ninety days. Now you can't buy the new house and you'll lose the $10,000 deposit it took you and your wife five years to save.

If this imaginary nightmare happened to you, would you

scream that the government had no right to do this to you? Would you protest that your house is your property and you have the right to sell it to whomever you wish, at whatever price you wish? Would you feel like you were in some Alice-in-Wonderland world, where an action you take in your own interest is labeled discrimination and becomes a crime? Would you think this kind of injustice couldn't happen in America, the one place on Earth where you thought your property was secure?

Well, look around. Government commits this injustice on a massive scale, not to homeowners (not yet), but to business owners. The name of this injustice is *affirmative action.*

AFFIRMATIVE ACTION

Affirmative action is a term used by the Equal Employment Opportunity Commission (EEOC) to describe regulations designed to stop employers and school boards from discriminating against minorities and other groups.

Government creates affirmative action laws to give minorities an equal opportunity to get jobs or an education. And since everyone has a "right" to equal treatment, liberals claim that government should force employers to hire, or colleges to enroll, more minority workers or students. But to achieve this goal, affirmative action regulations violate our property rights and discriminate against everyone who isn't a minority member. In reply, liberals say, too bad—the end justifies the means.

Affirmative action and antidiscrimination laws violate our property rights. A company pays employees with the money it earns by selling its goods or services to the public. This money is part of the company's assets and property. A company has lost its property rights if it can't say who and by what standards it will hire or fire employees.

The same principle applies to a privately financed school or college. Entrepreneurs risk time and money to create private schools. The owners have the right to decide which students to admit or which people to hire, based on whatever standards they choose.

A government agency has no right to violate a homeowner's

property rights, as described earlier in our imaginary story. Yet many government agencies have almost unlimited legal powers to violate the property rights of business people. Worse, bureaucrats believe their actions are legal and highly moral.

Why are business owners treated differently than home owners? Why do the courts and the public allow government to strip business people of the same inviolate rights other citizens enjoy?

The answers are profoundly important. Property rights are the hallmark, the foundation, and the protector of other individual rights. The attitude a society holds toward property rights determines whether it stays free or becomes enslaved.

The reason we treat business owners as second-class citizens is that most Americans have accepted two disastrous doctrines: first, that helping others is our moral and political duty; second, that minorities and other groups have an economic right to a job, education, and so on.

Welfare-state liberals claim that our highest moral duty as citizens is to help our fellow human beings. They also claim the right to control or confiscate our property to achieve this goal. They say that helping minorities overcome past discrimination justifies discriminating against white people.

Just as entitlement programs redistribute our income, affirmative action laws redistribute jobs and education through preferential quotas. Just as entitlements confiscate our money to give unearned benefits to others, so affirmative action laws violate our property rights to give unearned benefits to minorities.

Liberals claim that we need preferential quotas. They say that businesses and schools discriminate against minorities and therefore deny them the right to a job or college education. This alleged discrimination therefore hurts minorities and should be stopped.

DISCRIMINATION: THE ASSAULT
ON PROPERTY RIGHTS

The claim that schools and businesses discriminate against minorities rests on a false and twisted definition of discrimination. Discrimination only happens when *laws* deny people the freedom to pursue their goals because of sex, race, religion, skin color, and so on. When the Declaration of Independence stated that all men are created equal, it meant equal before the law. Anytime government makes a law that denies one group the same rights and freedom as everyone else, it's committing illegal discrimination.

But discrimination should *not* apply to private property. It should not apply if a property owner denies someone the use of his property because of the person's sex, race, religion, and so on. Property rights means that we have the right to use our property as we wish. A right only protects our freedom to act. It guarantees our right to work for or trade with other people, *but only if these other people agree to the transaction.* A right guarantees your freedom to ask as many people as you want if they will trade with you. It doesn't guarantee that anyone will want to. A right doesn't guarantee you success and it doesn't give you the right to force someone to give you what you want.

For example, say there's an imaginary town where most business owners hate women and French people. This is a sick town, but follow my story. Suppose a very bright French woman is foolish enough to live in this town. She needs a job, so she applies to every business in town. Now a right means that she has the right to go to every business owner and ask for a job. In contrast, the town council has *no right* to pass a law that forbids French women from working in town. That would deny her the freedom to act. But each business owner has the absolute right to refuse to hire her, even though the owner is a stupid bigot who is losing a good worker. Each owner has the right to do what he wants with his property, which includes the right to choose who he does or doesn't want to hire.

The French woman has the right to be furious with the business owners. She has a right to call them stupid bigots. But she has no right to force them to hire her. Her only alternative, if she still choses to live in this town, is to keep making the rounds. She has the right to keep trying until she finds a business owner who is not a bigot and recognizes her intelligence. If she tries hard enough, she will find such an owner. If she can't, then she should find another town or city where stupid bigotry isn't a rampant disease.

A trade requires that both parties agree to the terms of that trade, and each person must respect the other's property rights. Therefore, you have no right to a job if the employer doesn't want to hire you. Likewise, an employer has no right to your labor unless you agree to work for him. Your labor is *your* property. You also have no right to a house if the owner doesn't want to sell to you, or to a college education if the school doesn't want to admit you, and so on.

A right applies to all people, or it's not a right. Just as *you* have the right to choose your school or employer, so the school or employer has the right to choose who they educate or hire. You can't claim freedom of choice and property rights for yourself, but then deny these same rights to other people or businesses.

If a person doesn't want to trade with you, for whatever reason, you're free to trade with someone else. If one bigot doesn't want to trade with you because of your sex or race, you're still free to act. That person can't stop you from trading with someone else who is not a bigot. *Only a law can stop you, and laws come from government, not individuals.*

There's only one basic way that someone can violate your freedom to act: by physical force. In a free society, government has the legal right to use force. A private citizen who uses force against another person is a criminal, and the law can punish him.

In a free society, only government has the legal right to restrict our freedom to act. The Civil Rights movement of the 1960s fought legalized discrimination against blacks by *state and local governments*. These governments had enacted racist laws that violated the political rights of blacks.

It was the police power of southern states that denied blacks the right to vote, to eat in white restaurants, to go to white public schools, or to sit in white seats on a city bus. It was the police power of the state that enforced apartheid in South Africa and murdered six million Jews in Nazi Germany.

Only government can legally forbid economic freedom to a whole race, religion, or sex (women were denied the right to vote by federal voting laws). Only government can impose a legal economic monopoly over an entire city, state, or country that denies minorities or any other group the freedom to act. In the former Soviet Union, and in Cuba and China today, government controls the entire population. If a communist government fires someone because of his religious or political beliefs, he can starve to death because he has nowhere else to go: the state is the only employer.

A private group, business, or individual can't legally restrict your freedom to act. A private citizen has no right to kill you, threaten you, lock you up, or stop you from getting what you want from others. If he tries, he becomes a criminal and can go to jail. In a free society that protects individual rights, only government can use force against you, and it has to justify that force in a court of law.

A private citizen has no right to use force against you, but he does have the right to refuse to let you use his property. Such a refusal is not discrimination; he's simply exercising his right to use his property as he sees fit. He may refuse to deal with you because he's a bigot, but *he has the right to be a bigot with his own property*.

An apartment house owner who refuses to rent to someone who is old, black, or has children is within his rights. That apartment house is his property and he has the right to rent apartments to whomever he chooses. The person he refused is still free to rent an apartment from another landlord who isn't a bigot. The first owner didn't restrict that person's freedom to act; he simply denied him the use of his property. In the same way, if a private school refuses to enroll a child because of the parents' race, color, or religion, that family is free to look for another school not run by bigots.

In these situations, the would-be tenant's or parent's rights weren't violated. *They had no right to that apartment or school in the first place.* They had no right to tell the landlord or school owner how to use his property. In such cases, there's no discrimination involved. You may feel hurt and insulted by a bigot's actions, but even a bigot has a right to his opinions.

America is rich, diverse, and full of opportunity. If one bigot refuses to deal with you because of your race, sex, or the way you part your hair, it's not the end of the world. You can always find other people, employers, or schools who will work with you, if you look for them.

Most decisions we make in life require discrimination in the only reasonable definition of that term: we discriminate when we make judgements or choose between options. We choose the option that best meets our needs, values, or preferences.

When we choose the car we like, the house we live in, the man or woman we marry, the friends we socialize with, the people we do business with, or the toothpaste we brush our teeth with, we discriminate. Personal freedom means we have the right to make choices with our life and property, even if other people think these choices are prejudiced. The notion that we discriminate when we decide what to do with our property is not only wrong, it also attacks our liberty and free choice.

Liberals use a trick to justify affirmative action: *they switch the meaning of discrimination from government laws to private actions.* Liberals claim that you discriminate if you refuse to let someone use your property because you don't like his or her sex, age, race, religion, health condition, sexual preference, or a growing list of other criteria.

Yet when government makes laws that give special privileges to minority groups, laws that necessarily discriminate against others, liberals say this is not discrimination or that it's "justified" discrimination. Therefore, the Constitution that originally protected our property rights has been turned completely upside-down.

Our property rights are now up for grabs. Anyone who wants to use our property can now yell discrimination if we refuse, and get the law to back him up. Government, on the other hand, now has almost unlimited power to discriminate in favor of some groups and against others.

Once we say that discrimination means refusing to let someone use our property, there's no limit to government's power to violate our property rights. Special-interest groups keep pressuring reelection-minded congressmen to dream up new rights that we can't discriminate against. First we couldn't discriminate based on race, color, or religion. Now we can't discriminate based on age, sex, health, disabilities, marital status, sexual orientation, and many more. The list keeps growing every year.

Antidiscrimination laws now extend to drug addicts and alcoholics. An employer who refuses to hire someone who was an alcoholic can get slapped with a lawsuit, because the Disabilities Act protects recovering alcoholics. Federal antidiscrimination laws even protect alcoholics who haven't cured their drinking habit, as long as they don't drink on the job or violate work rules.[1] This policy is not only outrageous, it's also dangerous.

Consider this hypothetical situation. You're the personnel manager for a passenger railroad, and you don't think it's good business policy to kill your customers. Therefore, you won't hire anyone who's had a record of alcohol or drug abuse, even if they say they've recovered. You sympathize with John Smith, a recovered alcoholic who applies for a job as conductor, but your first responsibility is to your customers' lives and safety. You refuse to hire him.

John Smith then files a discrimination lawsuit against you, and regulators force you to hire him. Six months later, John Smith has a relapse. He drinks on the job and wrecks a train, killing two hundred people. On board that train were your wife and children.

Would you ride on a train with John Smith as the conductor? Would you go to a dentist who was forced to hire a dental assistant with AIDS? Would you send your child to a school that was forced to hire a convicted, but "recovering" child molester? Antidiscrimination laws sometimes force businesses to hire people they consider dangerous or incompetent. When these laws violate a business owner's property rights, they also threaten your life and safety.

Consider how the government uses this switched definition of discimination in just one area of the economy—employment laws. An employer can't know in advance when he's breaking the law because courts keep expanding their interpretation of discrimination. Because discrimination is now defined as personal choices with private property, government can legally prosecute almost any employment policy.

Consider this imaginary situation: a company of 100 employees has 60 men, 37 women, 3 blacks, and no homosexuals. The company is already guilty of discrimination based on population statistics. Since 50 percent of the general population is women, then 50 percent of the employees should be women. Since about 6 percent of the population is homosexual, there should be six homosexual employees.

Also, 90 percent of management consists of white men over age fifty. This is clearly discrimination against women, blacks, and white males under age fifty. Also, most of the secretaries are young women, which is age discrimination against older women.

The company is located in a part of the city that is 90 percent Catholic, yet only 45 percent of the employees are Catholic. This is blatant discrimination against Catholics. There are also no Polish or Japanese employees, or men over six feet tall. This is outright national origin and height discrimination. The same applies to firing or promotion policies. The situation becomes ludicrous.

In the end, after spending months sifting through a company's employment records, the bureaucrat in charge of ferreting out discrimination claims that employee 'A' was hired instead of employee 'B' because the company discriminated against employee 'B'.

The employer says that he hired employee 'A' because this person was better qualified. When the bureaucrat then orders the company to hire employee 'B', he insults the business owner's judgment, tells him who he can or can't hire, and violates the owner's property rights. The bureaucrat, who probably doesn't have the talent or ambition to run a lemonade stand, presumes he has the right to dictate employment policies to a man who risked his time, money, and life to create a successful company.

A company's employment practices are an integral part of its business. The primary goal of a business is to make profits. A company usually hires, fires, or promotes employees based on competence. An employer judges an employee by his ability to do the job and by how much the employee contributes to the company's goals. A company's profits and future depend on its right to decide which employee is best for each job.

When government dictates hiring policies to employers, bureaucratic whim takes over. But the bureaucrat doesn't care about the company's health or profits; he only cares about making sure the employer hires the "correct" number of employees from each minority group. So government forces the employer to hire an applicant based on sex or race, instead of competence. Because there's no practical way to decide who to hire based on membership in a minority group, the bureaucrat uses arbitrary quotas. Antidiscrimination bureaucrats make employment decisions based on sex, race, age, and so on. But because they represent the government, they think there's nothing wrong with this policy.

Antidiscrimination laws create arbitrary standards that force employers to hire people they wouldn't hire if they had the choice. Since a company only has so many jobs available, the employer has to reject those applicants who are more qualified so that less qualified applicants get the job. *When government gives special privileges to one group, it necessarily violates the rights of others.*

Affirmative action liberals sometimes admit that their regulations violate other peoples' rights. But they claim that we need this policy to make up for past discrimination against blacks and other minority groups. They claim that it's perfectly moral to violate the rights of innocent people to correct past wrongs against a particular group.

Over three hundred years of slavery and government-enforced segregation kept blacks from getting the same job skills, education, and economic freedom that most of us take for granted. But this past discrimination was mostly political. State Jim Crow laws created and enforced discrimination. These laws violated blacks' political rights and restricted their economic freedom. When slavery was abolished and discrimination laws declared unconstitutional, blacks finally gained political and economic freedom.

This country committed horrible crimes against blacks. But it also committed crimes against American Indians, interned Japanese, Chinese laborers, and other minority groups through the years. In each case, government laws created the injustice.

The American *government* killed Indians and put them on reservations. The American government interned Japanese-American citizens. In the gold-rush days, the city of San Francisco passed laws that discriminated against Chinese immigrants.

Blacks and other minorities still feel angry about the wrongs done to them, and rightly so. But to our credit, America passed laws ending such discrimination. Politically, minorities are now equal with everyone else because laws now protect their rights.

In spite of past wrongs, equality before the law is all that anyone has the right to demand. But blacks and other minorities use affirmative action laws to get restitution from white people who never violated their rights. They use past government-created discrimination to justify violating the political rights of innocent people. Affirmative action laws punish a person, not for some wrong he's done, but for the collective guilt of his ancestors. Affirmative action is original sin, racialized.

An important legal principle of a just society is that a person is guilty or innocent based solely on his actions. To declare a person guilty, to punish him, to violate his rights because of what his dead racial ancestors did, is unjust and irrational. Yet we use this concept to justify affirmative action laws.

Based on the same theory, the following should also happen: Young Americans of German ancestry should have all their income and property confiscated to pay for the murder of six million Jews in Nazi Germany between 1933 and 1945. We should punish all white Americans living today for what their great-grandfathers did to American Indians a hundred years ago. Japanese-Americans today should pay reparations to the United States for the death and destruction Japanese people caused during World War II. We should punish Catholics living today for the Church's Inquisition in the fifteenth century, because their ancestors tortured and murdered Jews and Protestant heretics.

Does this sound crazy? Of course it does. Yet liberals use this theory to justify punishing white Americans for the sins of their great-great-grandfathers.

WITH GOVERNMENT AS YOUR FRIEND, WHO NEEDS ENEMIES?

On the surface, what I've said up to now may seem harsh and uncaring toward minorities. It's not meant to be. In fact, an important reason I'd like to end most taxes, regulations, and entitlements (including affirmative action and antidiscrimination laws), is because the Welfare State hurts minorities worse than any other group.

Minority groups won't get their fair share of the American dream by demanding more entitlement programs. Why? Because the Welfare State's systematic violation of our liberty and property rights eventually wrecks the economy and sends everyone (except bureaucrats) to the poorhouse.

Socialism and communism are political systems that either control or destroy property rights. The more socialist or communist a country is, the poorer its people. It's no accident that Americans enjoy a high standard of living, while the people of India, China, and Russia live in poverty.

Very few Americans, including minority groups, would prefer to live in India or China today. Yet liberal politicians burden us with a mountain of taxes and regulations that suffocate our economy and destroy millions of jobs. In their blind quest to help minorities, liberals don't care that they're turning America into another socialist hell-hole that hurts the people they allegedly want to help.

Minorities, like everyone else, want jobs and a future. But an economy destroyed by liberals has few jobs and no future, except for bureaucrats. Just ask the Russian people. It's much easier to find a job in a free economy that's healthy and growing than in an economy strangled by ever-increasing taxes and regulations. It's much easier to bypass a bigoted employer if there are many other companies who are desperate for workers.

To create more jobs for everyone, we should slash taxes, end regulations and entitlement programs, and dismantle the Welfare State. Business owners would then be free to reinvest their profits and triple their production. Our economy would explode with new jobs for everyone. *This* is the kind of affirmative action we need.

Instead, we're going in the opposite direction. In the name of being a friend and protector of minorities, government increases taxes, creates more entitlement programs, and tightens the noose around our necks with ever more regulations.

How does the Welfare State hurt minorities?

TAXES

High taxes hurt minorities. A minority member in a low-income bracket pays close to 30 percent or more of his income in total taxes. These taxes include not only federal, state, and local income taxes, but also sales tax, Social Security tax, and miscellaneous others. That's hard-earned money he can't afford to lose.

It's money he could have used for school tuition. If he was better educated, he would have more skills for the job market and a brighter future. The money could pay for medical insurance so he isn't wiped out when he gets sick. It could pay for his child's education. He might even save the extra money to start his own business. Or, he could simply put the money in the bank for retirement. He would have the option to use his money for his own life, not have it taxed away by government.

Business taxes also affect minorities. Every penny of tax that a business pays to government adds to the cost of doing business. These include sales, corporate, real estate, commercial use, disability, worker's compensation, unemployment insurance, Social Security, and federal, state, and local income taxes.

These taxes are a major expense for companies. Businesses simply add the taxes to the price of everything we buy, raising retail prices for everyone. These price increases make it harder for low-income minorities to pay for food, rent, and other basics.

Business taxes and regulations also destroy jobs. The Welfare State strangles the economy. When everyone is struggling to keep their heads above water, there's a limit to how much businesses can increase prices. If they can't increase prices, and taxes keep going up, the only way to stay in business is to cut other expenses. They do this by firing people or substituting machines or computers for workers. That's what's happening in the economy today. Hundreds of big companies are firing thousands of workers, even though the economy is out of the recession.

Social Security taxes hurt minorities in another way. They prevent minorities from closing the income gap between rich and poor. A low-income couple, working to age 65, could save a nest egg of close to $300,000 if they could put their Social Security taxes into a personal IRA account.[2] They could pass this money on to their children. The nest egg would give the kids a big push up the economic ladder and help close the gap between rich and poor in this country.

Assume for a minute that we dismantled the Welfare State and phased out all entitlement programs. Let's say by doing this we reduce the federal tax bite from the current $1 trillion to a mere $200 billion a year. This would put $800 billion a year back into taxpayers' pockets. Most of this money would go into personal bank accounts, and banks would recirculate this $800 billion back into the economy.

Can you imagine the explosion in our economy, in the jobs created, and in our standard of living if this happened? The expanding economy would create so many new jobs that employers would be desperate for workers to fill all the positions opening up. Most employers couldn't *afford* to be stupid bigots and discriminate—they would hire anyone who could do the job. In a free, dynamic economy the color most business people care about is green, the color of money.

This isn't just theory. Sioux Falls, South Dakota is a boom town with a 1.9 percent unemployment rate, the lowest in the nation (as of May 1994). It's a boom town because it's friendly to business. South Dakota has no corporate or personal income tax and fewer regulations than most other states.

As a result, new businesses are popping up like mushrooms. There are growing numbers of manufacturing plants that are begging for workers to fill all the jobs, and companies keep raising their wages to attract workers away from their competitors or other states. John Morrell & Company, a packing plant that employs 2800 workers, has to pay a starting salary of $9 an hour to attract enough workers.[3]

The intense demand for workers in the booming Sioux Falls economy gives native Americans and other minorities good paying jobs. Sioux Falls business owners don't care about a job applicant's race or color because workers are too much in demand.

Imagine if we dismantled the Welfare State and the entire country was on fire like South Dakota. Competition and a booming economy would create millions of new jobs, and wages would go up. Minorities could get their piece of the American dream without regulations, affirmative action, or antidiscrimination laws.

THE DEFICIT

The huge deficit takes away billions of dollars of precious capital that could circulate back into the economy for job-creating investments. Most taxes saved by eliminating the deficit would end up in bank savings accounts. Banks could then lend this money to minorities who want to buy a home, start a business, or send their children to college. Other businesses would get loans to expand in an exploding economy. This would increase jobs for minorities and create fierce new competition that lowered prices for everything from bicycles to health care.

The deficit discriminates against minorities because, like heavy taxes, it strangles the economy, pushes up interest rates, and becomes a time bomb for our children. Without growth, the economy stagnates and job opportunities disappear for minorities and everyone else.

Now let's see how regulations hurt minorities.

Zoning Regulations

Zoning regulations often stop minorities from moving into established residential neighborhoods. These regulations set minimum lot and house sizes, pushing home prices beyond the reach of low-income families. And zoning regulations often prohibit apartment houses in many residential areas, which restricts low-cost housing. These restrictions make it difficult for lower-income families to find reasonably priced apartments to rent in good neighborhoods. That, in turn, keeps these families from sending their children to better public schools.

Environmental Regulations

Environmental regulations raise the cost of thousands of products, from houses to plastic toys. Home builders now have to file environmental impact statements on large projects, which delays construction by years and adds thousands of dollars to the cost of a home. Logging restrictions to protect owls sharply increases lumber prices, which also adds thousands of dollars to construction costs. Higher prices make it difficult for low-income minorities to afford a home.

Environmental regulations that protect so-called wetlands, endangered species areas, or coastal preservation areas, take millions of acres of land off the market. This raises the price of buildable land areas, which again raises house prices.

Federal and state governments own millions of acres of land in this country. The state government owns more than half the land in California, and the federal government owns more than 90 percent of the land in Alaska. The same applies in many other states. This cheap, government-owned land could be used for building homes, apartment houses, and shopping centers, but environmental regulations keep this land off the market. In turn, apartment rents and house prices in built-up areas increase because regulations restrict the supply of land for new houses and apartments. Elitist members of the Sierra Club get to enjoy the fresh air and beautiful views in these restricted lands. But minorities who desperately need a decent environment for their kids, can't live in these areas.

Environmental regulations increase the cost of oil and electric power. Thousands of products are made from oil, including plastics, clothing, gasoline, and so on, and everyone uses electric power. These regulations add thousands of dollars to car prices, inflate our electric bills, and increase the price of almost every product we buy. As we noted earlier, higher prices hurt low-income minorities on tight budgets.

Rent Control Laws

Rent controls don't benefit low-income minorities. Wherever they apply, builders and apartment house investors stay away. Investors are afraid to build in areas where rents are controlled, and owners often let their existing buildings deteriorate because controlled rents are too low. This situation reduces new apartment house construction. In turn, the supply of decent apartments decreases and rents increase for everyone else.

New York City is a case in point. Fifty years of rent controls have restricted the supply of decent apartments and increased the rent of decontrolled apartments. Low-income minorities can't afford the high rents in decontrolled apartments, which forces them to stay in crime-ridden, rent-controlled ghetto slums.

In most areas of the country without rent controls, there's an abundance of apartments at reasonable rents. When there are no controls, apartment house investors keep building until the market is saturated. The sharp increase in apartments then lowers rent levels. The free market takes care of the problem.

Minimum Wage Laws

Minimum wages hurt minorities by eliminating jobs. When government increases the minimum wage, low-income employees are often thrown out of work. Minimum wage laws discourage companies from hiring young people, minorities, those with little education or experience, or immigrants who can't speak English. Businesses are willing to hire these people, but only at lower wages. That's because the employees have poor job skills, language problems, or little education. Minimum wage laws prevent minorities from getting entry-level jobs where, if they work hard and are conscientious, they could learn a useful trade. Government creates minimum wage laws *because* many people would work for below-minimum wages to get a job. In effect, minimum wage laws stop people from working as much as they discourage companies from hiring them.

If someone wants to work for below-minimum wages and employers will hire them, why does government have the right to interfere? Immigrants, teenagers, and minorities, those who find it most difficult to find jobs, are shut out of many jobs by these laws.

Like Mexican laborers who cross the Rio Grande at night to work in the fields of California, other minorities would work at low-paying jobs because it benefits them. *No one forces anyone to work.* No one works at a low-wage job unless he wants to and unless he gains by it. Again, what right does government have to interfere in an arrangement where both parties benefit and want to work with each other?

Occupational Licensing Laws

Occupational licensing laws put up roadblocks against minorities who want to work for themselves or start a small business. For example, let's look at how taxi license regulations affect minorities.

The number of taxis in Los Angeles is only about one-fifteenth the number of taxis in Washington, D.C.. But Los Angeles is over seven times the size of the nation's capital. If Los Angeles had only five times more taxis than it does under restrictive licensing, thousands of low-income minority members could have jobs. Since there are about 3,000 licensed occupations, license regulations have a devastating effect on minorities.[4]

Most cities own and operate municipal services such as bus lines, garbage collection, and fire protection. These are city-run monopolies that stop competition by law. What if private enterprise ran these services? A city resident could then choose his private bus, garbage collector, or fire protection company like he chooses his grocery store.

Minorities could then start businesses to supply these services. If you had a used car, you could open a taxi service. With a van, you could start a local bus route. If you had a small truck, you could start a local garbage pickup business, and so on. City workers would no longer have a monopoly on these jobs, and customers would pay less for the service because of increased competition.

Drugs

Drugs kill, destroy peoples' lives, turn children into criminals, and spread AIDS from contaminated needles. Drugs create a culture of inner-city violence that murders thousands of young men and tears minority communities apart. Government regulations cause this havoc.

Drugs cause violence *because they're illegal*. Make drugs legal like alcohol or cigarettes and much of the violence would fade away. If drugs were legal, they would be cheap. You could buy them in a pharmacy over the counter like a pack of cigarettes. If they were as cheap as cigarettes, young pushers couldn't make big profits selling them on street corners. Organized crime would quit the drug business, just as they quit the booze business when Prohibition ended. The free market would drive them out.

Much of the violence in inner cities comes from drug users who commit crimes to support their habit. If drugs are cheap, legal, and freely available, drug users won't need much money to support their habits. Do people commit robbery to get money for aspirin? It would be the same with drugs.

This is not just theory, because legalization worked in England. Legalization in the form of medicalization, where doctors give drugs to addicts, kept England free of drug-related crime for 50 years. Then in 1971, the British prohibited drugs and imposed severe jail sentences for drug pushing and possessing. Result: Drugs have become Britain's No. 1 crime problem.[5]

Even under prohibition, British doctors are allowed to set up programs to supply drugs to addicts. Dr. John Marks started such a program in Liverpool in 1982. What happened was extraordinary.

"The crime rate among addicts went down 96 percent," doctor Marks said in an interview. "Even more surprising, astonishing really, is the number of new addicts decreased geometrically. We compared our results with a nearby town that has prohibition and their rate of new addicts was twelve-fold higher than ours."[6]

If drugs were legal, drugstores or medical clinics could sell cheap, clean, disposable needles. We would prevent many deaths and the spread of AIDS because drug users would not have to use dirty needles anymore. Users could take drugs under the supervision of a local doctor. That doctor could prevent deaths from overdose and try to wean users off their habit.

Here's what happened in Dr. Marks's Liverpool drug addict clinic: "Because the needles are clean, there have been no AIDS cases in Dr. Marks's clinic and no deaths from overdoses or polluted narcotics."[7]

Illegal drugs create violence, and violence breeds violence. Drug users and pushers buy handguns to commit crimes, and other kids then buy guns to protect themselves. The guns and killing escalate until it becomes an epidemic.

If drugs were legal, many guns would disappear because fewer people would need them. The drug pushers would go out of business and the drug users wouldn't have to rob anymore. Drug-related gun use and crime would diminish. The circle of violence would be broken.

I am *not* saying it's good to take drugs. It's stupid and dangerous. But there's little difference between drugs, alcohol, or cigarettes. Many people kill themselves with alcohol and cigarettes. Alcohol kills thousands of people in car accidents, and smoking kills people by causing lung cancer and other diseases.

But we have a right to wreck our bodies if we want to. It's *our* bodies. Personal freedom means that we have the right to make choices about our lives and our bodies. The right to make choices also means the right to make the *wrong* choices. This is the essence of personal freedom.

If someone has the right to kill himself with alcohol or cigarettes, which kill far more people than drugs, what twist of logic or morality makes it right to ban drugs? No matter how much we may hate the idea of people taking drugs, government has no right to tell us what we can or can't do to our own bodies. No one has the right to be morality dictator with other peoples' minds and bodies.

To repeat: Drugs kill people because they're illegal. They're illegal because of government regulations. Remove the regulations and we'll stop most of the killing.

Birth Control

For many reasons, low-income minorities often have more children than middle-class families. They know less about contraceptives, have less money to pay for abortions or birth control pills, and many live under a welfare system that rewards them for having children. Having too many children locks minority parents (very often single mothers) into a lifetime of poverty.

Yet many regulations put obstacles in the way of family planning. Right now, many state legislatures are trying to pass laws that restrict a woman's right to an abortion. *This hurts minority women most of all,* because they can't afford to travel to another state to get an abortion.

For years, FDA regulations have kept the French abortion drug RU-238 from being sold in America. French women have been using the drug for ten years. It induces abortion with a pill, providing a cheap, simple, and nonsurgical way to have an abortion. Yet government regulations prevent minority women in this country from using it.

Worst of all, welfare programs that give aid to unwed mothers and their dependent children have disastrous effects on minorities. These programs give unwed mothers incentives to have more babies, and turn the mothers into dependents of the state. Having too many children that they can't support ruins the lives of millions of young girls. It destroys their independence and their future.

Health Care Regulations

Health care regulations make life harder for minorities. Medical licensing laws restrict the number of available doctors, squash price competition among doctors, restrict the procedures that nurses or physician-assistants can do, and raise the cost of health care for everyone.

Government regulations that control hospitals raise the cost of treatment, restrict free-market competition, and reduce the number of hospitals. Regulations on the health care industry sharply increase health insurance premiums. Low-income minorities are not able to afford these high premiums.

As a result, many poor minority patients without insurance use hospital emergency rooms for their health care needs. Waiting can literally kill them because they often have to wait many hours before seeing a doctor.

Government-Run Schools

Public education is state run, like the Post Office. That's why many inner-city schools are war-zone children killers. Besides drugs, violence, and the schools' horrible physical condition, the quality of education stinks. Inner-city children in such schools are lucky if they get out alive, especially young boys. They're lucky if they learn anything other than how to survive in a violent, hostile world.

We can change these conditions by getting government out of the education business—*by ending its monopoly on educating our children.* School vouchers are only a first step. Government-run school systems should be phased out and turned over to free enterprise.

Entrepreneurs in minority communities could be at the forefront of this change. If there was a free market in education, anyone could open a school. In the past, minority entrepreneurs tried to start their own schools or teach their children at home, but were stopped by state regulations. State bureaucrats closed the schools. Why? Because the teachers weren't licensed by the state, the local teacher's union objected, the school didn't meet the accreditation standards of the local Board of Education, or compulsory education laws required the kids to attend the local approved, drug-infested high school. In short, regulations and bureaucrats stopped minority entrepreneurs from opening schools in their own neighborhoods.

In America, there are over thirty million people who are functionally illiterate. This means they can't read a want ad properly, fill out an application for a job, or do simple arithmetic problems.[8] Ghetto, government-run schools foster illiteracy and add to the problem. If education is a way out of the ghettos and the road to a better future, then public schools have left minorities in the gutter. The way to solve this problem is to separate education from government.

If private enterprise ran education, we would have thousands of storefront schools popping up all over our inner cities, providing low-cost, innovative education for local kids. The schools would run the gamut from local neighborhood tutors, to computer education centers, to huge education companies that open local neighborhood branches.

Minority parents understand that education is crucial to their children's future. Good education is a huge unfulfilled need. Entrepreneurs would meet that need by creating thousands of new schools. These schools would give kids a low-cost, no-frills education that concentrated on the basics of reading, writing, and arithmetic. Fierce competition would drive down tuition costs to a level that low-income parents could afford.

> Take East Palo Alto, California, for instance—a very poor black community of 19,000. Dismayed by the failure of public schools to teach and maintain discipline, Gertrude Wilks founded the Nairobi Day School in 1966. The school's 55 pupils pay only $60 per month tuition— $540 per school year. Students at Nairobi work hard, and nearly all succeed. The school's methods are so successful, in fact, that Wilks *offers a money-back guarantee for those who fail to learn to read within the year* (emphasis added).
>
> Similarly successful is Marva Collins Westside Preparatory School in Chicago. Begun in 1975 in a poor, black area, the school teaches minority children, many of who have been classed as "slow learners." At Westside their achievement levels improve dramatically, thanks to Collins's blend of individual attention, 3-Rs basics, and the classics.[9]

Many local governments force children to stay in high school until age sixteen. The violent troublemakers who don't wan't to be in school make life miserable for the other students. If we ended compulsory education laws, free-enterprise schools could kick out violent troublemakers. Children would learn in a safe environment.

So a major way that government regulations hurt minorities and destroy their children's future is through government-run public schools. We should abolish them.

I could list many more regulations, but I've made my point. Regulations hurt minorities in so many ways that minorities should be screaming to abolish them. As I wrote in the title to this section: "with government as your friend, who needs enemies?"

A BRIGHT FUTURE WITH A FREE ECONOMY

Minorities are desperate to find a solution to their problems. They grow angry and frustrated at the violence and poverty in their communities, and they see no future for themselves or their children. They think the system is against them.

And it is, *but not in the way they think.* The system that's against them is not the free market. We don't have a free market in this country. We have a Welfare State that taxes and regulates us into poverty. It's the Welfare State that ruins the lives of blacks and other minorities.

In contrast, a totally free economy would be their best friend. If we abolished the Welfare State, the economy would explode. Jobs for minorities and everyone else would be plentiful. Housing would be low-cost and plentiful. There would be less violence in minority communities because drugs would be legal. Free-market education would be safe, inexpensive, and high-quality.

Welfare could be phased out completely, which would make minority families stronger. With welfare, food stamps, and similar programs ended, the only road to a better future would be through education and hard work. Young women wouldn't get money for children born out of wedlock. Contraceptives and abortion would be safe, cheap, and readily available, especially with the RU-238 abortion pill.

If we ended subsidy and entitlement programs, taxes would be reduced to almost ground zero. With income taxes and Social Security taxes eliminated, minorities would have more money to start a business, educate themselves, and save for retirement, medical expenses, or their children's future. The gap between low-income minorities and the middle class and rich could start to close. Minorities would get their share of the American dream, as they rightfully deserve.

CHAPTER 4

REGULATIONS—DO THEY REALLY PROTECT US?

Welfare-state bureaucrats think we need protection from evil, sloppy, or malicious business people who might cheat us, pollute our air, sell us harmful products, and so on. To allegedly protect our health and safety, government creates a suffocating web of regulations that strangle our economy.

Thousands of agencies on the local, state, and federal levels control every part of our lives. Government regulates wages, land use, health care, education, product safety, transportation, food production, drug development, communications, labor relations, employment standards, building construction, occupational licensing, and much more.

We spend enormous sums to run the agencies and pay the bureaucrats. Regulations cost businesses hundreds of billions of dollars in lost profits, constant aggravation, decreased competitiveness, millions of hours in lost time, and inflated product prices.

It's estimated that federal regulations alone cost taxpayers over $400 billion a year, of which $100 billion goes just for paperwork.[1] Why do we endure this burden? Why do we have so many regulations? Do they accomplish their purpose? Is their $400 billion (and rising) price tag worth it? Lastly, does government have the right to impose these regulations in the first place?

Why do we have regulations? Let's examine this question first.

"DO SOMETHING ABOUT IT!"

Regulations come from our understandable desire to help people who are in trouble. A regulation usually starts with an alleged problem. The problem usually starts with a group of angry and vocal people claiming that some industry or corporation has hurt them in some way.

They could be patients complaining that a pharmaceutical company sells drugs with bad side effects, workers complaining that a corporation doesn't pay decent wages, tenants complaining that their landlord charges too much rent, consumers complaining about the high cost of health insurance, or environmentalists complaining that kangaroo rats need protection. The list is endless.

A cry for action goes out, demanded in the name of the public interest. Angry voters put political pressure on reelection-minded legislators to pass a bill that will solve the problem. Then Congress creates or expands a regulatory agency, and gives it powers to enforce the new laws. The legislators, feeling a glow from helping their constituents, then go on their merry way to pacify the next group screaming for laws to solve its problem.

Meanwhile, the regulatory agency goes to work on the first problem. Those industries affected by the regulations either find a way to get around the new laws or try to influence the regulatory agency for their own benefit. Or even worse, the regulatory agency "solves" the problem, only to find that its solution creates far more serious problems.

It costs millions of dollars to comply with these regulations, and the regulated industry has to pass these costs on to consumers. Thousands of regulations in hundreds of industries raise consumer prices across the board.

The new laws also create an entrenched bureaucracy. Bureaucrats have a vested interest in expanding the regulations because their generous pensions, paychecks, and cushy jobs would end if the regulations were eliminated.

We then get a catch-22 situation: either regulations don't solve the problem, or they solve it at the expense of consumers, the regulated industry, and employees that the industry has to fire to cut expenses. But instead of repealing the original regulations, bureaucrats become more vindictive toward the producers. Congress gives bureaucrats the job of regulating industry to protect the public. When regulations raise consumer prices and destroy jobs, bureaucrats blame producers for being greedy or selfish. Bureaucrats and congressional committees then try to "persuade" producers to lower their prices. In a recent example, a congressional subcommittee tried to persuade the chairmen of five pharmaceutical companies to lower their drug prices.

When persuasion doesn't work, bureaucrats create *more* regulations or impose multimillion dollar fines on the industry. Government administers more poison as an antidote to the first regulatory poison. Today, a constant stream of new regulations, imposed on a widening circle of industries, robs consumers, causes chronic, long-term inflation, strangles our economy, and throws millions of Americans out of work.

But instead of blaming government for these problems, we blame the free market. We make producers and business owners into scapegoats. We believe liberals who say that the producers' duty is to serve the public, not to make profits, and that government should force producers to do their duty. This welfare-state philosophy destroys our liberty, ruins the economy, and makes producers the slaves of bureaucrats.

I'm not trying to scare you with exaggeration. The process I described happened in pre-Nazi Germany, precommunist Russia, and many countries in Asia, Africa, and South America that are presently fascist, socialist, or welfare states. These countries' citizens endure tyranny and poverty as a way of life.

WHAT ARE REGULATIONS SUPPOSED TO ACCOMPLISH?

Congress usually creates regulations after people have been hurt by a company's product or service. One notorious example is the deformed babies born by mothers who took the drug Thalidomide. Other examples are defective cars killing drivers, health insurance companies' refusing to insure people with preexisting conditions, and a collapsed building killing people because a contractor used shoddy materials. Bureaucrats claim that regulations protect us against such defective products and unscrupulous business practices.

The harm regulators want to stop usually affects relatively few people. Often there's no harm involved, and the regulations simply promote liberals' political agenda. Yet regulations shackle an entire industry to prevent future problems. For example, bureaucrats strangle the entire pharmaceutical industry to prevent future Thalidomides.

Regulations try to protect us from the pain and suffering that life, the free market, or other people cause. Bureaucrats presume that we have a right to this protection, and that they're the only ones who can provide it. Both premises are wrong.

In a free market, force is banned by law. Trade requires the voluntary consent of the parties involved and no one has the right to use force to gain something from others. In trading, each person respects the other's property. Anyone who uses force or fraud is not a trader but a criminal who is subject to the penalty of law.

We have the right to expect that people abide by their agreements with us. We also have a right to be protected from violence and fraud. The police and our criminal law system give us that protection. If you believe that someone polluted your water supply, or made a drug that hurt you, or cheated you in a business transaction, you could take them to court. In such cases, all you need is the right to prove your claim. If the jury agrees with you, they'll award you damages.

Our civil and criminal law systems aren't perfect, because we can only use them *after* we've been hurt. But no one has a right to damages for an alleged wrong unless he can prove that wrong in court. Otherwise the defendant might be punished for something he didn't do.

But regulations are preventive law—they punish whole industries for alleged future crimes that usually never take place. Regulations don't right actual wrongs; instead, they try to eliminate *potential* harm. They try to legislate away the dangers of nature and human weakness. But in their never-ending quest to take the risks out of life, regulators violate our political rights and personal freedom.

REGULATIONS ARE IMMORAL AND ILLEGAL

We base our legal system on the principle that a person is presumed innocent until proven guilty. Therefore, government has no right to fine, arrest, or imprison someone unless that person has been properly accused, indicted, and tried by a jury of his peers in court. In criminal proceedings, it's the plaintiff's responsibility to prove guilt beyond a reasonable doubt based on facts presented in court.

The law can punish someone only when he causes actual physical or psychological harm to another person. The law can't punish a person for an act or crime he never committed. It can't punish him for the actions of another person or group, or for the possible consequences of his actions. *Yet regulations break these fundamental rules of law*: they punish companies for the actions of others, for acts they never commited, or for the possible consequences of their actions.

Remember, people create businesses, so businesses should have the same legal rights as you and I. Yet regulations punish business owners by restricting their freedom and forcing them to spend huge sums to comply with the regulations. Government presumes that the owner of a company is guilty of a crime he never committed, simply because his company is part of an industry it regulates. The company then has to *prove its innocence* to the regulatory cops. A legal system that forces someone to prove his innocence to power-hungry bureaucrats belongs in a fascist or communist country, not in America. Yet that's the legal system behind regulations.

For example, the FDA forces pharmaceutical companies to spend up to seven years and $100 million to test new drugs. The FDA *assumes* that drug companies would deliberately sell unsafe drugs, without having to prove this in court. In effect, the FDA punishes drug companies because they *might* sell harmful drugs or because thirty years ago, some company sold Thalidomide.

Congress creates affirmative action laws that force employers to hire minority employees. These laws punish business owners and violate their property rights. Government bureaucrats dictate employment policy to a business owner who committed no crime. They punish the owner because he *might* discriminate or because other employers discriminated in the past. Worse, discrimination *should not be a crime in the first place.* As we saw earlier, owners have a right to "discriminate" with their own property.

Big companies who want to merge often have to get Federal Trade Commission (FTC) approval. The FTC arbitrarily *assumes* that the merging companies intend to create a monopoly. It then assumes that this alleged monopoly would overcharge us or force smaller companies out of business. The FTC assumes that customers have a right to the companies' products at a "reasonable" price. It also assumes that small companies have a right to stay in business, even if big companies are more efficient. But neither customers or small companies have such a right.

The merging companies are *presumed guilty* of trying to stifle competition and must prove their innocence to FTC bureaucrats before they can merge. The companies commit the crime of trying to become more efficient. As punishment for this crime, the FTC violates their liberty and property rights. It also forces the companies to wait sometimes years for the bureaucrats' *permission* to merge.

In late 1993, Bell Atlantic Corporation announced plans to buy Tele-Communications Inc., the country's biggest cable-television company. This merger will speed up the data superhighway link between telephone systems and cable television, bringing huge new benefits and services to consumers.

What was the government's response? It created a regulatory nightmare that will delay the merger for years. The companies need the direct approval or acquiescence of Congress, the FCC, the FTC, and the Justice Department. At the state level, the merger has to be reviewed by public utility commissions in Bell Atlantic's telephone service areas. At the local level, the merger will face the review of about 1,600 city council franchise authorities.[2] Here we have two giants of the communication industry wanting to merge and bring us wondrous new services that we never had before. Yet government makes them go through a regulatory nightmare.

Even if this merger created a monopoly (which it won't, because there's so much competition), so what? No monopoly ever lasts very long in the free market. The free market is one giant arena of companies trying to beat their competition in one way or another. That's the *essence* of the free market. If consumers like a new product or service, other companies soon enter the field and destroy a company's attempts to create a monopoly.

These companies are giving us a service we never had before. They have the absolute right to merge and charge whatever they want, without having to get a bureaucrat's approval. Instead of blessing these companies, government violates their property rights and hurts consumers.

We don't need bureaucrats to protect us. Consumers are king (and queen) in the marketplace. Consumers decide who succeeds or who doesn't, and they're ruthless. If the companies charged monopoly prices for their new service, they would be in trouble. They would have few customers, or high profits would bring in competitors who charged lower prices. Monopoly prices would create the competition that destroyed the monopoly.

Electric power companies also go through a regulatory nightmare to build new power plants. They have to file environmental impact statements with the EPA. The grotesque premise here is that we have to protect fish from warm water that power plants eject. Adding insult to injury, regulators presume that utilities are guilty of hurting the fish before any charge, proof, or court proceeding takes place. Utility companies bring us life-giving electricity that heats our homes and cooks our food. Yet eco-cops violate the property rights of utility companies because power plants give fish a warm bath.

DO REGULATIONS PROTECT US?

Imagine the following: there's an outbreak of food poisoning in a big city. Investigators discover a toxic substance in the bread sold by a large supermarket, and many customers become deathly ill. The voters write angry letters to their congressmen to do something. "Protect us!" they demand.

But the problem is that no one knows which farm grew the tainted wheat used in the poisoned loaves. No one knows which farmer mistakenly used the wrong chemical fertilizer on his wheat crop.

So the bureaucrats come up with a brilliant solution. To stop the food poisoning, they confiscate all wheat supplies and close down every wheat farm in the United States. Would you say the regulators solved the problem? Well, of course they did. They stopped the outbreaks of food poisoning, didn't they?

But millions of Americans are now starving because all wheat has been confiscated and there's no bread in the stores. As usual, the regulators' "solution" created far more serious problems than the relatively minor one they set out to solve.

Let's look at another hypothetical situation. Suppose a patient has a cancer growth on his nose which could spread and kill him if not treated. The patient's doctor, trained in the Washington School of Medical Bureaucracy, comes up with the perfect solution—he amputates the patient's head. When the patient's relatives scream at the doctor, he can't understand why they're so angry. He stopped the spread of the cancer, didn't he?

Do you think these imaginary stories have no relation to reality? Think again. These kinds of "solutions" are the essence of government regulation.

At first glance, regulations may seem to accomplish their purpose. The FDA may occasionally stop a harmful drug like Thalidomide from being sold. The FCC may sometimes keep "objectionable" television programs off the air. FTC food inspectors may sometimes stop bad chickens from coming to market.

But regulations have devastating consequences. They usually inflict far more damage on many more people than their short-term, temporary benefits are worth. Regulations are like snow. One snowflake can't hurt us, but billions of them in a blizzard can bury a town.

For the past two years, Congress has been threatening drug companies with price controls because voters have been complaining about high drug prices. Price controls is a regulatory blizzard that would bury new drug development.

In 1993, for example, brokerage companies cancelled more than $500 million in public and private stock offerings for new drug and medical-device companies because of the threat of price controls. Worse, if Congress passes drug price controls, new drug development will slow to a trickle. That's because drug companies will be afraid to invest millions of dollars in research.

> Schering-Plough spent $100 million for a plant to make alpha interferon when that drug was known only to help a rare cancer. Under price controls such an effort would not be made—nor the discovery that the drug treats 15 other diseases.[3]

The regulator, like the entitlement-program liberal, believes that the end justifies the means. He thinks his regulations are just and moral because his goal is pure—he wants to protect us. To achieve this end, he'll use any means available. He sees nothing wrong in violating the property rights of whole industries or strangling the economy with his regulations.

For the same reason, he also arrogantly disregards the devastating effects of his regulations. These regulations increase the price of everything we buy, and bankrupt businesses, throwing thousands of people out of work. In the last ten years, 168 sawmills shut down and over 30,000 people lost their jobs because environmental regulations shut down logging in the northwest's old-growth forests.[4] *This is the effect of just one regulation from one federal agency.*

Why do laws with good intentions wreak havoc with our lives and the economy? Because regulations kill our desire to work and shoot a poisoned arrow into the heart of the free-market system. When regulations strangle the free market, they ruin our ambition.

HOW REGULATIONS KILL AMBITION

Productivity depends on technology. Technology creates the machines and production systems that build our cars, houses, and television sets. A worker without tools produces only what his muscular strength and endurance allow, which isn't very much. Machines increase his output.

A blacksmith two hundred years ago might have worked an hour to shape a few bars of iron into horseshoes. A technician in a modern steel plant can produce thousands of horseshoes in the same time by pressing a few buttons. In India, a typical peasant works from sunup to sundown to plow a few acres of land. In America, a farmer can cultivate thirty acres a day without walking a step because he uses tractors instead of oxen. Before we had modern textile machinery, a woman spent weeks of painstaking labor to weave the cloth for her daughter's dress. Today, that same woman can control machinery that turns out thousands of bolts of fabric in a day.

The economy expands when machines (technology) take over dirty, repetitive, and labor intensive jobs. Increased production lowers the price of everything we buy. That's why greater productivity creates a better standard of living for everyone.

But increased productivity doesn't happen by itself. First someone has to invent the machinery; then an entrepreneur has to risk his money to build the industrial plants that produce the product. Because people, not robots, invent our life-giving technology, we have to be deeply concerned about why they do this. What motivates investors and entrepreneurs to risk their money on new ideas and technology? What pushed Henry Ford to make millions of cars, or Steven Jobs to produce millions of computers? What lights an entrepreneur's spark and fans his ambition despite risks, problems, and setbacks? The answer is: freedom and rewards.

People must be free to create, and they want to know they'll get rewards if they create something others value. Edison expected rewards for inventing the light bulb and the phonograph. George Eastman expected rewards for producing affordable cameras. Blue-collar and office workers expect a reward (paycheck) for their contributions in producing their company's car, airplane, or computer.

If we can't keep what we earn, if bureaucrats steal our rewards and control our property, then we lose our energy and ambition. Work and reward have to be inseparable, for several crucial reasons.

Psychologically, we get great pleasure from creating something good and useful. When we're productive, our self-esteem rises. We enjoy learning and growing, and we gain a sense of pride and accomplishment. If we get no reward for our efforts, we feel that no one appreciates us. We lose our desire to keep working. When we're denied rewards it's like being slapped in the face.

The link between work and reward also affects our standard of living. Rewards act like a ship's rudder: if we're succeeding, we know our actions and judgment have been correct. If we're not succeeding, we change course. Poor results force us to plan better and redouble our efforts to reach our goals.

Rewards are the gold ring on the carousel—they spur us on and keep us going. If, after all our efforts, regulations confiscate our gold ring, we feel enraged and stop trying.

A *New York Times* article about Californians hurt by the recession clearly illustrated this point. It discussed how heavy-handed environmental regulations pushed many California business owners to move out of the state, taking jobs with them.[5]

In the article, Rosemary Ruiz, the owner of Independent Forge, an Orange County company that makes metal parts for airplanes and other uses, said, "I could set the world on fire, but the state [of California] could douse it out."[6] California regulations are such a burden that she's afraid to expand her business. Multiply her frustration by millions of other business owners who are choked by regulations, and you can imagine what regulations do to our economy.

Morally, the link between work and reward tells us that this world is just and fair. The link confirms the principle that we should get rewards, *not punishment*, when we produce things that other people value. If we work hard, take risks, and persevere, we have a right to keep the money we earn.

Politically, the link between work and reward tells us that we have a right to our life, and that government's job is to protect that right. It confirms the principle that our freedom and hard-earned money don't belong to society, the public, the majority, savings and loan bankers, or any other special-interest group that wants to steal from us.

Government regulations, and taxes that regulate our income, cut the link between work and reward in principle. They tell us that we have no *right* to what we earn and that bureaucrats can control our rewards and our lives. They choke our desire to work and achieve, and threaten our standard of living.

Anyone who values his own judgment and believes he has a right to what he earns will resent bureaucratic controls. Independent people stop working when bureaucrats choke them with regulations. They strike back by retiring, folding their business, or moving to another state or country. That's why thousands of American businesses now move their operations overseas, taking jobs with them. They move to a country that doesn't tax or regulate them to death.

GOVERNMENT-MADE MONOPOLIES

Government also strangles the economy by creating monopolies. This has been going on for a long time and it's usually done in the name of protecting the public. Government-created monopolies got into high gear after the Civil War, when railroads spearheaded an explosive expansion of the economy. Corrupt politicians looking for bribes created monopolies for corrupt businessmen looking for a fast buck.

One notorious example was the Central Pacific railroad in California. In the early 1870s, state legislators gave the Central Pacific a monopoly on commercial railroad traffic in the state. The monopoly lasted for over thirty years. During this time, many other railroads tried to build competing lines in California but were stopped by law.

The Central Pacific took advantage of its monopoly by charging exorbitant freight rates that wiped out farmers' profits. But the railroad could fleece farmers only because state legislators gave it that power. If the Central Pacific didn't have a monopoly, farmers would have shipped their produce with competing lines offering lower freight rates. It wasn't free-market capitalism that injured California farmers, but state *interference in the free market*. Yet the free market took the blame.

Government-created monopolies still thrive today. Con Edison and Brooklyn Union Gas in New York City are monopolies, and many other cities give monopoly franchises to utility companies.

74

Amtrak is federally subsidized. In 1992 alone, Amtrak received more than $300 million in subsidies from American taxpayers to cover operating losses.[7] Until recently, AT&T had a government-created monopoly on telephone service.

There were few regulations on the taxi industry before the 1930s. Anyone with a car and ambition could go into the taxi business. This situation soon threatened the established taxi fleets and existing public transit systems. As a result, in the name of protecting the public, cities throughout America created public transit systems and restricted entry into the taxi business.

The result? We sometimes have to wait on icy street corners for an hour because our town or city runs the bus system. Or if we're lucky enough to have some extra money, we can pay overpriced taxi fares to a monopoly-licensed and approved taxi driver. Approved cabs have no legal competition from gypsy cabs, private vans, or private bus lines that city regulations outlaw.

Most government-run services such as city sanitation departments, the federal Post Office, and public education systems are monopolies run by bureaucrats. Regulations either totally ban or severely restrict private competition. Because government monopolies don't have to complete for our business, the quality of service declines and the costs increase.

These monopolies are run by civil-service employees, many of whom can't be fired because of tenure. If the government monopoly loses money because of poor service or bad management, it doesn't go out of business as it should. Instead, it holds out its hand and gets more tax money to cover its losses. The federal Post Office is an example.

Government monopolies exist to provide "essential" services, not to make profits. Profit is a dirty word to most bureaucrats. Public schools are prime examples. Bureaucrats who run the schools claim that education is too important to be left to the private sector.

But the opposite is true. Education is too important to be left to incompetent or power-hungry bureaucrats who have monopoly control over your children's education. A free-enterprise school has to give your child a good education, or you'll take your business elsewhere. Bureaucrats who live off government paychecks keep their jobs whether your child gets a good education or not. Who would you rather entrust your child's education to?

Government monopolies are immoral and illegitimate because they violate our freedom of choice. Government forces us to deal with bureaucrats, rather than with fiercely competing private companies whose survival depends on giving us high-quality products and services at reasonable prices.

Think about your daily activities for a moment. Which products and services are you happy with and which give you constant aggravation? The car, food, house, clothes, computer, or college education you buy in the free market is usually a high quality product at a reasonable price. If you don't like one company's product or service, you can buy from dozens of other companies. Fierce competition forces companies to continually strive to give you better products at lower prices.

Now think of how aggravated you get when you deal with the Post Office, public schools, or other government-run services. If you don't like using the Post Office or sending your child to a substandard government-run school, too bad. You have no choice because government forces you to deal with them.

Ask yourself, *by what right*? Why should you be forced to deal with bureaucrats? By what right does government deny you the freedom to choose your postal company or child's elementary school? There's nothing more important to you than your child's education. You can choose your grocer and accountant. But you have no right to choose the best school for your child because government has outlawed a vibrant free-market school system.

Like most people, you can't afford local school taxes and tuition for a private school at the same time, so you send your children to a government-run school. Government forces you to put your children's future into the hands of bureaucrats and civil-service employees. If you don't like how they teach your children, you can't do much about it. State-run, public school monopolies reveal the moral essence of all regulations—compulsion. They violate your freedom to choose. Such regulations don't belong in a free society.

Another government monopoly creates high drug prices. The Orphan Drug Law gives special tax breaks and a seven-year monopoly to pharmaceutical companies who produce specialized drugs for rare diseases such as Parkinson's disease and severe anemia. These drugs are called orphan because the diseases they treat only affect a relatively small number of people. Most pharmaceutical companies wouldn't develop drugs for such limited markets because of the high costs involved. To solve this problem, government gives the companies a seven-year monopoly to induce them to invest millions of dollars to develop the drugs.

Here's a typical example of twisted government policy in action. Many pharmaceutical companies won't invest in development costs for orphan drugs because the FDA approval process takes so long and costs millions of dollars. Eldepryl, a drug for Parkinson's disease, cost Somerset Corporation $10 million to develop, for a potential market of about 12,500 people. Epogen, a drug for severe anemia, cost Amgen Corporation $150 million to develop, for a potential market of 50,000 to 100,000 people.

What happens after the company develops the drug? They often charge high prices for the drug because there are no other competitors making similar drugs. Parkinson's disease sufferers currently pay about $2 a pill for Eldepryl, and a severe anemia patient pays about $4500 a year for Epogen.[8]

Do I blame the drug companies? No, I don't. Drug companies have the right to make as much profit as they can, because they take the risks and invest millions of dollars. These drugs have high prices only because the FDA gave the companies seven-year monopolies. If other pharmaceutical companies produced these drugs or cheap generic substitutes, free-market competition would drive prices down.

The real problem is that the FDA makes it risky to develop these drugs. The real problem, therefore, is that the FDA *exists in the first place.* If we abolished the FDA, drug companies wouldn't have to spend years and tens of millions of dollars to get a drug approved. They would develop orphan drugs without needing a special monopoly. Fierce free-market competition would then drive prices down.

THE UNBELIEVABLE COST

Most bureaucrats are totally indifferent to the mess they create.

If regulations force producers to spend a few extra dollars, they say, then companies can just pass these extra costs on to consumers. That's exactly what has happened. Regulations have sharply increased the price of cars, houses, education, health insurance, and thousands of other products and services Americans need but now find hard to afford.

We noted earlier that federal regulations alone cost taxpayers over $400 billion a year. If we merely double this figure to account for the cost of state regulations, this adds up to $800 billion a year. If we divide the United States population of about 250 million people into this figure, we find that state and federal regulations cost at least $3,200 per year for every man, woman, and child in this country. Now add the thousands of regulations imposed by thousands of towns, cities, and villages throughout the country. The costs could easily double again to a conservative $6,400 per year.

Regulations hurt consumers, but they also place a staggering burden on producers. An example is the steel industry, which has to comply with hundreds of regulations by the Labor Department, Environmental Protection Agency, Occupational Safety and Health Agency (OSHA), and many other federal agencies. Regulations control safety standards, building codes, worker's compensation, health and pension plans, employment standards, labor relations, environmental impact statements, mining and transportation, and many more. The steel industry also has to comply with hundreds of state and local regulations. And these are the regulations on just one industry!

Regulations increase the price of every product made with steel. They also put American steel producers at a competitive disadvantage to foreign producers. That's one reason why our steel companies lost business in world markets and had to lay off thousands of workers.

Regulations destroy millions of Americans' dream of owning their own home. The housing industry must comply with a mountain of city, state, and federal regulations. These regulations include zoning, rent controls, environmental impact statements, expensive utility hookup fees, worker's compensation laws, out-of-date building codes that restrict the use of newer, cheaper materials, and many more. Many towns and cities throughout the country force builders to pay for playgrounds or park improvements as the price for necessary approvals. In effect, builders sometimes have to pay extortion money to local governments before the bureaucrats *allow* them to build.

> These delays are expensive. In some California communities, according to Brookings Institution economist Anthony Downs, the first $30,000 of the cost of a new home is directly attributable to government permits and fees. . .
>
> The permit maze sometimes stops housing altogether. In West Windsor Township, New Jersey, the developer of a proposed 2,600-unit subdivision discovered that he needed 11 different approvals from nine separate agencies before construction could begin. But after four years of pursuing permits, the market had disappeared, and the housing project was suspended.[9]

This choking noose of regulations increases the price of new homes. By reducing the supply of new homes, the regulations also increase the resale price of existing homes. It's estimated that regulations increase the price of the average house by as much as 35 percent.[10] This figure doesn't even account for long-term inflation caused by government regulations over the last forty years.

Did you know that in the 1940s, you could buy a modest-sized house in the heart of Beverly Hills, California, for between $50,000 and $85,000? I remember my father telling me that the average price of a house in 1945 was about $25,000. Today the same house would cost about $160,000. In California, the price of an average house is almost $200,000. How does this affect the American dream of owning a home?

> According to the Census Bureau, 57 percent of families—56 million Americans—can't afford to buy a median-priced home where they want to live. Nine of ten renters are, in effect, frozen out of the market for median-priced houses. The situation is particularly acute in California and the northeast corridor between Boston and Washington, D.C.. But it's spreading fast to states like Florida, Ohio and Illinois.[11]

Regulations remove the housing industry from the benefits of the free market. Free-market competition usually increases the supply and lowers the price of products that are in great demand. Look at the price history of products that are *not* regulated. The price of computers has plummeted over the last six years. The computer I'm writing on cost me $2,000 six years ago. Today, the same computer costs about $300.

Prices have dropped sharply because there's fierce competition, and the computer industry has much fewer regulations to comply with than older industries like cars, house construction, or pharmaceuticals.

We can clearly see the effect of regulations when we look at the automobile industry. Fifteen years ago, the average car price was between $7000 and $8,000. Today, it runs closer to $15,000. Why have car prices doubled, even with fierce competition from the Japanese, while computer prices have plummeted? Again, regulations are the culprit.

Hundreds of safety and pollution-control regulations have increased car prices over the last ten years. Car manufacturers, like the steel industry, are also hit with hundreds of other city, state, and federal regulations. Under such conditions, how could car prices *not* escalate?

Environmental regulations increase electric power costs. EPA regulations reduced smokestack emissions, but at a staggering price to utility companies. One study estimated that electricity production costs would increase by $4.8 billion by 1995 because of the 1977 Clean Air Act amendments.[12] This $4.8 billion means higher utility bills for all of us.

When the Welfare State ruins the economy, companies find it harder to pass the cost of regulations on to consumers. When companies can't raise prices, and new regulations keep increasing their costs, they are caught in a terrible bind. They either have to lower costs, or go out of business.

Guess how they lower costs? As we saw earlier, they either lay off workers, or move overseas to countries that have lower labor costs and fewer taxes and regulations. In either case, thousands of American workers lose their jobs. That's exactly what has happened in the past five years. Though the economy is out of the recession and doing better, hundreds of large companies have fired thousands of workers or moved part of their operations overseas. Regulations add hundreds of billions of dollars to the cost of doing business in America. They depress profits, increase unemployment, add to the welfare rolls, put companies out of business, and stop investment and expansion plans.

That's why we have an astonishing situation today: young Americans are now afraid of the future. They're struggling harder to make a living, and are afraid they'll have a lower standard of living than their parents. If you thought that you couldn't end up poorer than your parents, think again.

When regulations choke profits and violate our freedom, consumers no longer dictate what should be produced. Instead, bureaucrats arrogantly dictate what consumers should want. When bureaucrats force us to buy nonpolluting cars, government-approved houses, and drugs that are effective and absolutely safe, government violates our freedom to choose.

To see where our regulation nightmare is leading us, look at a socialist or communist country. In India, many industries are state-owned and operated, and a great weight of taxes and regulations strangles the economy. The Indian people are intelligent, vigorous, and hardworking. But the socialist planners of India deny their people the life-giving power of the free market and condemn them to poverty. The same is true of every socialist country around the world.

A communist country is a totally regulated economy, where the state owns all property. When Russia was communist, the ever-suffering people waited for hours on bread lines. They waited to buy nonexistent consumer goods from stores with empty shelves. The Russian peoples' dismal standard of living after seventy years of communism should be a great lesson to us. It's a gruesome and frightening example of what happens when government regulates the economy.

If government tells you that you don't own your paycheck or profits, but that farmers, welfare recipients, or savings and loan banks do, why should you keep working? If government strangles you with regulations and loots your hard-earned money, why should you continue to produce? If your work doesn't support your life and make it better, why should you continue to strive? The answer is that you should not and would not.

When an economy is totally regulated, it goes to ruin because most people produce little beyond what they need to stay alive.

In the former Soviet Union, famine was the main crop of collective farms. But each farmer worked like a mule on his own little private plot of land. Any form of socialism, from the mildest welfare state to communism, eventually leads to economic disaster.

Even if the Welfare State causes economic disaster, many bureaucrats claim that regulations are justified if they save just one person's life or keep one person from being injured. Regulations violate the freedom of 250 millions Americans to allegedly protect a relatively small number of people who *might* be injured without the regulations.

Liberals distrust freedom and the free market. They think the free market can't be trusted, that its underlying goal is to hurt people. As a result, they prefer using government force to "protect" us. Consumer-protection regulations clearly reveal liberals' basic attitude toward people. They think that human beings, and business people in particular, are irrational brutes who operate on the range-of-the-moment. They think that business people risk their time, effort, and sometimes life savings for fly-by-night schemes that hurt millions of Americans.

Consumer protection regulations reveal liberals' ignorance of the moral values and practical skills needed to succeed in business: honesty, integrity, perseverance, intelligence, long-range vision, and the willingness to take risks. A free economy brings out the best in people and makes them live up to their highest potential. Welfare-state liberals presume they have the right to control this moral, dynamic economic system with snooping bureaucrats and regulations backed by force, threats, and massive fines.

Liberals often justify regulations by claiming that they protect the health and safety of millions of people, and therefore achieve the greatest good for the greatest number. Let's look at some facts. Today, the average American lives to the ripe old age of 72. In 1900, the average life span was 47.3 years. The life expectancy today in India is 50 years, in East Africa—45 years, in the Middle Ages of preindustrial Europe—30 years.[13] Freedom, technology, and industrialization gave us the gift of longer life, and *therefore better health and safety*.

We can clearly see the life-giving benefits of technology and industrialization when we look at countries that don't have these benefits. In underdeveloped countries, misery, squalor, disease, hopelessness, and backbreaking labor is a way of life for millions of people.

Regulations violate our freedom and loot profits. As a result, entrepreneurs eventually say, "The hell with this. Why should I risk my money and work like a mule so government can loot me and regulate me to death?" They stop producing the technology that makes us safer and healthier. They stop creating the technology that cured diseases, put food on our tables, and almost doubled our lifespan.

In short, government regulations don't protect us. Instead, by strangling technology and the free market, they *threaten* our health and safety and cause great harm to millions of people. Regulations may bring temporary, short-term benefits to a few people, but they eventually ruin the economy and destroy our lives.

WHY REGULATIONS CAN'T WORK – THE BUREAUCRATS' STRANGLEHOLD

In a shocking, powerful book, *Government Racket: Washington Waste From A to Z*, the author, Martin Gross, describes government programs that waste hundreds of billions of dollars a year.

One example is the Department of Agriculture and farm subsidy programs. In 1901 this agency employed about 3,000 people to supervise subsidy programs for five million farmers throughout the country. By 1935, the number of farmers had increased to 6.3 million, but the number of agency employees had increased to 20,000. In 1993, there were only about 2.1 million farmers, yet 60,000 people now worked for this agency.

Between 1901 and 1993 the number of farmers *decreased* by over 60 percent but the number of Department of Agriculture employees *increased* over 2000 percent. It's estimated that current farm subsidy programs cost about $56 billion a year and over $190 billion in subsidies have been paid out since 1980.[14]

This is just one instance of government waste. Mr. Gross's 270-page book is filled with many other examples. Worse, the Department of Agriculture is not a freak case of one agency out of control; it's just the tip of the iceberg, and typical of most government agencies. Any government-run agency or entitlement program inevitably creates the same waste because the waste is built into the system. Why is this so?

Government *by its nature* is wasteful and incompetent. It's structurally programmed to waste taxpayer money on a vast scale. Human nature drives bureaucrats to increase the size, scope, and power of their agencies. Any attempt to stop this process is doomed because we haven't solved the root problem—that regulatory agencies and entitlement programs exist in the first place.

To understand why government waste is inevitable, let's look at the crucial difference between the profit motive of a business and the bureaucratic motives of a regulatory agency. This difference will explain why businesses operate efficiently and make profits, while government regulatory agencies are incompetent and lose billions of dollars a year.

People go into business to make profits. No one risks investing their money for the fun of it (although business can be fun). It takes time, money, effort, perseverance, and constant supervision to make a successful business.

In business, there's a constant drive to lower costs and increase efficiency. If an entrepreneur makes no profits, all his efforts are for nothing and he might as well be working for someone else. The owner must be eternally vigilant or his business will fail.

In contrast, a regulatory agency is not in business to make profits. Its function is to *spend* money to achieve its legislated purpose. A bureaucrat is doing his job only if he spends every penny Congress gives his agency. Efficiency in the business sense does not apply to bureaucrats. They have no competition, don't have to make profits, and have a built-in monopoly for their services.

Bureaucrats are motivated by four goals:

First, they want to increase their budgets. A regulatory agency, unlike a private company, can't prove its worth with profits. It makes no profits. Its primary road to status is through size. Perks, salary levels, and political influence increase when an agency grows.

An example is the EPA. Between 1971 and 1980, the EPA's annual budget grew about 44 percent a year, which included a one-year growth rate of 264 percent in 1971/1972.[15] The EPA's political influence increased as the agency became more powerful.

Second, bureaucrats want to expand their jurisdiction. An agency's size depends on the reach of its regulatory powers. The farther its tentacles spread, the more industries or areas of the economy it regulates, the more it can justify its existence. Agencies constantly have to justify their existence to congressional committees who fund them. *No justification means no money.*

Third, bureaucrats want to increase their regulatory activity by increasing the number of companies or industries they investigate. Because an agency can't use profits to prove that its production has increased, its only other proof of usefulness is its activity.

To increase activity, an agency has to create problems when it can't find them, or find problems when it can't create them. Again, the agency needs to justify its existence to congressional committees that fund it. If there were no problems, there would be no need for regulations and therefore no need for any regulatory agency. If Congress dismantled an agency, then goodbye to the bureaucrats' power, cushy jobs, and high salaries.

Here's an example of an agency creating problems to justify its existence:

> The EPA will seek out as many varieties and sources of pollution to the maximum extent possible, short of damaging credibility. The members of Congress will not be interested in pouring millions of dollars, year after year, into agency research that produces no grave environmental damages.[16]

If there were no widespread dangers from pollution, then we wouldn't need EPA bureaucrats. So the EPA must find or invent pollution problems to justify its budget and existence.

Similarly, the FDA assumes that new drugs are lethal and dangerous until proven otherwise. This assumption justifies the FDA's existence, its funding from Congress, and its control over pharmaceutical companies.

The bureaucrats' fourth major goal is to make no mistakes that would anger Congress, and therefore threaten their funding. The

EPA, or any other regulatory agency, doesn't like to make mistakes. It doesn't like being blamed for errors that hurt people. For example, the FDA didn't like the public outrage against it after it allowed drug companies to sell Thalidomide. When people get hurt because of an agency's mistakes, the public and Congress get angry. This anger threatens an agency's future funding.

To prevent this possibility, an agency will be extremely cautious. For example, the EPA sets pollution risk levels at zero for the most susceptible people in the population, such as the elderly with lung problems. These strict pollution standards mean big trouble for a company planning to build a new factory or power plant. The company has to reduce emissions to extremely low levels by installing very expensive antipollution equipment. The zero-risk policy sharply inflates the cost of the plant and often makes it impossible to build. Without the new plant, local towns lose factory and construction jobs, and consumers lose products the plant would have produced.

But EPA bureaucrats could care less. They protect themselves from making any mistakes by setting impossible clean air and water standards. The air in nearby towns may be arctic clean, but new factories won't be built because EPA regulations make them too expensive to build. The local residents won't have jobs, but spotted owls and unemployed workers will have super-clean air to breathe.

Other regulatory agencies don't like to make mistakes, either. That's why the FDA forces pharmaceutical companies to spend up to seven years testing new drugs. It wants to make sure that drug companies discover every side effect of a new drug. It doesn't want to be embarrassed by another Thalidomide. As a result, the FDA delays new drugs that could be saving the lives of millions of people. FDA delays have been accused of killing people:

> In the professional literature in the 1970s, the FDA was accused of responsibility for 10,000 heart-related deaths a year because it kept beta-blockers off the U.S. market long after they had proved successful in Europe.[17]

But FDA bureaucrats don't care, because few people notice drugs that don't make it through the regulatory mine fields. Few people blame the FDA for drugs that never came into existence or took seven years to get approved.

Here we see the true danger of regulations. A private company that sells a harmful product, whether purposely or by accident, hurts a relatively small number of people. The error is quickly discovered and corrected because the company gets bad publicity and the victims file massive, class-action lawsuits. The company usually takes the product off the market or corrects the defect. That's the extent of the damage.

The recent bad publicity on movie-theater popcorn illustrates this point. A study came out that a bag of movie-theater popcorn made with butter and coconut oil had more fat than four cheeseburgers. Within a week the United Artists movie chain was offering and advertising low-fat, air-popped popcorn to its movie customers. This is a typical response of private companies whose profits depend on customer satisfaction.

But when agencies like the EPA or FDA make nationwide policy decisions, they can do massive, widespread, and long-term harm to millions of people. Over 30,000 loggers, mill workers, and construction workers lost their jobs because of EPA spotted-owl regulations. Thousands of sick people suffer and die because FDA regulations keep lifesaving drugs off the market for years. Millions of Americans can't afford a home because of massive layers of regulations that increase house prices. Worse, we can't correct these problems because arrogant civil-service bureaucrats can't be sued and have no competition.

Always remember that bureaucrats spend other peoples' money. How would you act toward money if you operated under the following conditions: Government gives you billions of dollars of other peoples' money to spend. You don't have to make a profit. You won't be accountable for how you spend the money, and no one will blame you if the billions you spend are totally wasted. And the more you spend, the bigger your agency gets. As your agency grows, you have a better chance for a promotion, higher salary, and juicier retirement benefits.

Under these conditions, would you care about how you spent the money? Would you be concerned about efficiency? Would you give back money you didn't spend? Would you keep asking your Congressional oversight committee for more money and power?

If your answers were no, no, no, and yes, you now understand why human nature makes regulatory agencies *inevitably* grow into the monsters they are today.

We have a regulation nightmare in this country because of human nature, bureaucrats' built-in goals, and their need to spend taxpayers' money without regard for profits or results. A bureaucrat's perks, career, pension, status, and salary depend on increasing the size, reach, and activity of his agency and its regulations. That's why it's almost impossible to dislodge bureaucrats once they're entrenched. They fight tooth and nail to protect their power, privileges, and elite status.

Bureaucrats sometimes admit that their regulations have bad effects, but they say, "Don't worry—we can fix the problem. We can streamline the regulations." This is one of their favorite fantasies. Ever since the Welfare State started in the 1930s, bureaucrats have been trying to increase government's efficiency. We all know the results. For a reminder, I urge you to read the book by Martin Gross that we discussed earlier. Without the profit motive and competition, bureaucrats have no reason to be efficient, and every reason to spend and waste taxpayers' money. You can't change human nature.

But the situation gets worse if bureaucrats do become more efficient. An efficient bureaucrat does his job better, which makes him even more dangerous. If he's more efficient, he's able to hurt more people who have to obey his regulations. An efficient regulator can force more people to act against their judgment and waste more billions of dollars on his regulations. Regulators don't produce anything. Their job is to point legal guns at us and command us to obey their regulations. Remember, the Nazis were efficient in killing Jews. They created assembly-line killing factories called concentration camps. Don't ever ask for efficient bureaucrats, or you may get your wish.

FREE-MARKET MAGIC

Many Americans agree that regulations are destructive. But most of us would hesitate to end them completely because we would be afraid to live without government protection. Who would stop businesses from cheating or making products that harm us? How would we protect ourselves from polluters or manufacturers of unsafe toys, drugs, or food? Big corporations care about profits, not people, don't they? If we have no regulations, wouldn't America turn into a dog-eat-dog society, where everyone hurts everyone else?

These are the understandable fears of millions of Americans who have lived under the security blanket of regulations for so long that they're afraid to live without them. They don't know there are better alternatives to government watchdogs. They're afraid of the free market and don't understand how it would protect them.

It's true that businesses only care about profits, but *that's exactly why they have to care about people.* A company makes profits by selling goods or services we want. If we don't like a product, we won't buy it. If we think the product is unsafe, unhealthy, or doesn't work, we won't buy it. If we hear bad things about it from family, friends, or consumer reports, we won't buy it. We'll buy from another company that makes a better version of the same product. As consumers, we're smart and merciless. We decide which companies will fail or succeed by our purchase decisions. In a truly free market, the consumer is king (or queen).

In a free economy, competition is always fierce. It's therefore in a company's *self-interest* to offer a safe, high-quality product. The company's profits and survival depend on consumers choosing its products over those of its competitors.

For example, a drug company's most important asset is its reputation. If the company produces unsafe drugs that cause harmful side effects, it will get a bad reputation. Doctors, hospitals, and individual consumers won't buy its drugs anymore. Its profits will plummet or lawsuits will drive it out of business.

A car manufacturer that makes unsafe or poor quality cars will lose business quickly for the same reasons. That's why Americans were buying Japanese cars instead of American cars. If a builder makes houses that are unsafe, shoddy, or overpriced compared to his competitors, he'll soon find himself without customers.

Lincoln said, "You can fool some of the people all of the time, and all of the people some of the time, but you cannot fool all of the people all the time." This observation is especially true in a free market where consumers have so many sources of information to help them judge product quality. These sources include books, newspapers, television, consumer reports, comparison shopping, relatives and friends, and your common sense.

A business owner's time, effort, investment, and future success depend on his company's reputation, on his ability to produce the kinds of products that consumers demand. If he fails to do this, his *whole life's work can be destroyed.*

It takes a business person many years of consistent, excellent service to the public to build a reputation that's a financial asset to his business. And he can't relax for a minute. He has to continually improve his product or service so it's better than the competition. He can't afford to ruin his reputation with one faulty or unsafe product because too much is at stake.

New companies coming into the field can't immediately compete with established companies. They have to spend years of hard work to earn their own reputation. Companies at every level of the free market compete for the best reputation for their products or services because their profits and survival depend on this. Competition for reputation is built into the free market and is the consumers' most powerful protection against dishonest businesses. Competition also increases the quality of everything we buy. The producer's self-interest and his passionate desire to succeed are the best and most consistent protectors of our health and safety.

Does this mean some companies won't be unscrupulous or make honest mistakes? Absolutely not. There are no guarantees when it comes to the products that human beings create. But the self-interest of companies in business for the long term would keep harm down to a minimum.

In a free market without regulations, we would also be careful consumers. Knowing that big brother isn't protecting us anymore, we would depend even more on a company's reputation. We would ask friends and neighbors about which products they liked and which to avoid. We would rely on outside resources like *Consumer Reports* magazine to give us quality comparisons of products and companies. Consumers would demand quality, and companies would make every effort to keep improving their products.

Cars and computers are two good examples. Over the years, their quality has improved because of fierce competition. The Japanese forced Detroit to shape up or lose business. Computers get better, cheaper, and more powerful every year. Quality sells.

The number of products that harm consumers is relatively small compared to the overwhelming number of quality products we buy. A product you buy may not live up to your expectations, but ask yourself when was the last time you bought a product that actually hurt you?

If a consumer is hurt by a product, he can sue the company. If he proves his case, the court awards him damages. If many people are hurt by a product such as a defective car, they can bring multimillion-dollar, class-action suits against the manufacturer. Such lawsuits, along with the bad publicity, are usually enough to make the offending company correct the defect.

Compare a business owner's motivation to that of a bureaucrat who's supposed to protect our health and safety. The bureaucrat lives off government paychecks; the business owner gets paid by consumers who buy his products. A bureaucrat's paycheck doesn't stop if a product is unsafe; the business owner can go bankrupt and lose his life savings if he sells a product that hurts his customers and ruins his reputation.

A bureaucrat has no personal self-interest in protecting us. He'll keep his civil-service job and salary whether he protects the consumer or not. Bureaucrats don't care about us because our spending decisions don't affect them in the least.

A business owner's success and future depend on his reputation. But regulations *undercut the value of reputation* in the marketplace. Regulations place the fly-by-night new business on the same footing as the reputable business that's been around for many years. Regulations imply that all companies are suspect, and that one company is no better than another.

Regulations grant an automatic but unearned guarantee of safety to products that meet minimum standards. They therefore imply that all companies meeting these standards are the same. That gives new companies instant credibility. Regulations tell consumers they don't have to judge products for themselves or bother with reputation anymore, because bureaucrats will do our thinking for us.

For example, a medical license doesn't necessarily guarantee a doctor's competence. A doctor, architect, hot dog vendor, or building contractor gets a license by meeting government-set minimum standards. Most consumers believe that anyone with a license is competent. The license creates an instant reputation that didn't have to be earned.

Very often, a regulation's minimum standards become the maximum standards in the marketplace. If licenses and regulations make competitors equal in the eyes of consumers, then it doesn't pay for a company or professional to go much beyond the minimum standards. He gets little competitive advantage from doing so.

Regulations also make consumers drop their guard. If two doctors have licenses or two banks have FDIC insurance, we believe they're both equally competent or safe. We think government has checked them out thoroughly. Human nature being what it is, people are often lazy. If government does our checking for us, why should we be careful? And we aren't. How many of us check our doctor's credentials or our bank's financial statements?

Because regulations decrease the value of reputation in the marketplace, they *lower,* not raise the safety and quality of the products and services we buy.

JUST GIVE US THE INFORMATION

Regulations not only strangle producers, they also restrict our freedom of choice. If some drugs have bad side effects, why not just require clear labels so doctors and consumers know the dangers?

If air pollution in a manufacturing plant might cause lung problems, workers should be free to choose between working in the plant or being unemployed. Rather than closing down the plant with expensive pollution regulations, the manufacturer should simply be required to post a warning notice of the potential side effects of the pollution.

Instead of regulations that take a product off the market, companies should give consumers the information they need to make their own common-sense decisions about the product. Product warnings would be similar to those on cigarette packages that say *SMOKING CAUSES CANCER.*

Federal and state governments have used his method, and it works. In 1987, California passed Proposition 65, a law that required companies to place warning labels on products that contained any one of three hundred toxic chemicals. The law didn't ban the toxins, regulate the companies making them, or create a huge new tax-supported bureaucracy.

Instead, it simply required companies to disclose if their products contained any of these toxic chemicals. Such disclosure laws have a powerful effect. For example, one company removed the toxins from its typewriter correction fluid rather than risk bad publicity from disclosure.

Another similar disclosure law was the 1986 federal law that created the Toxic Release Inventory (TRI). The TRI is a list of companies that use and release large amounts of certain toxic chemicals into the environment. Like Proposition 65, it had a powerful impact on companies emitting these toxic chemicals. When the law took effect in 1987, a big chemical company was alleged to be a major polluter. To avoid bad publicity and a tarnished reputation from disclosure, the company volunteered to cut its worldwide air pollution emissions by 90 percent within five years. It accomplished that goal.[18]

Disclosure of harmful products or practices, either by a government agency or by private consumer-protection groups, can be a powerful free-market force. It can protect us against negligent producers. It can make companies remove harmful products, and improve the quality of their products. With safe, high-quality products, companies don't have to worry about embarassing disclosures.

Disclosure laws also protect our freedom of choice. We have the right to know if someone is selling us something that can hurt us. But we also have the right to use that product, though we know it can hurt us. We have a right to our lives and our bodies. We therefore have a right to sniff glue, take drugs, smoke cigarettes, or bungee-jump off a cliff if we want to. *We have the right to know, but we also have the right to ignore what we know.* Government should have no control over our choice.

CONCLUSION

Regulations strangle the economy, throw thousands of people out of work, cost us hundreds of billions of dollars, and violate our property rights and freedom of choice. Yet every year, Congress and local and state governments keep passing more regulations. We keep giving bureaucrats more power over us.

Why do we let government get away with this? Why do we keep making regulations that wreck our lives and strangle our economy? I'll answer these questions in the chapter, "Why Do We Go Along?"

CHAPTER 5

DANGEROUS NONSENSE: THE ENVIRONMENTAL MOVEMENT

The human race is heading for ecological disaster because of its increasing and all-pervasive assaults on our air, water, and land. Pollution is everywhere. Our industrial civilization is heading toward environmental collapse, and mankind's fate hangs in the balance.

Does this scare you out of your wits? It's intended to do just that. This scenario from a second-rate horror movie is passed off as scientific fact by a new breed of doomsday prophet, the ecologist. Here are more of his prophesies. Read and take heed—the end is near:

> . . . the present course of environmental degradation, if unchecked, threatens the survival of civilized man.[1]
> Yet the evidence is overwhelming that the way in which we now live on the earth is driving its thin, life-supporting skin, and ourselves with it, to destruction.[2]

Environmentalists' doomsday predictions would be comical, if

95

it wasn't for the fact that these scare stories have frightened local, state, and federal legislators into creating a massive, poisonous layer of regulations. Environmental regulations violate our property rights, restrict our personal liberties, threaten our standard of living, and throw thousands of Americans out of work.

Environmentalists concoct end-of-the-world scenarios all the time. These predictions are calculated to scare us. As we'll see, most of them turn out to be pure fantasy, exaggerations, or deliberate distortions of the facts.

DOOMSDAY STORIES AND REALITY

Oil Spills

One environmental scare story involves the alleged dangers of oil spills. Ecologists have exaggerated the damage from oil spills to justify regulations that restrict oil exploration. Yet natural oil seeps spill more oil into the oceans than all manmade leaks put together. And the oil that nature or oil companies leak into the oceans does little, if any, long-term harm.

After the Santa Barbara oil leak in 1969, liberal media coverage showed the usual pictures of seals and ducks coated with oil. Yet most biological studies showed that the crude oil that washed ashore affected existing fish and plant life only slightly, if at all. These findings were confirmed by the Water Quality Office of the Environmental Protection Agency in 1971.[3]

At the time of the blowout, the usual dire predictions were in the air. Local newspapers commented that offshore pollution could kill plankton and other marine life. A local columnist forecast that the spill would ruin sport and commercial fishing and repel migratory fish for years. A marine biologist claimed that the oil would kill all fish along twenty miles of coast. These predictions turned out to be the usual exaggerations.

In a January 1993 storm, the oil tanker Braer crashed against the cliffs of Shetland Island and broke apart. Over 630,000 barrels of oil spilled into the sea, more than twice the amount spilled off the Alaskan coast in 1989 by the tanker Exxon

Valdez. Was there an environmental disaster? No, there wasn't. The storm that drove the Braer into the cliffs created churning seas that dispersed the oil and broke apart all but the heaviest slicks.[4] Of course, environmentalists couldn't admit that the Braer tanker oil spill was a meaningless nonevent that caused no lasting damage. In a typical doomsday prediction, a spokesperson for the environmental group Greenpeace darkly prophesied that the oil spill would have long-term "devastating" effects on the Shetland Islands. Environmentalists claimed that 700 birds, 2 seals, and untold (meaning unknown) number of fish were killed. What actually happened? Within a few months, it was hard to tell there had ever been an oil spill.[5]

Then there was the mother of all oil spills. During the Gulf War in 1991, Iraq deliberately discharged at least six million barrels of oil into the Persian Gulf, by far the largest oil spill in a nearly closed body of water. In spite of frantic and hysterical predictions of ecological doom for the Gulf, what really happened?

Scientists conducted a hundred-day expedition in the Mount Mitchell, a research vessel of the National Oceanic and Atmospheric Administration that had been operating in the Gulf since February 1992. The scientists concluded that while hundreds of miles of beaches lay under thick layers of oil, sea life in deeper waters was healthy and undamaged. In other words, the mother of all oil spills had little effect on the Persian Gulf, which is practically a closed body of water.[6]

Studies show that oil spills are relatively short-lived because the ocean breaks them up naturally in a few weeks. Most of the oil evaporates, becomes decomposed by bacteria into water and carbon dioxide, or dissolves in the sea water and quickly fades away.

Look at a map of the world and note the size of the oceans—they cover three-fifths of the Earth's surface. If the oceans had a sense of humor, they would laugh at human oil spills. The effects are just too puny to be concerned with.

Air Pollution

Over the last twenty years, EPA regulations have forced industry to spend over $30 billion to reduce levels of carbon monoxide and other air pollutants. The 1992 amendments to the Clean Air Act will force industry to spend another $12 billion a year to reduce air pollution levels even further.[7]

Car makers, electric power plants, and hundreds of other industries pass these costs on to us, the consumer. Auto and electric utility industries affect the entire economy. Air pollution regulations therefore force us to pay sharply higher prices for cars and thousands of other products.

But over the last thirty years, studies have not shown a significant relationship between public health and air pollution. In 1968, John R. Goldsmith, a member of the California Air Resources Board, studied the problem. He found no correlation between pollution and higher levels of lung cancer and other respiratory diseases.[8]

Of course, heavy air pollution can be a health hazard to some people. Also, a recent study has shown that even fine particle emissions from cars and power plants may sometimes be hazardous. But we're spending hundreds of billions of dollars to eliminate every last speck of air pollution.

The EPA costs cities millions of dollars by forcing them to reduce carbon monoxide (CO) levels in the air. Carbon monoxide is toxic to human beings, but only at very high concentrations. Studies show that carbon monoxide levels of 120 parts-per-million (ppm) affect our red blood cells and impair our ability to act. CO levels of 60 ppm only affect us slightly. At CO levels of 48 ppm, the studies showed no convincing evidence of harmful affects. Yet the EPA sets maximum CO levels at 9 ppm![9]

Let me repeat this. Scientific studies show no harmful effect to human beings at CO levels of 48 ppm. Yet the EPA takes thousands of dollars out of your pocket to pay for regulations that reduce CO levels to 9 ppm. According to the studies, carbon monoxide levels in cities could be 500 percent higher than EPA standards and still not hurt us.

In 1995, anyone buying a new car will pay thousands of dollars more because of regulations that do nothing for our health. The only thing these regulations do is give employment to EPA bureaucrats.

EPA regulations also force industries to reduce pollutants that create ozone in the air. Yet many studies show no connection between ozone levels and health problems. Because of special climate and atmospheric conditions, Los Angeles often experiences high ozone levels. For the last forty years, ozone levels in that city have been above EPA maximum limits for between 100 and 200 days every year. Yet studies have shown no difference between the health of Los Angeles residents compared to residents of other American cities without ozone problems.

In fact, weather and other natural causes alone create more ozone in Los Angeles than EPA standards allow. In other words, if all cars, people, and industry were removed from the state, California would still be violating EPA standards![10]

The Oceans Are Alive and Well

EPA regulations now ban waste dumping in the sea. Ocean dumping is supposed to be bad for our health. The facts don't support this. Oceans can absorb huge quantities of waste without disturbing their ecological balance. Municipal sewage is mostly water, containing less than 1 percent of nontoxic, biodegradable, suspended human waste. The sea's huge volume of churning, oxygen-rich water breaks down the waste through diffusion, convection, and biological action.[11]

Fecal coliform bacteria counts are used to roughly measure human waste pollution. Right after a barge dumps its sludge, coliform levels are higher than normal in the dump site. After about one hour, the sea disperses and breaks down the sewage, and coliform counts return close to normal.

The oceans are so huge that every human being on Earth has more than twelve billion cubic feet of sea water available for waste disposal. Sanitary engineers say that it takes only two hundred parts of seawater to purify one part of sewage because of seawater's biological action on garbage. In effect, oceans are natural purifying plants.[12]

Waste dumping has little affect on the oceans and provides food for sea life. It's also the least expensive way to dispose of waste. New York's Nassau County used to dump wastes at sea for about one-third the cost of other methods. It's been estimated that landfills and incineration cost three to five times more than barging the waste out to sea.[13]

Some environmentalists have made fantastic pronouncements about the oceans dying. Yet studies show that the oceans' overall productivity has actually increased, partly because of waste nutrients dumped into the sea. In the past thirty years, in spite of all the wastes dumped into our oceans, the world's catch of fish has doubled.[14]

The whole ocean dumping issue is a farce. In the hot summer of 1988, garbage, trash slicks, and used syringes washed up on beaches all along the Eastern shoreline. When local governments closed the beaches, outraged voters put pressure on congressmen to outlaw ocean dumping. In a typical knee-jerk response in the fall of 1988, Congress caved into the pressure and banned ocean dumping. Now municipalities have to put garbage in stinking landfills that pollute water supplies, and they're running out of land for the garbage.

But guess what? The garbage that washed up on shore in the summer of 1988 had nothing to do with ocean dumping. The garbage and used syringes came from overtaxed municipal sewage systems![15] Today, local governments tax you to pay for landfills that cost three times the cost of ocean dumping. Yet municipal sewage agencies caused the problem in the first place!

Pesticides

What about the dangers of using pesticides like DDT? Don't they poison us? Before its ban, there was little evidence showing that DDT harmed human beings. In 1970, studies showed that people carried about twelve parts per million of DDT in their fatty tissue.[16] But no studies showed any harm or link to diseases coming from such small concentrations.

They also overlook the fact that pesticide residues on food are well below the levels set as safe by the FDA and are effectively negligible. No fatalities, no serious illness, and no cancer has resulted from the approved use of pesticides. Dr. Robert Scheuplein, the respected food-safety microbiologist with the FDA, concluded that the effective cancer risk from pesticide residues in food is 0.0000076. That means that less than five hundredths of one percent of all cancers might be caused by pesticide residues.[17]

And natural pesticides are a much bigger risk than manmade ones. Dr. Bruce N. Ames is a biochemist and molecular biologist at the University of California at Berkeley, and director of the National Institute of Environmental Health Sciences Center at Berkeley. Dr. Ames is also a member of the National Academy of Sciences, and has received many prestigious rewards for research excellence. He had this to say about pesticides, cancer, and environmentalists: "People fret about pesticide residues, but 99.99 percent of the pesticides Americans consume are natural constituents of plants, Dr. Ames said. He has calculated that the typical American eats about 1500 milligrams a day of natural pesticides, which is 10,000 times the average daily consumption of 0.09 milligrams of synthetic pesticide residues."

Dr. Ames also said: *"I think pesticides lower the cancer rate"* (emphasis added). Dr. Ames believes that antioxidants in fruits and vegetables fight cancer. Pesticide use increases crop yields, making it easier for millions of Americans to eat healthy foods that fight cancer. This respected scientist also had this to say about pollution and environmentalists:

> Pollution seems to me to be mostly a red herring as a cause of cancer.
> Environmentalists are forever issuing scare reports based on very shallow science.
> Standard animal cancer tests done with high doses are practically useless for predicting a chemical's risk to humans.[18]

To "prove" cancer risks from pesticides and other synthetic chemicals, EPA scientists stuff rats with huge doses of these chemicals, find tumors, then declare the chemicals cancer risks. The doses given to lab rats are often hundreds of thousands of times more than the doses people are exposed to. Many scientists have criticized the EPA's testing procedures as ludicrous, and its cancer fears over pesticides as grossly exaggerated.

About these EPA tests, Dr. Ames said:

> "The dose makes the poison," Dr. Ames said, quoting a maxim of toxicology. "At some level, every chemical becomes toxic, but there are safe levels below that. You cannot extrapolate linearly from a high dose to a low dose and end up with a realistic risk estimate. A

101

tenfold reduction in dose would produce much more than a tenfold reduction in cancer risk."[19]

EPA testing methods are similar to the following imaginary procedure: EPA scientists force-feed a lab rat with 2,000 pounds of bread, and the rat dies of shock and bulimia. The EPA then declares that bread is harmful to our health and asks for regulations to shut down all wheat farms.

The EPA uses these ludicrous lab tests to justify laws that ban DDT and other chemicals that fight disease or increase our food production. This is a tragic mistake, because DDT and other pesticides save lives. DDT has been used worldwide to increase food production, and to fight malaria, encephalitis, and yellow-fever. Between 1944 and 1974, it's estimated that DDT saved at least five million lives and greatly increased food supplies all over the world.

Pesticides fight hordes of insects that destroy our crops. Studies show that despite using pesticides, insects destroy between $3 billion and $20 billion worth of crops a year in America. Without pesticides, it's estimated that crop and livestock output would be reduced by about 40 percent, wiping out exports and increasing our food prices by 50 percent to 75 percent.[20]

"Fragile" Forests

Another doomsday story involves the "fragile" forests ecologists want to protect from logging companies. Three hundred years ago, forests covered about 42 percent of the land within the continental United States. Today, in spite of all the housing tracts and increased population, forests still cover about one-third of the land. Alaska, twice the size of Texas, is almost completely wild, and about 33 percent of its land is forested. These figures don't include lands that logging companies reforest to insure future tree supplies. Even today, less than 5 percent of American land is urbanized, with the rest being suburban, farm-land, and wilderness covered with trees.[21]

Most of us naively accept ecologists' claims that we're destroying our forests. In 1920, lumber companies were depleting our forests, but they've gotten wiser since then. Common business sense made them realize that if they cut down all the trees and didn't replant, they would eventually be out of business. As a result, lumber companies now plant two trees for every one they cut down, and the growth of new timber exceeds yearly logging by 33 percent. Today, we have an estimated 230 billion trees, the most trees we've ever had this century.[22]

And what's the real value of forests? They don't support large animal populations. Most forest animals are small because forests don't have the lush vegetation found in open plains and savannahs. Forests also kill off grasses and small plants near the ground by blocking life-giving sunlight. And how many Americans visit forests as a religious experience? Most of us are content to limit our contact with nature to our lawns, local parks, and golf courses.

Why should we care so much about forests? I personally prefer open country with rolling hills spotted with trees here and there, like in California. To me, vast forests are dark, brooding, and not very inviting. And they're pretty boring (except maybe for Sequoia trees). Why should we lose valuable timber, loggers' jobs, and new oil fields because elitist environmentalists like hiking through forests?

And natural causes destroy more forests than people do. In 1941, more than 190,000 natural fires destroyed over 26 million acres of forest. By 1965, brave firefighters, risking their lives, had reduced this destruction down to about 2.7 million acres using firefighting techniques like sprays and firebreaks. Today, natural fires account for only about 5 percent of all timber destruction. In spite of logging, human beings have been a friend and protector to our forests.

By far the greatest enemy of trees are insects, not people. Insects are responsible for over 40 percent of tree acreage losses. With the help of environmentalists, government banned insecticides like DDT. As a result, millions of trees have been needlessly blighted and destroyed by insect pests. The infamous gypsy moth has ravaged timber areas throughout the eastern United States.

Forests supply little food for people. In contrast, grasslands supply nourishment for huge herds of deer, buffalo, and antelope. Open grasslands are far more valuable to plants, animals, and people, supplying nourishment for all. By clearing forests, people also create new farmland that helps feed the world.

In short, forests are not that valuable for man, beast, or plants. Their primary value is for lumber. Should we let forests alone so they stand there useless, rather than using trees to build our homes and factories? Shouldn't we use them to support human life, rather than worrying about spotted owls? No owl or forest is worth destroying the jobs of thousands of loggers, mill workers, and construction workers.

The Ozone Hole

The ozone hole is one of our ecologists' favorite scare stories. Environmentalists say that manufactured chemicals are punching holes in the ozone layer, and these holes let high levels of cancer-causing ultraviolet radiation reach the Earth. If this scenario was true, ultraviolet radiation levels on Earth would be rising.

> The only problem with this theory is that ultraviolet radiation levels on the Earth's surface are going down, not up. According to scientists from the National Oceanic and Atmospheric Administration, the University of Colorado, and the National Center for Atmospheric Research, the amount of ultraviolet radiation reaching the Earth has, in some urban areas, *decreased* (emphasis added) by 5 to 18 percent . . . Measuring instruments set up across the U.S. in 1974 by the National Cancer Institute show that over two test periods–1974-79 and 1980-85–the amount of ultraviolet "B" (UVB) reaching the Earth actually decreased by an average of 0.7 percent per year since 1974.[23]

If ultraviolet radiation levels are going down, then how can we be losing ozone? If recent measurements show temporary or cyclical decreases in ozone levels, then factors other than ozone must affect UVB radiation levels. Again we have eco-pseudoscientists using flimsy facts and unproven theories to scare us.

As usual, other reputable scientists say that changes in ozone levels could have a natural cause. "Some (of these changes) have been correlated to solar activity, stratospheric weather patterns, intense cold, and the presence of chloride and/or nitrogen . . . or cyclic patterns."[24] Scientists at the American Geophysical Union in Washington State recently reported that ozone levels over North America have increased over the last two years.[25] This finding seems to confirm that ozone levels change because of natural causes.

Yet because of ozone eco-babble, the federal government has passed laws that will ban freon, halon, and other important CFCs (chlorofluorocarbons). Why are freon and halon important to us? Freon is the gas in our refrigerators that keeps our food cold. It's nontoxic, nonvolatile, and not harmful to living organisms. When invented in 1930, it replaced dangerous chemicals previously used for refrigeration, such as ammonia, methyl chloride, and sulphur dioxide. These chemicals used to kill people when they leaked from refrigeration systems. They were also inefficient compared to freon.

The cost to replace freon is going to be astronomical. Just replacing refrigeration systems to transport food across America will cost over $150 billion. One estimate says that the cost of banning freon for refrigeration would be $800 a year for every man, woman, and child in this country.[26]

Banning freon and other CFCs has frightening consequences. Without these superb refrigerants, food will spoil and there could be increases in food poisoning and stomach cancers. Other experts estimate that banning CFC refrigerants in food transportation systems could kill millions of people around the world.

Robert Watson, head of the Ozone Trends Panel (a strong supporter of banning CFCs), has admitted that "probably more people would die from food poisoning as a consequence of inadequate refrigeration than would die from depleting ozone."[27]

So people might die, have less food to eat, and get more stomach cancers because of environmentalists' nonfacts, unproven theories, and scare tactics.

Global Warming

Last but not least, we have the mother of all doomsday stories.

For over twenty years, environmentalists have scared us with this one. It seems that car exhausts, forest clearing, power plants, and other industrial activities increase carbon dioxide levels in the atmosphere. Increased carbon dioxide will allegedly create a barrier in the atmosphere that traps the Earth's heat, creating a "greenhouse effect." As a result, the Earth's temperature will rise, causing glaciers to melt, seas to rise, worldwide flooding, and calamity to the human race.

As expected, there are many reputable scientists who think this theory is nonsense. Other scientists have their own theories that totally contradict global warming.

Kenneth E.F. Watt, professor of environmental studies at the University of California at Davis, theorized that an excess of carbon dioxide in the atmosphere should lead to global cooling, not warming. Watt argued that carbon dioxide will heat tropical oceans, leading to additional evaporation. This will produce denser and more widespread clouds at high elevations, which will decrease the amount of sunlight that penetrates the atmosphere. Some scientists believe that the Earth is warming, but attribute the change to causes other than carbon dioxide production. Frederick Seitz, past president of the National Academy of Sciences, suggested that solar activity may have caused global warming, and Reid Bryson, director of the Institute of Environmental Studies at the University of Wisconsin, Madison, believes that dust and smoke are the primary causes of climate change.[28]

There are also scientists who question whether the Earth has gotten warmer over the last hundred years.

Temperature measurements may be biased by the effects of urbanization; weather stations are located in urban areas, where heat-absorbing buildings and pavement can raise the readings one to two degrees above the surrounding atmosphere. After correcting for the "urban" effect, a study by the National Oceanographic and Atmospheric Administration concluded that there was *no statistically significant evidence of warming in the United States* (emphasis added). Andrew R. Solow, a statistician at Woods Hole, pointed out that because monitoring stations tend to be located on land rather than oceans and more are in the Northern than in the Southern Hemisphere, temperature readouts are not really global at all. Ten years of weather satellite data have also shown *no evidence of global warming* (emphasis added).[29]

There's no valid evidence of global warming. Instead, there's solid evidence that the Earth has *not* been warming. Since 1978, a temperature-measuring satellite called Tiros II has been orbiting the Earth 24-hours a day. Guess what? The satellite's measurements showed no significant increase or decrease in the Earth's temperature. Scientific temperature measurements from Tiros II show no global warming trend in the last fifteen years.[30] In other words, global warming is a myth.

Many eminent scientists agree that global warming and other environmental scare stories are just unproven theories. Prior to the Earth Summit meeting in Rio de Janeiro in June 1992, scientists from around the world issued the Heidelberg Appeal. In the Appeal, scientists asked government leaders at the summit to be careful. They asked the leaders not to make serious environmental decisions based on pseudoscientific arguments or false and nonrelevant data. More than 250 scientists, including 27 Nobel prize winners, issued the Appeal on June 1, 1992.[31] Today, 2,300 scientists from 79 countries, including 65 Nobel prize winners, have signed the Appeal .[32]

Former governor of Washington and former chairwoman of the Atomic Energy Commission, Dr. Dixy Lee Ray, also thought that global warming is nonsense. In her wonderful 1993 book, *Environmental Overkill: Whatever Happened To Common Sense?*, she said that it was unlikely that carbon dioxide would cause any significant changes in worldwide temperatures. Jeffrey Salmon is executive director of the Washington-based George C. Marshall Institute. In the July 1993 issue of Commentary, he flatly stated that he found no valid scientific evidence to prove that manmade gases are causing the Earth to warm from a greenhouse effect.[33] In short, you are being conned. Government takes money out of your pocket to enforce environmental regulations that, in most cases, protect you from *nothing*.

I could describe many other eco-scare stories, but I think I've made my point. These doomsday prophesies are either distortions or exaggerations of unproven facts. Unfortunately, environmentalists and the liberal media spout this eco-nonsense so often that we start to believe them. That's the problem and the danger. Panicked, short-sighted congressmen believe the scare stories and pass environmental regulations that strangle our economy. According to studies by the U.S. Congress Joint Economic Committee in 1992, it costs us over $115 billion a year just to administer the regulations.[34]

Later we'll see why eco-radicals spread their scare stories, desite their flimsy facts and groundless theories of doom.

NATURE'S POLLUTION

Contrary to popular belief, human beings are not this planet's main polluters—nature is. Earthquakes, ice ages, erosion, forest fires, volcanic eruptions, living organisms, and climate catastrophes have spewed massive amounts of pollution into the environment. Compared to nature, our pollution is puny.

Pollution by nature continues today. During an International Indian Ocean Expedition in the early 1960s, oceanographers discovered an area of sea twice the size of Portugal that contained 40 to 50 million metric tons of dead fish. This amount of fish equaled the yearly world catch at the time. Since little human industry existed close by, only natural causes could have killed the fish.[35]

Rain that falls over the United States carries 2.5 million tons of sodium sulfate, the same amount of calcium salts and carbonates, and thousands of tons of naturally occurring sulfuric and nitric acids (from natural, not manmade pollution sources). Although human beings create new poisons, nature pollutes our water and food supply with rock minerals like lead, mercury, and sulphur.[36]

Natural springs are often loaded with salts, acids, and radioactive particles leached from surrounding soils and rocks. Natural oil seeps release tons of crude oil on land and into the oceans. These seeps along the California coast continually bleed about one hundred barrels of oil a day into the Pacific Ocean, a rate greater than the Santa Barbara oil spill.[37]

Living organisms are also major polluters. Many plants emit hydrocarbons. Trees emit terpenes, which are hydrocarbon compounds often forming a haze above conifer forests. Methane, or swamp gas, is naturally produced by plants disintegrating in lakes, rivers, and swamplands around the world. It's estimated that nature generates 1.6 billion tons of methane a year; human beings create less than 100 million tons of methane a year.

The California Department of Environmental Research estimates that volcanos and natural emissions discharge about 220 million tons of sulphurous gases into the atmosphere. Humans discharge only about one-third of this amount. People put about 50 million tons of nitrous oxides into the air, but nature pumps 500 million tons of nitrogen dioxide, 5.9 billion tons of ammonia, and one billion tons of nitrogen into the air. Natural lightning creates ten times more airborne nitric acid than people do.[38]

The point is: we contribute to pollution, especially with our cars in big cities, but human pollution is insignificant compared to nature's pollution. The Earth is millions of years old. It's been bombarded with thousands of volcanic eruptions, ice ages, and massive climate changes. Human beings have had heavy industry and polluting technology for about 150 years, which is a drop of water in the ocean of time. Nature has polluted the Earth for millions of years, yet the planet and human beings have managed to survive and prosper. So where's the crisis? Simple. It's manufactured by radical environmentalists.

We do have some pollution problems, but they're usually small, localized, and correctable. For instance, a few cities like Los Angeles and Mexico City have serious car exhaust pollution. The problem comes from geography and the local terrain. Both cities are located in a valley that's surrounded by mountains. As a result, restricted air circulation causes layers of stagnant, polluted air (smog) to accumulate. The smog causes problems for some people with lung problems, but most city residents seem able to tolerate the pollution.

I'm not saying that air pollution in some cities isn't a problem. Smog can be nasty and irritating. But as we saw earlier, no studies have ever shown that air pollution even hurts most people. Air pollution is a problem, but it's a relatively minor one compared to the costs required to clean it up.

Moderate air pollution can sometimes be good for us, strange as this sounds. A group of scientists from the Finnish Forest

Research Institute in Helsinki came to the conclusion that man-made air pollution is good for our forests. After analyzing data from several studies, these scientists concluded that from 1971 to 1990, the rate of tree growth on the European continent increased 30 percent, and total volume of wood in tree trunks increased by 25 percent.

The scientists listed several possible reasons why the forests grew: the climate got warmer; airborne nitrates fertilized the forests; and increased concentrations of atmospheric carbon dioxide, which plants need to manufacture food, nourished the trees. Nitrates and carbon dioxide are both produced when oil, coal, and natural gas are burned.[39] It seems that moderate man-made pollution helps our forests grow.

GOVERNMENT-CREATED POLLUTION

Government is a major polluter in this country. Federal, state, and local governments dump millions of tons of raw sewage, toxic chemicals, and radioactive wastes into oceans, land fills, waste dumps, estuaries, and local waterways. Government sewage, sanitation, toxic waste disposal, and water treatment agencies have total control over how, when, and where these wastes are disposed. If bureaucrats in charge of these agencies make mistakes, we all suffer the effects of the pollution they create.

But the big difference between government and privately created pollution is that it's hard to sue the government. If a private company pollutes your water supply or dumps toxic material on your doorstep, you can sue them for millions of dollars. What can you do if government is the polluter? The U.S. Defense Department may dump toxic or radioactive wastes that pollute your water supplies, or a local sanitation department may create stinking land fills near your home. It's almost impossible to sue government agencies, and bureaucrats have unlimited resources for legal fees.

To solve this problem, we should turn over waste management to private enterprise. Private waste management would reduce costs, improve efficiency, and make companies liable for pollution damages. A civil-service bureaucrat who can't be sued or fired cares little about pollution he causes; a private company that can be sued into bankruptcy cares very much.

The federal government owns about one-third of the land in this country. The land is managed by the Forest Service, National Park Service, Bureau of Reclamation, Bureau of Land Management, and others. As a result, bureaucrats can mismanage these lands or cause enormous environmental damage without being accountable to anyone. Special interest groups also pressure Congress and these agencies for subsidies and "pork-barrel" legislation that hurts the environment.

The U.S. Bureau of Reclamation, the agency that oversees water resources and federal dam construction, is a prime example. Over the years, dam projects have wreaked havoc on millions of acres of land:

> The effects of irrigation on wildlife are amplified when rivers and natural lakes are dewatered by subsidized federal water projects. In Nevada's Pyramid Lake and in the Stillwater National Refuge, for example, water levels have receded to unprecedented low levels. A system of dams and canals on the Carson and Truckee rivers has caused the drawdown by diverting water to irrigators in Nevada's Lahontan Valley. The water level at Pyramid Lake, home of the endangered cui-ui fish and the threatened Lahontan cutthroat trout, has dropped by sixty feet. The Stillwater Refuge, which in good years harbored 200,000 ducks, 6000 geese, and 8000 tundra swans, has lost almost 68 percent of its productive marsh. In 1938, Winnemucca Lake, once a paradise for waterfowl on the Pacific Flyway, dried up. The same fate may be in store for Pyramid Lake and Stillwater Refuge.[40]

Environmental destruction in Nevada and California was the by-product of federal "pork-barrel" legislation. During the last eighty years, the U.S. Bureau of Reclamation has spent billions of taxpayer dollars bringing subsidized irrigation water to western farmers. Farmers get interest-free loans and pay only a fraction of the market cost of having this water stored and delivered to them.

Federal land management policies cause much environmental damage. They flood thousands of acres of land, destroy wildlife refuges, waste precious water because farmers get generous subsidies, and cause pollution contamination when natural water systems are disrupted.

Farmers and other special-interest groups would not get special treatment or pork-barrel favors in the free market. If we sold all federal lands to private owners, none of this could happen. In the free market, entrepreneurs would build massive dams and water projects only if they made economic sense. Market-priced water would encourage farmers to be more efficient. Entrepreneurs building water projects would be liable for damages for pollution that they caused to neighboring private lands, including privately owned wildlife refuges.

In a free market, property rights and strict liability laws would protect the land. The sale of all federal lands would also generate hundreds of billions of dollars in revenues that could reduce the federal deficit.

Government water control and irrigation projects have damaged federally-owned land. For over sixty years, federal farm policy has had equally devastating effects on almost 300 million acres of private farmland. Ecologists complain about farmers who destroy wetlands and use too many pesticides. Yet government is the culprit here. The federal government gives farmers direct subsidies, crop price supports, and subsidized insurance to increase crop production and support farmers' incomes.

That's one reason why farmers use so much pesticides and drain millions of acres of wetlands. If government pays farmers to increase crop production and eliminates most of their risks, why wouldn't they? It makes business sense. Farmers get more income and crop supports by putting more land under cultivation and using pesticides to increase the output per acre. Without government support, most farmers wouldn't drain and cultivate poor-quality wetlands. They do this because of federal subsidies. Federal agricultural policies cause heavy environmental damage, but farmers and pesticide manufacturers take the blame.

Environmentalists criticize the free market for producing so much abundance and garbage. Thousands of private and government sanitation trucks dump millions of tons of garbage a day into landfills. These stinking landfills cost hundreds of millions of dollars, ruin surrounding residential neighborhoods, and sometimes contaminate underground water supplies.

They also make life miserable for city dwellers. In New York City, apartment house owners used to incinerate garbage. Then the City Council passed a law that forbid this practice. Building owners now have to install compactors that collect and compress the garbage in the basement. The result? A whole city swarming with cockroaches because building owners can't burn garbage.

Many local governments forbid garbage incineration because the resulting air pollution might violate strict federal clean-air regulations. But there are modern scrubbing devices that clean incinerator exhausts. Smokestack pollution is a relatively minor technical problem easily solved by private incineration plants.

We have smokestack emission technology that solves the problem, but many state and city governments forbid garbage incineration. As a result, cities dump millions of tons of garbage in land fills. That costs taxpayers hundreds of millions of dollars, and fouls our land and water supplies. Worse, we pay taxes for *nothing*. As we noted twice already, most studies have shown that air pollution doesn't cause health problems to most people.

These programs, policies, and regulations are just some of the ways that government causes pollution and damages our land, water, and air resources. We could end these problems by repealing environmental regulations, ending all subsidy programs for farmers, turning over waste disposal to private companies, and selling off all federal and state-owned land.

THE EFFECTS OF ENVIRONMENTAL REGULATIONS

Lost Jobs

To "save" the northern Spotted Owl, the federal government restricted logging on almost seven million acres of federally-owned forests in Oregon, Washington state, and northern California. In 1990, the owl was designated a threatened species under the protection of the Endangered Species Act. EPA bureaucrats predicted that regulations designed to save the owl would throw about 33,000 logging industry workers out of jobs in the northwest.[41]

Did this massive loss of jobs bother environmentalists? Not in the least. In fact, they complained that the plan didn't go far enough, that it wouldn't insure the owl's survival, and that half the remaining owls would still die.[42]

The Federal Clean Air Act required 1994 cars to emit 98 percent less exhaust pollutants by 1994 than cars emitted in 1968. At these levels, auto exhausts will be cleaner than the air in many forests. Trees and plants in coniferous forests emit terpenes, nitrous oxide, and carbon monoxide, similar to the organic gases emitted by car tailpipes (these gases create the haze over the Smoky Mountains).

The University of Michigan Automotive Consulting Group estimated that the additional cost for these stricter emission standards would be about $1,015 per car. California and twelve Eastern states are trying to force manufacturers to build cars with very low emission levels. To do this, Ford, Chrysler, and General Motors will have to produce and subsidize high-priced electric cars that most drivers won't buy. To cover losses on the electric cars, average car prices will go up another $2800.[43]

Stringent auto pollution regulations, added to thousands of other regulations car manufacturers have to comply with, have pushed average new car prices to about $15,000. Emissions and safety regulations alone add about $3400 to a car's price.[44] With prices this high, many Americans either can't afford to buy or go deeper in debt to pay for the car.

Take a deep breath when you walk out the door of your house. Do you smell any air pollution? If the air seems reasonably fresh and clean to you, too bad. The EPA's eco-cops don't think so. They want car emission levels so low that you'll have to pay an extra $3,000 for a new car, if you can still afford one.

Though cars are now selling like hotcakes, General Motors and other manufacturers have been closing plants and firing thousands of autoworkers. High car prices put manufacturers in a vulnerable competitive position, so they're downsizing to protect themselves from future recessions.

Environmental Regulations Kill People

Regulations make it increasingly expensive and unprofitable to strip-mine coal. As a result, coal mining is going back in time because more coal has to come from underground mines. Instead of working outside in the fresh air, more coal workers now suffer cave-ins, escaping gas, black-lung disease, mine entrapments, and deadly explosions. Thousands more coal miners will get sick, injured, or die because environmental regulations strangle open-air strip-mining.

One of these injured miners is Harry L. Morris. The New York Times interviewed him about his health and medical insurance problems. He worked in the mines his whole life, including nineteen years on his knees in front of a four-foot high underground coal seam. Because he breathed coal dust for many years, 64-year-old Harry Morris has to take seven pills a day for arthritis, stomach trouble, and black-lung disease. He contracted pneumonia many times, including twice in one month. At the time of his interview, his health insurance was running out and he was scared.[45]

But environmentalists don't seem to care about Harry L. Morris or thousands of others like him who work in underground mines. To eco-radicals, what's important is that we don't "scar" the land with strip-mining.

Environmental regulations ban DDT and other insect and disease-killing pesticides. This ban kills people who now have little defense against malaria, encephalitis, and other mosquito-born diseases. Fungicides protect the world's food supply from crop-devouring insects. Environmental regulations that ban fungicides cause bloated-belly hunger or death by slow starvation for millions of people.

Endangered species regulations protect disease-carrying rats and child-eating alligators. Cougar hunting is restricted in all states from the Rocky Mountains to the Pacific Ocean. As a result, mountain lions are becoming more common in the West. Worse, because humans can't hunt them anymore, they're losing their fear of people.[46]

In 1990, California passed a law that banned cougar killing. In April 1994, a cougar killed Barbara Schoener, a mother of two children. She was jogging on a northern California trail, 45 miles northeast of Sacramento. The cougar came up behind her, sank its teeth into the back of her neck, and killed her.[47] If environmentalists hadn't put cougars on the endangered species list, Barbara Schoener's two children might still have their mother. Wetlands regulations protect swamps that breed malaria-carrying mosquitoes. Most Americans think that malaria is only a problem in Asia, Africa, or other faraway places. That's not true. Malaria has killed or crippled thousands of Americans since colonial times. Up to the 1940s, malaria was one of our most threatening diseases.

We've always fought malaria by draining swamps and killing mosquitos with pesticides like DDT. But wetlands and pesticide regulations have taken these weapons from us. As a result, since the early 1970s, malaria has increased almost tenfold in this country. Throughout the world, over 400 million people suffer from malaria and almost four million people die from this disease every year.[48]

If you live near a wetlands area that's a breeding ground for mosquitos, you could contract malaria, or your child could die from encephalitis because of these regulations. If we value human life, we should be *draining* most wetlands, not protecting them.

Make no mistake about it. Environmental regulations are not fluff or a joke—they kill men, women, and children.

High-Priced Homes We Can't Afford

Millions of Americans now can't afford a home. All over America, environmental regulations stop or delay new house construction. Environmentalists are experts at using lawsuits to stop new construction on wetlands (swamps), drylands, highlands, lowlands, eastlands, and westlands—on any lands that are "delicate ecosystems." To eco-radicals, the entire Earth is a delicate ecosystem. Therefore, they try to stop new construction anywhere they find it.

In their quest to stop development in its tracks, environmentalists cite "wetlands" almost everywhere. They also take advantage of the 19-year-old Endangered Species Act.

In Riverside County, California, development has been restricted on 81,000 acres while authorities study how much of the area the

Stephen's kangaroo *rat* needs (emphasis added). In Walton County, Florida, in 1991, U.S. Fish and Wildlife Service concerns about the Choctawhatchee Beach mouse effectively shut down one large subdivision before it could get off the ground. And in scrubland along the Southern California coast, builders fear that the California gnatcatcher—described by a developer as "a tiny bird with a big attorney"—will go on the endangered list.[49]

This outrage is happening across America, over and over again. We used to think that we should exterminate rats and mice. Now it seems that disease-breeding vermin need protection from people. Environmental delays, lawsuits, and regulations add thousands of dollars to the price of already high-priced homes, making it impossible for millions of young couples to buy their dream house. Endangered species regulations consider kangaroo rats more important than people.

Inflated Prices for Everything We Buy

Environmental regulations restrict oil, coal, and nuclear energy production. Regulations have stopped or delayed oil drilling offshore and on government lands (including millions of acres in Alaska), coal strip-mining, and nuclear power plants.

These restrictions increase our fuel, gasoline, and electricity bills and discourage energy companies from developing new fields. By restricting domestic production, the regulations also force us to import more than 45 percent of our oil, mostly from the Middle East. Arabs love our environmental regulations.

Energy regulations hurt us in many ways. Energy is the pumping heart and motor of our civilization. Plastics, clothing, chemicals, and thousands of other products come from oil. Higher electricity costs increase the price of everything, from aluminum cooking pots to our monthly electric bills. These eco-regulations take money from your pocket and leave you less for food, shelter, and your children's education.

The Assault on Our Liberty

Environmental regulations are a frontal assault on our property

117

rights and personal freedom. Regulations have closed off north-west forests from logging, throwing thousands of people out of work. Regulations have forced farmers, cattlemen, lumber companies, mining companies, ski resort operators, and oil companies off their land. Wetlands and endangered-species regulations have blocked developers from constructing houses, factories, and shopping centers on their own land.

Power-hungry EPA regulators have expanded the legal definition of wetlands to such an extent that a wetland can now be almost any land that water touches. Under current EPA regulations, eco-bureaucrats can now classify prairie potholes, corn and wheat fields, vacant, weed-covered lots, and almost 60 percent of all land in the United States as wetlands.[50]

Environmental regulations now take precedence over private property rights. An eco-cop who declares your property to be a wetlands, a place inhabited by an endangered species, or a place where migratory birds might roost, can stop you from developing your land.[51]That means if you fill in potholes that collect water, divert a stream to irrigate your land, drain a mosquito-infested swamp on your farm to grow wheat, or build your house on land used by kangaroo rats or other "endangered" species, eco-cops can fine or imprison you. If eco-cops declare your land to be a wetlands, then swamps, rats, and birds have more right to your land than you do.

For over two hundred years, Americans have drained wetlands (swamps) to make a decent life for themselves. We drained swamps to build cities, create farmland, and fight malaria and encephalitis. We filled in swamps because we believed that we had a right to live on this Earth like human beings.

If we had wetlands regulations since colonial times, here's what would have happened: Almost 100 million acres of farmland in the Midwest and most land in the Mississippi Valley would be declared off-limits. That's because thousands of farmers drained the water on their land into the Mississippi and other rivers. Draining the water off their land allowed them to grow crops that feed us. New Orleans would not exist, because it was built on drained swampland. Finally, EPA bureaucrats might be out of a job because Washington, D.C. would not exist. Our capital city was built on a malarial swamp that was drained and filled.[52]

The Supreme Court seems to have forgotten the existence of the Fifth Amendment to the Constitution, which reads: "No person shall . . . be deprived of life, liberty, or property, without due process of law; nor shall private property be taken for public use without just compensation."

Environmental regulations are a blatant violation of the Fifth Amendment. In the name of protecting the Alabama Beach Mouse, Houston Toad, Desert Pup Fish, Kangaroo Rat, Puerto Rican Cave Cockroach, Puritan Tiger Beetle, and over 740 other snails, rodents, and bugs on the endangered species list, eco-regulations are ripping our precious liberty to shreds.

Here's how far environmentalists can go: a team of professors from Rutgers University put forth a program they called the "Buffalo Commons." They proposed that the federal government should force 400,000 people living in 110 counties in nine states off their land ("deprivatize" them). Why? So that buffalo could roam the land.[53]

I want you to imagine living on a farm in Kansas that your family has lived on for generations. Then some eco-cop comes by with an eviction notice. He tells you that the new "Buffalo Commons" regulations require you to vacate your land so buffalo can take over. How would you feel about that?

From the Revolutionary War to Desert Storm, hundreds of thousands of brave Americans have died fighting to defend our freedom. Yet today, with little protest, we throw our liberty into the gutter for the sake of rats, owls, and wetlands swamps.

I could list many other disastrous consequences from environmental regulations, but I think you get the point. Environmental regulations are dangerous to human life. They attack our liberty, destroy our property rights, strangle our energy, housing, and automobile industries, and inflate the cost of cars, fuel, houses, electricity, and hundreds of other products. These regulations also kill men, women, and children.

Does this mean pollution isn't a problem, that we shouldn't be concerned with it at all? Am I in favor of raping our lands, poisoning our air and water, and using chemicals that poison us? Of course not. I have to live on this planet, too. But I'm not concerned about pollution because the environmental crisis is a myth and a hoax.

SPECIAL TARGET—THE ENERGY INDUSTRIES

A good test of someone's motives is to see where his actions lead—to see how his actions affect the real world. If we look at America today, we see a curious set of conditions. The environmental movement has never been stronger. Environmental groups have blocked or delayed power plants, coal-mining operations, oil pipelines, offshore oil wells, and many other industrial enterprises. Environmentalists who claim they want to improve our quality of life have never had more opportunity to do so.

With the strong-arm help of the federal government, environmentalists have tried to regulate every major industry in this country, from chemical production to housing developments. But nowhere have their efforts been more fierce than against the energy industries—oil, gas, coal, nuclear, and even hydroelectric power.

I believe environmentalists have made these industries a special target because energy is the heart of our industrial civilization. All our steel mills, factories, automobiles, and electric power plants would be dead hunks of metal without fuel to run the motors and generate the power. Just as food keeps us alive, so energy is the life force of our industrial society. Stop the flow of energy and the motors stop, the roads grow empty, the factories close, and therefore we control pollution.

In spite of energy's crucial importance to our lives and well-being, ecologists try to restrict the development, exploration, or production of oil, coal, nuclear energy, and even hydroelectric power.

The Alaskan Pipeline

In 1969, Exxon, Atlantic Richfield, and a consortium of other oil companies proposed building a 789-mile pipeline from Prudhoe Bay on Alaska's North Slope to the ice-free port of Valdez, on Alaska's south-central coast. The estimated cost was $3.6 billion. Beneath the North Slope field lay the largest oil field ever found in North America—over 24 billion barrels of high-quality crude oil.

Environmental organizations filed a lawsuit against the pipeline and forced the U.S. Interior Department to spend over three years preparing an environmental impact statement. It finally took four years to get the project approved with major design revisions. Only now, the estimated cost of the pipeline had jumped to $6.5 billion. It then took another four years before oil companies completed the pipeline and oil started flowing from Prudhoe Bay.

Eco-radicals blocked the Alaskan pipeline for four years because they claimed that oil development would cause environmental disasters to this "vulnerable" land. The land they called vulnerable is a miserable frozen wasteland—millions of square miles of ice packs, howling winds, frozen tundra, and sub-zero temperatures. This vulnerable land that ecologists worried about is a nightmare land, not fit for human habitation. What were the potential disasters?

Environmentalists worried that oil machinery and equipment would litter the Arctic wasteland. They claimed that putting a pipeline over the frozen tundra would be like cutting a knife through living flesh. They were also afraid that because oil moved through the pipeline at a temperature of 140 degrees, the permafrost under the pipeline might melt and the pipeline might break. If the pipeline broke, thousands of gallons of oil would spill over the ground.

Even if some oil leaked, so what? Who cares if a broken pipeline spills a little oil in this nightmare wilderness? Are millions of Americans lining up to go on cruises to the Arctic in the dead of winter? Only a few polar bears live in this God-forsaken lunar landscape. Besides, the oil company would quickly mend the pipe and stop the leak because they lose oil and money while the pipe is leaking.

What other disasters were possible? Because the pipeline would be above ground over half its length, ecologists feared that the pipeline could block caribou migrations, that jeeps and other vehicles that serviced the pipeline would scar the land, and that the pipeline would be a scenic eyesore.

Eco-radicals seem to believe in animism, which projects life and feelings onto inanimate objects. Ice packs are described as if they're living skin. Roads scar the land and cut a knife wound through living flesh. Environmentalists often describe wetlands, arctic tundra, and sand dunes as "fragile" or "delicate."

If roads scar the land, what about farms? Do farmers cut a knife wound through living flesh when they plough their fields? Do ecologists want to shut down all our farms because plowed fields are a scenic eyesore?

This kind of eco-babble delayed the development of an oil field holding almost 24 billion barrels of oil and 26 trillion cubic feet of natural gas; and this is just the tip of the iceberg. In 1964, Congress passed the Wilderness Act that permanently removed nine million acres of federal land from oil exploration. Today, wilderness regulations have locked up over 89 million acres of land. If we add the lands removed because of wilderness-study classification, the total increases to over 222 million acres. If we then add all national parks, wildlife refuges, Alaskan set-asides, and other federal lands to the total, over 319 million acres have been blocked off from exploration. This represents about 45 percent of all lands owned by the federal government.[54]

How much oil and gas could we find on the 319 million acres of federal land that are now locked up? My guess would be enough to make us totally independent of foreign oil.

Offshore Oil

Undiscovered offshore oil fields have been another special target of environmentalists. Soon after President Reagan proposed a five-year offshore leasing program in 1982, Congress passed moratoriums that removed millions of acres off New England and California coastlines from the program. Since then, lawsuits by environmental groups have removed millions of potentially rich offshore acres from exploration.[55]

The federal offshore leasing program started in 1954. Since then only about 30 million acres, or 3 percent, of total federal offshore acreage has been leased. Compare this to other countries. Since 1964, England has leased 66 million offshore acres (including the huge North Sea oil field), and Canada has leased about 900 million offshore acres.[56] Canada has a population of about 15 million people compared to our 250 million, yet they've leased thirty times more acreage than we have.

Oil companies have drilled almost 19,000 offshore wells in the past twenty-five years. These wells have produced almost seven billion barrels of oil and thirty-three trillion cubic feet of gas, and we're just beginning to tap the potential here. Yet offshore exploration is being stopped by the same eco-radicals who tried to block the Alaskan pipeline.

Ecologists claim they're afraid of oil spills from offshore wells. We noted earlier that bacteria, evaporation, and the ocean's cleansing action quickly break up and eliminate oil spills in open seas. Environmentalists have exaggerated the danger of these spills. Of the almost 19,000 offshore wells drilled in the past twenty-five years, only six have had oil spills that caused serious pollution. The spills were cleaned up quickly, with little harm done to anyone except a few fish or birds.

Why this excellent safety record? Because oil companies don't like losing money. They lose millions of dollars worth of oil from a spill, and pay out millions more for cleanup costs and lawsuits by fishermen and environmentalists.

In spite of this extraordinary safety record, California Standard Oil was barred from drilling new offshore wells along the coast of Santa Barbara. Regulations still forbid offshore drilling along much of California's coastline today.

What environmental cataclysms can an offshore oil well create? An oil spill could wash up on shore, dirtying some beaches and killing some fish. When such a spill happens, oil companies clean the beaches fairly quickly. If they didn't, tourist and fishing industries would hit them with heavy lawsuits. As for the fish, life is resilient in the sea; they quickly come back in force.

Again, eco-regulations strangle a major energy source, not because oil wells threaten human life, but because they "defile" nature. Oil that powers our cars and lights our homes doesn't flow because we're supposed to value fish more than human beings.

Western Coal

America's untapped energy resources are not limited to offshore oil. We also have vast amounts of low-sulphur coal under several million acres of federally-owned land in Utah, Montana, Colorado, and South Dakota. The reserves are so rich and the seams so thick (some go to fifty feet and more), that an estimated 350 square miles of these reserves could supply America's entire energy requirements for the next two hundred years.

Recoverable coal reserves are estimated to be 800 times current annual production. Coal accounts for over 90 percent of our fossil-fuel resources but produces less than one-fifth of our energy. Why aren't we using more of our vast coal reserves?

Electric utility power plants are big users of coal, and environmental regulations limit the sulfur content of smokestack emissions from these plants. As a result, it becomes too expensive to purify millions of tons of high-sulphur coal from eastern states. Are environmentalists enthusiastic about using billions of tons of clean, low-sulphur coal from western reserves? Guess again.

Coal mining companies have leased almost one million acres of western reserves, yet have mined only a small fraction of these acres because of pollution taxes and regulations. Strip-mining laws enacted in 1974 imposed a land reclamation tax of 35 cents a ton on all coal mined on federal reserves. This surtax and other regulations reduced profits. Coal companies aren't sacrificial animals. They won't mine coal if taxes and regulations force them to produce at a loss or for sharply reduced profits.

What do ecologists have against mining this coal? Strip-mining would "scar" the land and pollute some streams. Should we lose billions of tons of low-sulphur, nonpolluting coal because mining defaces a few square miles of land and "scars" inanimate dirt?

Atomic Power

Radical environmentalists have also blocked atomic power. Nuclear energy seemed the great bright hope of the future when serious development began in the late 1950s. Environmental regulations have strangled that hope.

In the Calvert Cliffs Decision of 1971, the Supreme Court ruled that the Atomic Energy Commission was responsible not only for pollution and radiation safety in licensing a new plant, but also for thermal and aesthetic effects. This court ruling forced the Atomic Energy Commission (AEC) to completely reorganize their program to meet the severe new air and water standards set by the National Environmental Protection Act of 1969. The decision affected 110 nuclear power plants under construction, being planned, or currently operating. It also forced the AEC to stop licensing new plants for seventeen months.

New licensing procedures sharply increased the time needed to review and build a new plant. It now takes almost ten years to get a plant approved and built, if it gets built at all. What utility company in its right mind would be crazy enough to endure the time, risk, and investment required for a new plant? Not many, and that's why nuclear energy is almost a dead industry.

The atomic energy industry's safety record is extraordinary. No private citizen has been killed by radiation exposure from a commercial nuclear power plant. Over the past thirty years, there were only seven radiation-caused deaths in the AEC's own production plants.[57] When you compare this record to underground coal mines that ruin the health of many workers every year, you realize how good this safety record really is.

In spite of the proven safety record of atomic power, environmentalists didn't give up. They tried other tactics to block new plants, and the Calvert Cliffs decision gave them the ammunition they needed.

On December 6, 1973, the California Coastal Zone Conservation Commission blocked a $1.3 billion atomic power project because the plant would disturb scenic areas, block access to a public beach, and allegedly hurt marine life. In that same year, the AEC ordered New York's Con Edison to build a new cooling system at its second nuclear power plant at Indian Point to protect fish. Con Ed appealed the order and said the second cooling plant would cost $70 million a year to operate. The courts denied the appeal and cool water for the fish turned into higher electric bills for New Yorkers. Once again, eco-regulations "helped" animals by hurting human beings.

Hydroelectric Power

What about an energy source that's totally nonpolluting? Surely

125

environmentalists couldn't have any objections to that. Guess again. Environmental groups sued New York State to block nonpolluting hydroelectric power. They wanted to stop New York from buying huge amounts of cheap electricity from Quebec's James Bay hydroelectric plants. They claimed that these plants would allegedly hurt the wetlands and wildlife in the James Bay area.[58]

The Shell Game

No matter what energy source we want to use, no matter how nonpolluting it is, environmentalists dream up some excuse to stop it. If the energy comes from oil, gas, coal, nuclear, or hydroelectric power, if human beings take it from this Earth or produce it, then by definition it's pollution.

Ecologists play a shell game with us. Now you see it, now you don't. If they can't stop development with lawsuits over air pollution, they try water pollution. When that doesn't work, they try the Spotted Owl guilt trip. If that doesn't work, they give us the old "upsetting the delicate ecosystem" routine. If that fails, they bring out the big guns—their doomsday, science-fiction predictions of ecological disaster.

Environmental regulations take money out of our pockets, threaten our standard of living, restrict our freedom of choice, put huge tax and regulatory burdens on businesses, and throw thousands of workers out of jobs. These are the real effects of environmental regulations.

Yet ecologists claim that they're helping us improve the quality of our lives. Except for making our air and water a little cleaner at enormous costs, these regulations only hurt us. Since environmental regulations hurt us more than they help us, eco-radicals either live in a dream world or they're hiding something from us. If their regulations don't improve our lives, what are radical environmentalists really after?

ECO-RADICALS: WHO ARE THESE PEOPLE?

To understand the eco-radicals' goals, it's important to understand what makes these people tick. The average eco-radical is a combination priest, naturalist, and pseudoscientist. In the role of naturalist and pseudoscientist, he studies the complex interrelationships linking living species to each other and to the environment. As priest, he elevates nature to the status of God and worships it.

Ecologists think that humans are sinners at heart. We're sinners because we don't have humility in the presence of nature. The ecologist claims that mankind is an arrogant, selfish, and callous monster who willfully destroys nature with his infernal technology and so-called progress.

Human beings are arrogant, he claims, because they assume they have the right and ability to change nature—because they have ambition, self-esteem, and intelligence. Human beings are selfish because they value and try to improve their lives. They're callous because they think their lives are more important than sea urchins, kangaroo rats, and malarial marshes.

In short, ecologists condemn human beings because we're guilty of the original sin—that we're human. Our sin, however, is not against God, but against nature. Adam was condemned because he questioned the premise that God knows best. Today, ecologists condemn the human race because we question the notion that nature knows best.

Nature Knows Best

This premise has actually been turned into a scientific "law." It's Barry Commoner's Third Law of Ecology, described in his book *The Closing Circle*, and reads:

> Stated baldly, the third law of ecology holds that any major man-made change in a natural system is likely to be detrimental to that system.[59]

Translated, this means that nature is allegedly perfect and inviolate—don't fool with it. To ecologists, nature knows best means that nature knows better than people how to function for itself and we should therefore leave it alone. In effect, nature is sacred because a million years of evolution has made it infallible.

But nature is neither sacred nor infallible. Nature is the physical result of a constant process of evolutionary change over millions of years, change that continues to this day. Nature is inherently change itself—a complex set of varying relationships and interactions between all living things and the physical and chemical environment of the Earth.

New species gradually emerge, and existing ones either die or change in response to changing conditions. The winds wear down mountains, the seas still engage the land in an age-old battle, and volcanic action creates new islands and destroys others.

Nature doesn't know best—it "knows" nothing at all. "Best" implies a static, arbitrary, unchanging nature that doesn't exist. Nature is constantly changing, driven by time, chance, and its own innate character.

Time, floods, earthquakes, volcanos, and climate changes have extinguished more animal species than now exist on Earth. Like atoms, environments aren't destroyed—they merely change into other forms. Lakes become swamps, swamps become meadows, meadows become forests, grasslands become deserts, and so on.

No ecosystem is best or most natural because ecosystems are constantly changed by nature or human beings. When the first settlers came to America, they chopped down forests to clear the land for farming. Upper New York State is beautiful and "natural," yet what we see today are third generations of trees planted or pruned by local residents. The Midwest used to be endless prairies of wild grass. Today, the prairies are endless corn and wheat fields—just different kinds of plants.

The human race has also contributed to our planet's health. Over 200,000 plants have been introduced into America from around the world, including pears, rice, wheat, apples, and potatoes. People and our atmosphere benefit by cultivating these crops (which absorb carbon dioxide and give out oxygen). Are these plants "unnatural" because they weren't here when Columbus arrived? Should we destroy our wheat fields and apple orchards to preserve the pristine purity of nature?

People have also helped nature by building dams and other structures to prevent floods and erosion. Should we blow up our dams and live in the dark without electricity because dams diverted "natural" rivers?

In 1992, less than 5 percent of America's total land area was densely populated urban centers. Much of America is still the way it was when Columbus stepped ashore—forests, deserts, mountains, and open grasslands. Even suburban areas are mostly grass and trees. In other countries that are less industrialized, nature has been altered even less in the last two hundred years.

Throughout the centuries, ecosystems have changed drastically on this durable planet of ours. But the Earth is still here, and people are better off than they ever were. Since the turn of the century the average life span for Americans has increased from about 50 years to 73 years. If pollution and technology were killing us, why are we living so much longer?

As for the notion that nature is sacred, let's get serious. Should we get down on our knees and worship swamps, earthworms, and old-growth pine trees? Yes, nature can be beautiful, inspiring, and refreshing, especially for harried city dwellers. But is nature sacred? Primitive tribes worshiped nature and believed that trees and animals have spirits. They bowed down to these spirits and offered sacrifices. Is this what ecologists want us to do?

"Delicate" Nature

Ecologists say that we're destroying spaceship Earth, which is like saying an ant could massacre a herd of elephants. They claim that nature is the new God, not to be questioned, disobeyed, or tampered with. Who is mankind, they ask, to poke his dirty fingers into the intricate, delicate, and divine workings of mother nature?

We should address this question to the thousands of people killed each year by floods, earthquakes, tornados, hurricanes, and malarial mosquitos. Ask them whether nature is sacred and delicate. Nature killed these people without mercy. Far from being delicate, nature is brutal, violent, and overpowering.

Radical environmentalists also claim that nature is emotionally sensitive. It seems that human beings are continually hurting its feelings:

> Human society is designed to exploit the environment . . Thoreau's woods, Mark Twain's rivers, and Melville's oceans are today under attack . . . Environmental degradation largely results from the introduction of new industrial and agricultural . . technologies . . . productive technologies with intense impacts on the environment have replaced less destructive ones . . . all this "progress" has greatly increased the impact on the environment..[60]

The human race allegedly rapes, attacks, degrades, exploits, and plunders nature. Will nature, like some angry god, take this abuse indefinitely? Not at all. Ecologists say that nature will strike back—it will collapse, and destroy mankind:

> Why, after millions of years of harmonious coexistence, have the relationships between living things and their earthly surroundings begun to collapse? . . . Yet the evidence is overwhelming that the way in which we now live on the earth is driving its thin, life-supporting skin, and ourselves with it, to destruction . . .The environmental crisis is a signal of this approaching catastrophe.[61]

We don't know when or how this catastrophe will happen. All we know is this: if we don't mend our ways, if we don't curb our arrogance and selfishness, the end is at hand.

Human Beings—Freaks of Nature?

To many ecologists, human beings are more than arrogant and selfish—they're fundamentally unnatural. Humans are different from other creatures. We refuse to adapt to our environment like animals, and we stubbornly insist on changing it:

> One of the most pervasive features of modern technology is the notion that it is intended to "improve on nature"—to provide food, clothing, shelter, and means of communication and expression which are superior to those available to man in nature.[62]

People have a notion that we can feed ourselves better if we use tractors and fertilizers. We have a notion that it's better to live in a warm house than a cave. We have a notion that it's easier to manufacture our clothes instead of hunting animals for skins. We have a notion that it's easier to fly from New York to California in three hours, rather than get there by covered wagon in a year. We have a notion that nature won't automatically give us what we need to survive.

Human beings have to manufacture everything their lives depend on because our nature and method of survival are uniquely different from all other living species. Unlike all other animals, we're born without instincts to guide us. We also have no fur, fangs, claws, or great speed or strength to help us survive in a hostile environment. Our unique and most powerful tool of survival is our minds—our ability to think. We have to learn everything our lives depend on. We can't survive by adapting to nature like animals—we have nothing to adapt with.

Humans have to alter their environment. We have to invent and produce the food, clothing, shelter, and other things we need to survive. Many environmentalists evade or resent this fact. They believe that human beings are unnatural *because* we can think and because we have to alter nature to survive. To admit that humans are part of nature would sanction everything they seem to hate: progress, technology, and the free market.

We hear the hysterical ravings of our ecologists rising to fever pitch today: don't cut down those trees—it will upset the owls; don't build that power plant—it will pollute the air; don't build the Alaskan pipeline—it may break and spill oil over frozen Arctic wasteland; don't build that offshore oil well—it may spill some oil on the beach and hurt some sea urchins; don't build that electric power plant—it will spill warm water into the local river and disturb the poor fish; don't build those houses—you might have to drain a local swamp (wetlands). In effect, environmentalists say "don't touch nature," which means *don't live like human beings.*

Protect Nature Or The Human Race?

We have a high standard of living only because we act on the principle that nature does *not* know best, that people can and

131

must alter nature for their own benefit. Here's what our lives would be like if we went along with the eco-radicals' agenda: we would be back in caves, warming ourselves over a sputtering fire, with an animal skin on our backs and the freezing wind howling outside.

There was a period in history known as the Dark Ages when human progress was frozen. It was a time of plagues, starvation, freezing mud huts, candlelight power, and backbreaking labor. If this picture makes you shudder and thank your stars for living in the modern world, look twice. Millions of people in Asia, Africa, and South America still live like this. For most of these people, hunger, disease, and misery are a way of life.

Those who live in pre-industrial misery don't share our ecologists' reverence for nature because they live too close to it. Primitive or underdeveloped societies don't need environmentalists preaching to them. People in these countries think nature is their deadliest enemy. They don't care about protecting it—they just want to survive it.

Without the machines and technology of an industrial society, we're at the mercy of a hostile and merciless environment. Without modern medicine, we would succumb to disease. Without modern agricultural technology, we would look starvation in the face. Without modern houses and electric power plants we would shiver from the cold in stinking hovels.

The notion of protecting nature can only make sense in an industrial society. In a world of paved streets, automobiles, supermarkets, and department stores, nature fades into the background. It's tamed and made to serve our needs.

Instead of being an enemy, nature now gives us relief from the fumes, noise, crowds, and concrete of modern cities. Nature has been transformed. It's not a source of fear any longer, but a source of pleasure. As a result, we now want to protect nature, to keep our refuge safe, clean, and beautiful. That's why so many Americans move out of noisy, polluted cities into suburban areas. Most people like trees, grass, and fresh air. That's why the environmentalists' message has such a powerful effect on us, and that's where the danger lies.

The ecologists' call to protect the environment touches a deep sympathy in us. We assume they lobby for environmental regulations to protect our health and to preserve nature as a source of contrast and pleasure. But nature can give us pleasure only within the comfort and security of an industrial civilization. We can enjoy nature only when we conquer it.

A snowstorm is beautiful while we watch it through the window of our warm, cozy home. The deep blackness of night doesn't scare us if our home is brightly lit with electricity. A blistering desert is grand when we ride through it in a fast, air-conditioned train. Other people's hunger and disease in faraway lands is only a sad item in the news for those of us with supermarkets full of food, and modern hospitals.

But take away our electricity, warm houses, supermarkets, medical centers, and speedy air-conditioned trains and we're left naked and defenseless. Take away our machines and technology and nature is now a brutal and indifferent enemy to human beings. Without our oil and electricity, we would freeze to death in candlelit huts. Take away the air-conditioned train and we would be buzzard food in the desert. Take away agriculture and medical science and we would starve or die of diseases. Without technology we're back in the Dark Ages with nature as our deadliest enemy.

Technology helps us survive, protects us from nature's brutality, and improves the quality of our lives. Any attempt to protect nature by political policies that weaken or destroy a country's economic and technological foundations, threatens our lives.

Environmental regulations might make the air a little cleaner, but what value is that to someone who's lost his job? Cleaner air means little to a man whose family is starving and freezing in a cold-water flat because he can't find another job in a regulation-wrecked economy.

This fact is obvious to the wretched people who live in countries that don't have modern technology and economic freedom. The misery, hunger, and disease in places like Africa or India should make us almost worship the factories, power plants, and shopping malls that make our lives so prosperous. If not worship, then we should at least be deeply grateful to technology and those who create it. Technology's enormous benefits make the issue of pollution, by comparison, a minor, stupidly irrelevant technical problem.

THE ECO-RADICALS' REAL MOTIVES

Instead of worshiping technology, eco-radicals condemn it *because* it gives us so much abundance. They claim that abundance pollutes our air and water. Cars, beer cans, fast food, warm houses, air conditioners, electricity, and throwaway diapers are the culprits because they "pollute" the environment. To eco-radicals, our abundance and good life are the enemy.

Ecologists tell us that pollution from uncontrolled technology and industrialization threatens life on Earth. To avoid this catastrophe, eco-radicals say we have to stop or restrict technology, production, property rights, and the free market. That is, we have to stop living like free human beings.

But if we did that, our economy would collapse and millions of Americans would lose their jobs. Our lives would be reduced to the squalor and misery that existed before the industrial revolution. We would be back in the Dark Ages.

If eco-radicals told us we must live in squalor and disease to protect sea urchins, kangaroo rats, and swamps, we would laugh at them, as they deserve. Since no one in his right mind wants a wretched life, ecologists must use scare tactics to convince us. Like modern-day witch doctors, they shake their sticks at us and predict the end of the world and mankind's destruction if we don't heed their words. Just as religious fanatics warn us that God will punish us if we don't give up sex and drinking, so ecologists warn us that nature will punish us if we don't give up our cars, air conditioners, and disposable beer cans.

Most of us dismiss the prophesies of doom by religious fanatics, yet we believe the doomsday predictions of radical environmentalists. Why? Because ecologists do something religious fanatics can't do. They use the prestige of science to give respectability to their wild predictions.

As we saw earlier, environmentalists use questionable facts and studies to "prove" their scare stories. Because we respect science, we believe these stories. After all, if scientific "facts" show that the Earth is in danger, shouldn't we do something about it?

The problem is that it's easy to distort facts or blow them out of proportion. Eco-radicals are experts at making broad, frightening generalizations from unproven facts and theories. But most of us aren't scientists, or we don't have time to analyze ecologists' scare stories. So we believe them because they're scientists and because the liberal media keeps spreading their message.

To "protect" the environment, ecologists have to stop us from producing so many cars, houses, power plants, and thousands of other products. They can only do this by strangling the system that creates these products—the free market. The only way to strangle the free market is to regulate it to death. To do this, environmentalists turn to government.

Government is the only institution that has the power to violate our property rights and economic liberty. It's the only institution that can strangle industrial production with regulations. Without government, environmentalists would be powerless.

So ecologists have to convince Congress to act. They know that congressmen are sensitive to their constituents' fears. So they have to scare us. They do this with doomsday stories and end-of-the-world predictions of global warming, global freezing, destruction of our oceans, destruction of all life on the planet, and so on. If pesticides don't poison us, car exhausts will. If water pollution doesn't kill us, air pollution will. If the greenhouse effect doesn't get us, the hole in the ozone layer will. The scare stories are endless.

When environmentalists scare enough of us, we then pressure Congress into passing environmental regulations. These regulations then strangle our property rights, the free market, and human progress on this Earth.

Property Rights

In a free society, property rights protect freedom and human progress. People stop growing food, making cars, or building houses if government loots what they earn through heavy, progressive taxes. We stop producing if bureaucrats strangle us with regulations. Every socialist, communist, or welfare state in human history has proven this.

Eco-radicals know this. So they attack property rights with a vengeance. Earlier we noted how environmental regulations violate the Fifth Amendment that protects property rights. But the Fifth Amendment doesn't seem to mean much to environmentalists.

A former administrator of the EPA who helped shape the land-use philosophy of that agency, believed that we should question private ownership of land. He suggested that we repeal the Fifth Amendment so that government could more easily seize private land for environmental purposes.[63]

Eco-bureaucrats can confiscate your property, stop you from using your land, fine you up to $25,000 per day if you don't obey their orders, and jail you if you use your land for something they don't allow.[64] And if you want to fight them in court, you can go bankrupt paying legal fees.

The eco-radicals' attack on property rights is widespread. Their regulations restrict logging in forests, create wetlands restrictions that stop developers from building homes and shopping centers on private property, and restrict mining and oil exploration on millions of acres of land. The list goes on and on.

Brandt Child of Kaneb, Utah, got a taste of environmentalists' utter contempt for property rights the hard way. He wanted to build a recreational park and tourist stop on four hundred acres of land he owned. He was going to build the resort around three acquifer-fed ponds on his land. When he started to build, some eco-police from the U.S. Fish and Wildlife Service paid him a visit. They told him that the ponds were the home of the Kanab Ambersnail, an endangered species, and that he couldn't build his park. Brandt Child told them, "This is my land; I own it and I pay taxes on it." Guess what the eco-cops told him? They said, "You may own it and you may pay taxes on it, *but we control it*" (emphasis added).[65] Need I say more?

Eco-radicals must also attack the free market because it's the engine of economic progress. The free market is simply millions of people trading and cooperating to produce goods and services that make our lives safer, better, and more fulfilling. The free market is property rights in action.

Here are some typical environmental statements on the free-market economy:

Far more serious than such objections is the questions of whether a conventional "market place" economy is fundamentally incompatible with the integrity of the environment.[66]

Translation: the private enterprise system causes all our environmental problems. The car you drive, the home you live in, the electricity that lights your house, and the furnace that warms your family in winter are all "fundamentally incompatible with the integrity of the environment." By implication, let's think about ending private enterprise and replacing it with what? Eco-socialism? Eco-fascism? Mud huts lit by candles and warmed by burning cow dung? Here's another one:

> I think if we don't overthrow capitalism, we don't have a chance of saving the world ecologically. I think it is possible to have an ecologically sound society under socialism. I don't think it's possible under capitalism.[67]

Translation: Capitalism, property rights, and the free market are ruining the world "ecologically." They produce too much abundance for human beings. That's not ecologically sound. We must abolish capitalism and economic liberty, and substitute socialism in their place. Socialism will protect the environment. It will end the anarchy and selfishness of capitalism, and lead us to an ecological utopia ruled by eco-commissars who know what's best for us. Does this sound familiar?

In 1917, a Russian named Vladimir Lenin said much the same things. He wanted to tear down the evil (to him) capitalist, free-market system just starting to bloom in Russia, and replace it with a more "equitable" system that redistributed "society's" resources. Well, Lenin had his experiment for seventy-five years. We all know what happened to his utopia and to the lives of millions of wretched Russians forced to live under his more equitable society.

But the environmental movement is more pathetic and irrational than Lenin. It wants us to sacrifice our lives, our future, and our freedom, not to help human beings (the proletariat) or future generations, but to protect owls, swamps, and kangaroo rats.

And by the way, when communism fell in Russia and Eastern

Europe, Western observers were appalled by the putrid environmental mess that fifty years of communism had created. Communist rulers ruined the environment because they didn't have to bother with property rights or a free market.

Am I saying that all environmentalists are mad communists? Of course not. Most environmentalists are sincere, well-intentioned, but naive people who love nature and simply want to protect it. But I believe that eco-radicals who lead the movement make up doomsday stories to promote an eco-socialist political agenda.

Human Progress

This virulent hatred for a free economy is a driving force behind the eco-radicals' fierce efforts to strangle the free market with regulations. Yet behind this hatred is an even deeper one. To understand why they try to wreck our economy, you have to grasp the shocking fact that some eco-radicals seem to hate the human race and Western civilization. They hate the fact that you, your family, your friends, and millions of other human beings live and prosper on this planet.

Most of us are naive about the environmental movement. We believe that when eco-radicals say we should "protect the environment," they mean we should protect it for people. What they really mean is that we should protect the environment *against* people. People are the enemy. Rats, swamps, and old-growth forests must be protected against you, your family, and the rest of the human race.

To confirm this, just watch nature programs on public television. In every program I've seen, human beings are depicted as the enemy. These programs portray us as vicious, violent destroyers of birds, wildlife, forests, rivers, and oceans. Nature is seen as pure, fragile, and innocent (including child-eating hyenas and alligators). Ecologists or their sympathizers create these programs, so the programs reflect the environmental movement's deepest attitudes toward the human race.

If environmental groups valued human life, they wouldn't try to cut our oil supplies. They wouldn't ban the hunting of alligators that kill children. They wouldn't file lawsuits against housing developments to protect kangaroo rats. They wouldn't lobby Congress to ban DDT, the pesticide that saves the lives of millions of people worldwide. They wouldn't ban logging in northwest forests to protect spotted owls, a ban that destroyed over 30,000 logging and sawmill workers' jobs.

Here's what one environmentalist had to say about loggers losing their jobs:

> "Loggers losing their jobs because of Spotted Owl legislation is, in my eyes, no different than people being out of work after the furnaces of Dachau shut down."[68]

Here's how I interpret this statement: Forcing owls to move to another forest because you cut down trees they nest in, is just as evil as murdering six million people in gas chambers. Owls are as important as six million human lives. If loggers unintentionally kill a few owls, they're as evil as the murderers who ran the Nazi gas chambers. Therefore, we should have no sympathy for loggers who lost their jobs.

Here's another quote:

> "Somewhere along the line . . . we quit the contract and became a cancer. We have become a plague upon ourselves and upon the Earth . . . Until such time as Homo sapiens should decide to rejoin nature, *some of us can only hope for the right virus to come along* (emphasis added)." [69]

These are typical quotes by radical environmentalists. What do these quotes say about the environmental movement's respect for human life?

I knew that the environmental movement values swamps and kangaroo rats over human life, but I didn't realize how sick this movement really is until I read a shocking article in *The New York Times*. It seems that in Brazil, environmentalists helped create a twenty-five-year-old ban on hunting wildlife. This ban includes the dreaded jacaré, the Brazilian alligator.

The jacaré is a vicious, prehistoric, man and child-eating monster who inhabits the Amazon River Basin. The article talked about Francisca Ramos da Conceicào. In the high-water season, alligators infest the riverbanks near where Mrs. Ramos lives.

One evening in August, an eighteen-foot jacaré emerged from the lagoon to forage for food in waters flowing around the stilts of her house. This is what happened:

"Gilson (Mrs. Ramos's 17-year-old son) went down to tie up his canoe," said Sidecley Conceicào Andrade, a barefoot, 12-year-old neighbor. "In the dark, he thought he grabbed the canoe, but it was the jacaré's tail. It took him away and ate him up."[70]

Can you imagine the horror of being eaten alive by an alligator? Can you imagine the nightmares and searing pain Mrs. Ramos must feel when she thinks of her son? Well, Brazil's environmental regulations killed her son and hundreds of other innocent victims of alligator attacks.

Imagine that you lived in Florida and were the parents of a beautiful little girl. How would you feel if an alligator protected by the Endangered Species Act snatched your daughter and ate her alive? How would you like hearing your little girl crying for her mommy or daddy while the alligator ripped into her? I apologize for describing such a horror in detail, but I want to bring home the real meaning of environmental laws like the Endangered Species Act. If you want to picture the essense of the environmental movement, just remember what the jacaré did to Mrs. Ramos's son.

Radical environmentalism threatens our health and our lives. But environmentalists can hurt us only because most of us have fallen for their propaganda. The problem is that we're a good-natured, but sometimes naive people. We give everyone the benefit of the doubt, including environmentalists. But we can't be naive any longer. We have to judge eco-radicals by their goals and actions. The only way to stop them is to repeal most environmental regulations and abolish the Environmental Protection Agency.

THE FREE MARKET CAN
PROTECT THE ENVIRONMENT

Is pollution such a minor problem that we should have no regulations at all? I believe the answer is yes. Most pollution causes relatively minor problems that we can correct with technology. More important, the free market, our legal system, and the strict protection of property rights can reduce harmful pollution.

The Free Market

Many people will tolerate modest levels of pollution because, compared to their alternatives, they benefit by it. Pollution has a price value in the market, like everything else. For instance, many Americans will live and work in towns near an auto plant that produces some air pollution. Many workers jump at the chance to work in these plants, because they value a good job at high wages over a little pollution. The free market gives them a choice. But if the EPA forces an auto plant to spend millions of dollars on pollution controls, the company has to recover its heavy investment. It has to lower wages, increase the price of its cars (the Japanese love this), or close the plant and move to a friendlier state, throwing all the plant workers out of a job.

EPA regulators had no mercy for the middle class. They took away the workers' choice and their jobs. If the economy was free and growing, with many job opportunities at new, clean industrial plants, then the old polluting plants would soon have a hard time finding workers. Competition for workers would eventually force the plant to modernize or go out of business. The free market would have solved the problem while giving workers a choice.

The same applies to housing. An apartment-house free market creates thousands of new and decent apartments at reasonable rents. In such a market, if a slumlord doesn't repair his buildings, how is he going to get tenants? He'll have to modernize his buildings or go bankrupt. Competition will force him to clean up the "pollution" in his buildings.

If Los Angeles smog became so annoying that people and businesses started moving out en masse, then community and business groups would soon find ways to reduce the pollution without regulations. Pollution controls might be costly, but the investment would be worth it because peoples' homes and businesses would be at stake.

141

This hasn't happened yet because most Los Angeles residents are willing to live with present levels of pollution. They value living in Los Angeles more than the annoyance of smog, and obviously feel that pollution levels aren't bad enough to make them move out. If pollution became intolerable, they would vote with their feet. The free market gives them that choice.

Regulations revoke this choice. In 1989, Los Angeles county enacted stringent new environmental regulations that will impose personal and economic hardships on many residents. Los Angeles regulations will force residents to buy cars with costly pollution controls. Regulations will ban or restrict everyday products like gasoline-powered lawn mowers, aerosol sprays, and barbecue lighter fluids. And this is just the beginning. Pollution regulations will raise the price of cars, houses, electricity, and hundreds of other products.

Regulations destroy jobs. California is still suffering from a government-aggravated recession. High taxes, layers of regulations, a welfare-state mentality, and a general antibusiness attitude by state officials are driving thousands of businesses out of the state.

California, once a leader in creating new jobs, has slipped badly. It now ranks thirty-fourth among all states in job creation, and it lost 626,000 jobs in 1991 because of businesses going bankrupt or leaving the state. Businesses are leaving the state because California is a regulatory nightmare. Besides backbreaking income and worker's compensation taxes, businesses have to deal with up to eighty regulatory agencies in Los Angeles alone.

One company based in San Diego, Rohr Industries, wanted to build an addition to its plant. Because of San Diego regulations, the building permit process would take 3 1/2 years to complete and cost $750,000. Yet in Arkansas, the same plant addition could be approved and built in only eight months and cost $750 in fees.[71]

In southern California, the South Coast Air Quality Management District (AQMD) is a powerful board that controls pollution standards throughout the area. It has created strict pollution regulations on paints and solvents, stopping companies that use these chemicals from fulfilling defense contracts. These and similar regulations have severely limited economic development in southern California.

Environmental regulations and antibusiness attitudes hurt workers in southern California. Regulations deny people the right to choose between good paying jobs and a little pollution. Most Los Angeles residents would, of course, choose jobs. But the regulators don't care about jobs or free choice. They have utter contempt and no mercy for the middle class.

If pollution got too annoying, people and businesses would adjust. They would move to outlying areas beyond central Los Angeles and create new regional centers. That happened in New York, where dynamic new centers developed in New Jersey, Westchester, and upstate New York. People who were fed up with Manhattan moved to these areas to live and work. This movement reduced population, car traffic, and pollution levels in Manhattan.

And if a two-hour, bumper-to-bumper commute of polluting cars gets too annoying, Los Angeles residents would take high-speed trains to work. Competing modes of transportation can develop in a free market. That's what happened in New York. Most people who work in Manhattan come into the city by bus, rail, or subway, not by car (it's just too annoying, expensive, and time consuming).

Car traffic in Manhattan, while heavy, is mainly limited to hardy souls whose business forces them to drive in (supply trucks, etc.), local residents and businesses, or those people who hate public transportation (run by government, not private enterprise). As a result, Manhattan car traffic and air pollution leveled off. And even when pollution was much worse, most Manhattanites didn't care because they enjoyed the excitement and convenience of living in the city.

The same process would happen in Los Angeles if the commute and pollution got bad enough (it would have to get really bad, because Californians love their cars). The point is this: people use their common sense and self-interest to adjust to, or correct problems like pollution, without government interference.

Car manufacturers would also accelerate technological improvements, because this would be good for business. If pollution became intolerable, clean-running cars would sell big. If most people were worried about pollution, manufacturers would have perfected electric or natural gas cars long ago.

There's another important free-market mechanism that reduces pollution. Over the last hundred years, there's been a natural progression from dirty to cleaner industries. At the start of the industrial revolution in England, the predominance of coal and relatively primitive machinery created heavy concentrations of polluting factories. Today, we're in the computer, electronic, and information age. Older, more polluting technologies are growing obsolete by themselves because of natural technological progress. How much industrial pollution is there in Silicon Valley, California, where they manufacture computer chips? Not very much. The older, polluting factories will die out by themselves, without the interference of regulators.

Bureaucrats think everyone is as rigid and fearful as they are. They don't understand and deeply distrust the free market. They impose their rules and regulations on us, instead of letting ordinary people solve their own problems. Americans are smart and ingenious—it's in our blood. If pollution affects our jobs or health, we'll eventually solve the problem without the help of bureaucrats or environmentalists.

Property Rights

We can also control pollution by unleashing the power of property rights. A good example is the Nature Conservancy, an environmental group that uses property rights to protect the environment. It *buys* land it wants to protect, and is the largest, private nonprofit owner of nature preserves in the world. During the 1980s it bought almost one-half million acres of land. The Nature Conservancy is funded by donations from foundations, corporations, and individuals. Landowners also donate property to the group, or sell it land at below-market prices.

An example is Keith Lewis, who sold forty-three acres of rolling oceanfront property on Rhode Island's beautiful Block Island to the Nature Conservancy for $125,000, a mere fraction of its market value. He did this because he loved his land and wanted to preserve it.[72]

The Nature Conservancy is the quietest, yet most effective

environmental group in the country. Unlike radical environmentalists who use lawsuits and regulations to block development, the Nature Conservancy respects other peoples' property rights and the free-enterprise system.[73] Property rights could also protect offshore fishing grounds and estuaries from waste dumped in these areas. If fishermen could prove damage to their fishing grounds, they could sue the companies or local governments responsible.

In fact, New York commercial fishermen filed such a lawsuit. Manufacturing plants had dumped chemicals into the Hudson River for thirty years. As a result, New York State banned fishing for striped bass between 1986 and 1990. The fishermen sued the manufacturers for lost income. After an eight-year lawsuit, they won. The manufacturers agreed to pay $7 million to between three hundred and four hundred fishermen.[74]

Similar lawsuits would force industrial plants or local governments to stop dumping wastes, pay heavy fines, or develop new waste-control technologies. And if we sold fishing grounds to the highest bidder, ownership would be clearly defined and lawsuits would be easier to prosecute.

The same applies to pollution of streams, rivers, and other waterways. If we sold water rights to the highest bidder, clearly defined property rights would make pollution lawsuits easier to prosecute. Property rights could also protect ground water. If industrial plants polluted underground water supplies, owners who used this water could sue for damages. When property rights are clear, legal action is easier, and financial damages convince polluters to clean up their act.

Making highways private property could reduce auto pollution. So many people use highways because the highways are free or tolls are cheap. If private companies owned the highways and charged higher tolls, then many drivers would think twice about using them as much.

To reduce toll costs, many car owners might reduce their highway driving, start taking car pools, or even use public transportation more often. Higher tolls would give a boost to bus and railroad systems, which should also be totally private. Entrepreneurs would build new and more efficient bus and rapid rail lines because these lines would become cost competitive with cars. That, in turn, would further reduce car traffic and pollution on highways.

Protect the Environment With Nuisance Laws

Nuisance laws protect a property owner from outside interference. Unfortunately, these laws are sometimes difficult to prosecute. Say your neighbor builds a barbecue pit in his backyard, and the smoke from his luau parties peels the paint off your house. You can sue him for nuisance damages.

But the system breaks down with public nuisances. Suppose your neighbor builds a steel mill on his property, and the mill's pollution damages not only your house, but the houses of many other residents in your neighborhood. Here, the steel mill is a public nuisance, and private lawsuits are difficult to prosecute.

If we changed the laws so people could easily start class-action suits against polluters who created public nuisances, then things would be different. Polluters would pay heavy financial damages to thousands of people, making these lawsuits more of a deterrent.

The same principle could apply to water pollution problems. As a hypothetical example, assume a large paper mill is located upstream on a river and is polluting the downstream water supply. If people living downstream could easily bring a class-action suit against the mill for water contamination and cleanup costs, they would get quick action. Heavy fines would convince the mill owner to shut down, clean up his act, or compensate downstream residents for polluting their water supply.

If private class-action suits were easy to prosecute in public nuisance cases, plant owners would develop new technologies to reduce pollution to avoid future lawsuits. Nuisance and private property laws would reduce pollution without regulations.

Lawsuits by property owners are a great way to protect the environment. But if our courts are jammed and backlogged, the system breaks down. This logjam has to be broken. We can do this by using quicker, less expensive alternatives like arbitration to settle disputes. We could also repeal victimless crime laws that overload our courts.

Unfortunately, not many of us could take on General Motors in a court of law. But if we put more resources into our court system and promoted private courts and arbitration, then more people could afford nuisance suits, even against big companies.

Criminal courts spend 30 percent to 50 percent of their time on victimless crimes.[75] Drugs, gambling, and prostitution should not be crimes. Personal habits, however stupid or dangerous, are not government's concern. People have the right to take drugs, just as they have the right to smoke, drink, or bungee-jump. Our bodies are our property, not the government's. Personal liberty also means the liberty to hurt ourselves if we want to. As for gambling and prostitution, they're simply social activities between consenting adults. Government has no right banning these activities.

A study found that a medium-sized California county spent $6.3 million, or 33 percent, of its annual $19 million criminal-court budget dealing with victimless crimes.[76] In big cities, the figures are probably higher. If we decriminalized drugs, gambling, and prostitution, our courts would have more time and judges available. As a result, pollution lawsuits would be easier to prosecute, and wouldn't drag on for years.

CONCLUSION

We all want fresh air and clean water. But, in falling for ecologists' doomsday stories, we forget these important questions: Is what they're telling us true? Do environmentalists have ulterior motives? Who is more important, you, your family, and your neighbors, or rats and swamps? Don't human beings have a right to live on this Earth? At what price do we remove the last speck of pollution from our air or water? Should we destroy our freedom, our abundance, and our children's future with strangling regulations to "protect the environment?"

Let's reaffirm the fact that people are precious and more important than rats, swamps, and old-growth forests. Let's proclaim that we have the right to live on this Earth like human beings. Finally, let's reject the ecologists' intellectual pollution by eliminating environmental regulations and dismantling the Environmental Protection Agency.

CHAPTER 6

HOW TO SOLVE THE
HEALTH CARE CRISIS

America has a health care crisis. Health insurance costs are exploding. Over 35 million Americans don't have insurance, and major medical insurance for an average family now costs over $7,500 a year. Total health care costs exceeded $838 billion in 1992,[1] $939 billion in 1993, and easily exceeded $1 trillion in 1994.[2]

Skyrocketing costs have also led to many other serious problems. Many small businesses have canceled their employee group-insurance policies because they can't afford them anymore. And because most Americans get insurance through their employers, "job-lock" sets in. Job-lock is where an employee is afraid to quit his job because he'll lose his health insurance.

Escalating costs also force insurance companies to deny insurance to people with preexisting medical conditions. To control skyrocketing costs, Medicare and Medicaid now pay reduced fees to doctors and hospitals. Many doctors who resent these low fees won't take Medicare or Medicaid patients anymore, so older people are finding it harder to get good medical care.

We have a crisis because our health care system is part of the Welfare State. Medicare and Medicaid are out-of-control entitlement programs, and government regulations strangle the health care industry.

Our health care crisis was spawned by the socialist idea that underlies the Welfare State: that helping others is a moral and political duty, not a personal choice. Medicare and health-care regulations are sanctioned by the idea that we have a right to health care. That right implies that others have a moral duty to pay our medical bills if we can't.

Do we have a right to health care? Are we morally responsible for everyone's health? Does our understandable desire for good medical care justify stealing from some people to give health care benefits to others? Does government have the right to force us to pay for everyone's medical bills, or force others to pay for ours? *Is helping our fellow man a moral and political duty or a personal choice?*

This important question is the central issue of the Welfare State and the health care crisis. President Clinton's proposed health care plan was the classic welfare-state solution: a medical-welfare concoction that would socialize health care in this country. It's most fundamental principle was that all Americans have a right to health care, guaranteed by government.

Before we ask government to "solve" the health care crisis with more regulations, we better take a good, hard look at why we have a health care crisis. Before we give more power to the same bureaucrats who brought us exploding federal deficits, public school systems, and the savings and loan scandal, we better think twice, then think again. We can end the health care crisis only by seeing what caused it.

THE EXISTING MESS

The projected deficits of the federal government are alarming. The red ink in 1992 was about $368 billion. This figure is expected to increase in the second half of the 1990s, reaching about $423 billion by the year 2002.[3]

The explosive part of the deficit comes from Medicare, Medicaid, and Social Security. Recent projections by the Congressional Budget Office said that annual spending on Medicare is expected to rise from $128 billion in 1992 to $301 billion in 2000. In the same period, Medicaid costs are expected to increase from $68 billion to $180 billion. It's estimated that government now pays over 42 percent of health care spending in this country.[4]

Richard G. Darman, former director of the Office of Management and Budget under President Bush said, "Total U.S. public and private spending on health is literally on an unsustainable path—threatening to consume an impossible proportion of the G.D.P."[5]

Because of exploding health care costs, over 35 million Americans can't afford health insurance. Most people think the uninsured are poor, elderly, or unemployed. "In fact, eight out of ten uninsured Americans are in families headed by a full-time or part-time worker . . . The majority of uninsured Americans are simply workers and their families who don't get insurance on the job and can't afford to buy it themselves."[6]

As you can see, we have a very serious problem on our hands. But to find real and long-lasting solutions, we have to understand exactly why costs are escalating out of control.

HEALTH CARE AND THE FREE MARKET

Health care is no different from anything else we buy. Supply and demand determine the price of any commodity, including medical care. Normally, the wonderful self-regulating mechanisms of the free market lower the prices of most products or services.

A typical example is the car industry. When cars were first invented, very few were produced, they were very expensive, and only the rich could afford them. But the demand for cars made big profits for Henry Ford. These profits became a magnet for other pioneering manufacturers, and Ford was soon competing with the Chevrolet brothers and other car makers. Fierce competition forced each new manufacturer to invent a better, cheaper car that more people could afford. Soon millions of inexpensive cars were rolling off the assembly lines.

Strong demand for a product or service creates profits. Profits attract other entrepreneurs who want a piece of the pie, creating fierce competition that inevitably forces prices down. But prices drop for most products and services only if there's a *free* market. When government interferes with the market, that freedom goes out the window.

There are two basic reasons why the price of a product or service would explode as health care is doing. First, if there's a big demand, and supply can't keep up with that demand, prices will shoot up. Eager buyers will bid up the price of the product or service that's in short supply. Second, if there's a stable demand for a product, but the supply is limited, again you have more people wanting the product than the supply available. Restricted supply then causes prices to jump.

In today's health care industry, contrary to what most Americans might believe, *there is no free market.* Government controls have thrown a huge monkey wrench into the system and created the worst nightmare possible. Entitlement programs like Medicare and Medicaid have exploded the demand for health care, while government regulations have strangled the supply. The inevitable result is the health care crisis—skyrocketing health care costs and over thirty-five million Americans unable to afford health insurance.

There are two major areas where government policies have affected health care. The first relates to general welfare-state policies such as regulations, deficit spending, and entitlement programs. These policies distort and restrict the free market throughout the economy.

By doing so, they cause or aggravate crime, drug use, poverty, unemployment, general inflation, diseases such as AIDS, and unwanted pregnancies. These government-created problems directly influence and increase health care costs throughout the country.

The second general area includes regulations and entitlement programs specific to the health care field. These include tax policies, Medicare and Medicaid, government controls over insurance companies, control of medical care by organized medicine, and regulations on the health care industry.

Government created the health-care crisis by spawning the Welfare State, exploding the demand for health care, and strangling the health care industry with regulations. But before we examine how government got us into this mess, let's look at some general conditions unrelated to government that have increased health care costs.

Income and Cultural Differences

Americans have a high standard of living. According to conventional measurements like the per-capita Gross Domestic Product (GDP), the United States is a wealthy country and we spend more on health care than most other countries.

Common sense and many studies have shown that when people have more money, they spend more on their health care. When a person has more income, he or she will get more periodic checkups, get treated sooner and more frequently, and demand the latest high-tech medical care.

In 1987, Americans spent about $2,051 per person on health care. According to a study by Schieber and Poullier, the relationship between personal income and spending explained $1,651 of this $2,051.[7] That is, three-quarters of the difference in higher health care spending between the United States and other countries was caused by the simple fact that Americans had more money to spend.

The second reason for spending differences between countries is cultural. Every country has its own standards about what it considers good medical care for its citizens. Medical treatment in the United States is more aggressive than in other countries. For example, "Compared to Americans, British patients are half as likely to have surgery of any kind and one-sixth as likely to undergo bypass surgery. British doctors prescribe fewer drugs, perform half the number of X rays as U.S. doctors, and use half as much film per X ray. Pap smears and blood tests are recommended only once every five years."[8]

American doctors like to do as many tests as possible. They also use the latest, most expensive technology to treat a patient. Americans want this kind of care. Unlike citizens in other countries, we're more impatient and aggressive as patients; we won't wait on line for anything, no less for important medical care. Americans wouldn't tolerate a one-year wait for a cataract operation, which is common in England. This attitude is part of the American character, and the medical establishment caters to it.

As another example, many American hospitals have modern pediatric intensive-care units to treat premature babies. Medical ethics, the fear of lawsuits, and aggressive medicine push hospitals to make every effort to save these babies. But intensive care is very expensive. It costs about $158,000 to save one premature baby, and the United States spends about $2.6 billion a year on such care. Many other countries don't make the same efforts for premature babies, so our costs in this area are particularly high.

Lifestyles

Compared to other countries, many Americans have lifestyles that expose them to more disease and health problems. We eat bad foods, smoke and drink too much, and don't exercise enough. We also have a very high suicide rate.

These bad health habits cause cancer, heart disease, high blood pressure, and many other problems. Louis W. Sullivan, former Secretary of Health and Human Services, said that the top ten causes of premature death in America are greatly influenced by our lifestyle choices and personal behavior.[9]

We're Living Longer

Medical science has rapidly improved in the last thirty years, and Americans are living longer. The number of people over age sixty-five increased from 9.2 percent of the population in 1960 to 12.2 percent in 1987. By 2010 the figure will climb to about 13.9 percent. In the year 1901, average life expectancy was about fifty years. Today, it has increased to about seventy-two years for men and seventy-seven years for women. The number of Americans over age sixty-five is expected to double by the year 2030 to sixty-six million people. Currently the fastest growing segment among the elderly is those over age eighty-five.[10]

Older people get sick more often and need expensive, long-term treatment. Also, as people get older, they see doctors more often. As a result, health care costs for people over age sixty-five are about 3.9 times more than for people under age sixty-five. Almost 30 percent of Medicare hospital payments occur within the last year of a patient's life. That's because we spend huge sums of money to keep old and gravely ill patients alive.

This isn't done in many other countries. Gravely ill patients in the Netherlands can choose euthanasia as an option. The British government rations health care in part by not providing medical treatments such as kidney dialysis and hip replacement to patients over a certain age.[11] Both these countries have socialized medicine, and have made deliberate decisions to ration health care this way to keep costs down.

High-tech Medicine and Lawsuits

America leads the world in using and developing medical technology. For example, compared to Canada, we have eight times more magnetic resonance imaging and radiation therapy units, six times more lithotripsy centers, and three times more cardiac catheterization and open-heart surgery units.[12]

American consumers demand the best medical care available. New technology is especially important to people with life-threatening illnesses such as cancer or heart disease. Doctors use expensive procedures to treat cancer, kidney disease, and heart disease. New technologies have prolonged life and dramatically improved the practice of medicine.

Technology creates short-term upward pressures on health care costs. Studies show that half the increase in real hospital costs between 1977 and 1983 came from investments in medical technology.[13] But in the long run, technology dramatically lowers medical costs, as we'll see later in the chapter.

Our legal system also contributes to rising health care costs, much more than in other countries. Patients expect hospitals to treat them with the latest medical technology. To avoid lawsuits, hospitals therefore invest heavily in expensive equipment.

The threat of lawsuits has increased medical malpractice insurance. This insurance can cost anywhere from $5,000 to over $60,000 per year, depending on a doctor's specialty. Doctors pass the cost of this insurance on to their patients.

Americans also sue more often than other people. American patients sue their doctors five times more often than Canadian patients do. As a result, Canadian doctors' malpractice insurance averages about one-tenth that of American doctors.

High malpractice insurance and the threat of lawsuits push doctors and hospitals to practice defensive medicine. Physicians sometimes do too many medical tests to protect themselves against lawsuits. An AMA study estimated that defensive medicine increased health care spending in 1985 by $11.7 billion.[14]

The problems I've discussed until now relate to cultural, population, or economic conditions peculiar to the United States. But the free market can solve many of these problems, as we'll see later in the chapter.

HEALTH CARE AND THE WELFARE STATE

Welfare-state policies destroy jobs, strangle the economy, and fuel long-term inflation. As a result, thousands of middle-class Americans are pushed into poverty. Almost nine million people are now unemployed. One American in ten, over twenty-five million people, is now on food stamps. Since 1989 the average salaries of white-collar workers have been going down. The job market for new high school and college graduates is dismal.

The Welfare State leads to a host of problems that sharply increase health care costs. Let's look at a few.

Poverty

The Welfare State ruins the economy and throws people out of work. Unemployment then leads to poverty. Lack of proper food, clothing, and shelter make poor people vulnerable to disease. They also have less money to pay for annual medical exams, prenatal care, and other health problems. As a result, poor people often postpone treatment until a medical problem becomes serious and forces them to go to a hospital. By that time, the necessary treatment is often more expensive.

Poor people are more likely to have no health insurance. If

they get sick, they often enter hospitals through the emergency room. Treatment in emergency rooms is more expensive than walk-in clinics or general hospital admission.

Welfare programs also encourage an increase in births by unwed teenage mothers. The teenage pregnancy rate in the United States is about 2.5 times that of Canada and England. One in ten young women between age 15 and 19 becomes pregnant in the United States.[15] Many of these pregnancies result in premature births or babies born with defects caused by lack of prenatal care. Both mother and baby need extensive medical care, which increases medical costs.

Violence

Government-created poverty aggravates crime. Poverty and despair often turn into violence, as the riots in Los Angeles showed us. Male homicide rates in the United States are more than twelve times that of Germany and five times that of Canada. The United States had more than three hundred times the number of rapes, robberies, and homicides than Japan did in 1987. This violence spills over into the health care system because most violent-crime victims are treated in expensive hospital emergency rooms.

Drugs

Drugs are a growing monster in our country. Poverty and profits have exploded drug use and placed a terrible burden on our health care system. The National Association of Public Hospitals, which represents the biggest government hospitals in America, reported in January 1991 that about 29 percent of all emergency room visits involved illegal drugs, and that each hospital delivered an average of 104 cocaine-addicted babies each year.[16]

There are about 375,000 drug-exposed babies in the United States. The estimated cost of their treatment is about $63,000 per baby for the first five years or about $25 billion total. In Canada and most other countries, the problem of drug-exposed babies is negligible.[17]

Many people who are poor, unemployed, and without hope take drugs to escape reality. Government regulations make drugs illegal. This increases drug prices and forces many addicts to steal to support their habit.

According to FBI data, 1 out of 3 robberies and burglaries is committed to obtain money for high-priced, black market drugs. . .Up to 40 percent of the murders in major cities and 20 percent of the killings nationwide occur in the drug trade. Innocent children and police officers are often caught in the crossfire.[18]

Many drug users end up in hospital emergency rooms because they overdose. Crime victims of drug addicts and victims of violent drug wars often end up in the same place. Health care costs escalate because of drug use, and violent crime increases because drugs are illegal.

AIDS

With over 100,000 AIDS patients in this country and another 200,000 people infected with the AIDS virus, we have an epidemic of this dreadful disease. The United States has more than three times the AIDS cases Canada has and more than six times the cases West Germany has.

The cost to treat each AIDS patient over his lifetime is about $85,000, and the total estimated cost in 1991 was about $5.8 billion. One estimate projected the AIDS epidemic will cost us about $15.2 billion by 1995.[19]

Many drug users get AIDS from using dirty needles. We could end the spread of this disease among drug addicts if we legalized drugs and medically supervised the addicts. "1 out of 3 U.S. AIDS cases is traceable to the sharing of infected needles by drug users. Criminalizing these users and prohibiting access to clean needles worsens the deadly AIDS epidemic."[20]

The Right to Health Care

Over thirty-five million Americans face the risk of bankruptcy from a catastrophic illness because they can't afford health insurance. Thousands of people could die because they can't afford medical treatment or a desperately needed operation.

Yet·this situation goes against our traditional attitudes toward health care. Most Americans believe that everyone should have the best medical care, and that it's morally unfair to deny someone health care because they can't afford it.

This notion of a right to health care is just another example of the Welfare State's socialist premise: that we have an alleged right to health care because helping others is our moral and political duty. If some people can't afford insurance, then the rest of us are morally responsible to pay for this insurance. We do this through Medicare and Medicaid, two entitlement programs that are exploding health care costs.

HOW GOVERNMENT STRANGLES THE HEALTH CARE INDUSTRY

Organized Medicine

Through the ages, professional groups like the clockmakers of medieval London created monopoly guilds to protect their jobs, income, and status from the "curse" of competition. One such quasi-monopoly today is organized medicine. The American Medical Association (AMA) has extensive control over the practice of medicine in this country through its power to set accreditation standards for licensing, hospitals, and medical schools.

By doing so, AMA policies isolate the medical profession from free-market competition. State regulations and AMA accreditation powers restrict the supply of doctors, for-profit hospitals, and for-profit medical schools. Whenever the supply of a product or service is restricted, prices go up. Since medical care is labor intensive, AMA controls contribute to increased health care costs. If we want to lower costs, we have to bring medical care into the free market. To do this, we need to question organized medicine's right to control the medical profession.

A Brief History of Organized Medicine

For a brief, shining moment, America once had a relatively free market in medical care. Between 1830 and 1865 only a few states had medical licensing laws. Anyone who wanted to practice medicine could do so with few restrictions. The free market decided which doctors succeeded or not.

During this period, there were also many private, for-profit medical schools, and their numbers were rapidly growing. These schools would admit almost anyone who wanted to study medicine. Admission standards were lenient and tuition costs were reasonable. With affordable tuition, easy entry into medical schools and the medical profession, and an expanding demand for doctors by a growing population, guess what happened? The number of doctors kept increasing and competition forced doctors to keep their fees at reasonable levels. The system wasn't perfect, but the sky didn't fall without licensing laws.

With so many new doctors entering the profession, incomes began to drop from the competition. Many established doctors resented the loss of income and status. That's where the AMA enters the scene. The AMA, established in 1847 as a permanent national organization, soon became the official spokesman for orthodox medicine. Its stated goal was to raise the quality of care for patients and to protect people from charlatan doctors.

Behind this avowed purpose, another concern was also evident. In 1847, the AMA's Committee on Educational Standards held its first meeting in Philadelphia. The following excerpt is from that Committee's report:

> The very large number of physicians in the United States . . . has frequently been the subject of remark. To relieve the diseases of something more that twenty million people, we have an army of Doctors amounting by a recent computation to forty thousand, which allows one to about every five hundred inhabitants. And if we add to the 40,000 the long list of irregular practitioners who swarm like locusts in every part of the country, the proportion of patients will be still further reduced. No wonder, then that the profession of medicine has measurably ceased to occupy the elevated position which once it did; no wonder that the merest pittance in the way of remuneration is scantily doled out even to the most industrious in our ranks.[21]

Obviously, the AMA didn't like the free market. It didn't like low fees, competition, and the loss of status. To correct the situation, the medical profession had to isolated itself from the free market. So the AMA turned to government for protection. It lobbied state legislatures into giving it controls over the practice of medicine. Studies show that the AMA had three goals:

> Following an exhaustive study of the early development of medical licensing laws in the United States, Hamowy has concluded that the goals of orthodox practitioners in general, and of the AMA in particular, were threefold: (1) to establish medical licensing laws that would restrict entry into the profession and thus secure a more stable (and lucrative) financial climate for physicians than had existed under uninhibited competition; (2) to destroy the proprietary (for profit) medical schools and replace them with a few nonprofit institutions that would provide extensive, thorough training in medicine, with a longer required period of study and a smaller and more select student body; and (3) to eliminate heterodox medical sects, generally seen as unwelcome competitive forces within the profession.[22]

The first AMA Committee on Medical Education established educational standards for licensing future doctors. The AMA lobbied state legislatures to accept the *principle* of licensing. It also convinced legislators to use the AMA's educational standards as the basis for granting a license to practice medicine. In effect, license laws backed by state power gave the AMA control over who could or could not become a doctor.

The AMA claimed that we need licensing to insure quality health care and keep out incompetent doctors with poor training. Yet the AMA has fought attempts to require follow-up competency tests for doctors. Many states don't require physicians to prove that they've remained current with medical knowledge to keep their licenses. Also, once a doctor gets a license, many states allow him to perform medical procedures, including surgery and other treatments, that he wasn't trained for.[23] And only a few states consider incompetence grounds for revoking a doctor's license.[24]

The AMA lobbied for licensing laws from the start, but the health-care free market continued to expand. A growing number of medical schools were graduating many new doctors. In 1870 there were about 75 medical schools in America, most of them for-profit. The number of schools grew to 160 by the year 1900 and more than 5,000 new doctors graduated yearly.

The AMA then lobbied state legislators for the power to set accreditation standards for medical schools. It convinced legislators that states should only license graduates of "first-class" medical schools. State laws directed medical examining boards to grant licenses only to graduates of schools approved by the AMA's Council on Medical Education and Hospitals.

Once the AMA had accreditation powers, many for-profit medical schools throughout the country closed because they didn't meet AMA standards. As a result of the AMA's accreditation requirements, the number of medical schools in America dropped from 160 in 1900 to 77 by 1940. By 1990 there were only 125 medical schools in the country, though the United States population had more than doubled since 1900.[25]

The AMA's accreditation powers also restrict the supply of doctors. While the demand for physicians mushroomed after 1900, supply didn't keep pace. In 1900, the population per doctor was about 637 people. By 1970 there were about 602 people per doctor. In seventy years, the population per doctor had stayed about the same.[26]

If government didn't regulate medical schools, we would have more doctors today. Competition and a growing population could have created two or three times more doctors and medical schools per population today than in 1900.

This prediction makes sense if we see what happened in the nursing profession during the same period. The AMA didn't try to restrict the number of nurses or nursing schools. In 1900, there were 432 professional nursing schools. In 1970 there were 1,328 (a 300 percent increase). In 1900, there were 3,456 graduates from these schools. In 1970, there were 43,639 (a 1400 percent increase). In 1910 there were 55 nurses per 100,000 population. In 1970, there were 345 nurses per this same population (a 700 percent increase).[27]

When the free market in medical education was not restricted, the number of nursing schools and nurses per 100,000 people increased sharply. In the same period, the number of medical schools decreased and the number of doctors per population stayed about the same.

AMA control over medical schools also inflates the cost of medical education. Its accreditation restrictions have cut the number of for-profit medical schools. Fewer medical schools restricts competition and therefore raises tuition costs. As a result, many doctors graduate medical school with debts from student loans that can exceed $80,000. Add the high cost of medical liability insurance and you understand why many new doctors have to charge higher fees.

Organized medicine also stifles competition by discouraging doctors from competing aggressively. The AMA's Code of Ethics forbids member doctors from engaging in unethical or unprofessional conduct. Price cutting (competition) and aggressive advertising are examples of such conduct.

The Code of Ethics in many states restricts doctors from advertising prices for medical care. The Code considers aggressive price advertising to be unprofessional conduct and possible grounds for license suspension or revocation. So, in some states, incompetence is not grounds for revoking a license, but advertising lower fees is!

CONSEQUENCES OF AMA CONTROLS

License laws, controls over medical schools, and restrictions on physicians' ability to compete isolate the practice of medicine from the free market. Since medical care is labor intensive, AMA controls contribute to higher health care costs. If we had enjoyed a free market in medicine for the last hundred years, there would be more doctors competing aggressively with each other and with nurses and other paraprofessionals. Medical care would be more competitive and less expensive. That's because medical care is like any other service business. Competition prods all businesses to increase quality and lower costs.

Restrictions on Nurses and Physician Assistants

The AMA has tried to restrict medical procedures that nurses, physician-assistants, and other paraprofessionals are allowed to do. Most states today restrict the right of nonphysicians to perform medical acts. Medical practice statutes hold that "a person who in any way performs, offers to perform, or holds himself out to the public as performing specific functions—e.g., diagnosing, treating, operating, or prescribing for a disease, ailment, pain, or condition, must be licensed as a physician."[28]

State licensing boards set medical practice standards, and AMA state medical societies nominate doctors who serve on these boards. As a result, AMA-nominated physicians can bar health care professionals they feel don't qualify to practice medicine, such as nurses, pharmacists, chiropractors, physician assistants, and physical therapists.[29]

The AMA claims that we need these restrictions to stop improper medical care by unqualified people. Yet studies show that nurses can substitute for doctors in many areas of medical practice.

> Two decades of research, summarized last summer in the Yale Journal on Regulation, gives clear evidence that advanced-practice nurses provide care of comparable quality and at a lower cost than doctors do. . .
> Advanced-practice nurses can safely substitute for physicians for up to 90% of primary care needed by children and 80% required by adults. The Yale report concluded that significant financial, legal, and professional barriers prevent the effective use of nurses.[30]

If nurses could treat patients, doctors would have more competition, less control over medical care, and eventually lower fees. But low-income people and those living in poorly served rural areas would benefit if nurses could treat them. Nurses could give advice and medical care that only doctors are now allowed to give.

> Gale Walker, the administrator of the 30-bed St. Benedict's hospital in Parkston, 60 miles west of Sioux Falls, said: "Here, it's not do I have a choice? It is what do I do to find a doctor or a nurse practitioner?". . .Or, said Linda Guthmiller, the assistant administrator and laboratory chief at the 25-bed Landman-Jungman Hospital in Scotland, 24 miles southeast of Parkston, "Doctors have to start dropping their egos, and they have to let the nurses and the physicians' assistants do more."[31]

Nurses and other paraprofessionals are competent to do many procedures only doctors are now allowed to perform. This isn't just theory—it's becoming reality. Columbia-Presbyterian Medical Center in New York City recently gave its nurse practitioners admitting privileges. Nurses there can now perform physical exams on patients, order diagnostic tests, immunize and deliver babies, and even admit patients to the hospital. And this new system is working out fine.[32]

AMA Controls Over Hospital Accreditation

Like medical schools, hospitals have to be accredited (approved) to operate legally. If a hospital isn't accredited, the state can revoke its license to operate. The private organization responsible for accrediting hospitals is the Joint Commission on Accreditation of Healthcare Organizations. The Commission accredits more than 5,300 hospitals and has the power to decide if a hospital qualifies for Medicare and Medicaid reimbursements.[33]

An organization that can disqualify a hospital for Medicare and Medicaid payments has enormous power. Since many hospitals get almost 40 percent of their revenues from Medicare and Medicaid, a hospital would be in serious financial trouble if the Commission revoked its accreditation.

The Board of the Joint Commission is composed overwhelmingly of representatives of five leading medical societies, including the AMA and the American Hospital Association.

"They are merely a trade organization," said Charles B. Inlander, head of the People's Medical Society, a health advocacy group. "The Joint Commission has a terrible conflict of interest. *It's the fox guarding the chicken coup*" (emphasis added).[34]

Dr. Sidney Wolfe, the director of the Public Citizen Health Research Group, which has long challenged the medical establishment, said:

But it (the Joint Commission) continues to be a private sector, mainly secret creature of the AMA and the American Hospital Association. It just doesn't make any sense to allow it to be the regulator of hospitals.[35]

Once the AMA controlled hospital accreditation, it disqualified proprietary (for-profit) hospitals that didn't meet its standards, just as it had disqualified many for-profit medical schools. States and the federal government also passed laws that restricted for-profit hospitals and gave special tax benefits to nonprofit hospitals. Government regulations decimated for-profit hospitals and paved the way for nonprofit hospitals to dominate hospital care in this country.

In 1910 there were approximately 2,400 for-profit hospitals out of 4,360 hospitals in the country (about 56 percent of the total). By 1968, there were 769 for-profit hospitals out of 7,137 (about 11 percent of the total).[36]

It's no great mystery why organized medicine would dislike for-profit hospitals. These hospitals are business enterprises that try to maximize profits, and demand that their employee-doctors act according to this motive. Managers of for-profit hospitals control doctors' fees and procedures. That's because hospitals' profits depend on giving good service while lowering costs. The AMA doesn't like private managers controlling doctors' fees and procedures.

It's a commonly held view that for-profit hospitals only care about maximizing profits, and therefore won't care about providing quality health care. It's argued that these hospitals would cut costs and endanger patients' lives just to make a buck. But studies have compared for-profit hospitals with nonprofit hospitals of similar size, offering comparable services. The studies found no significant differences in quality of care.[37] If anything, hospital entrepreneurs built many for-profit hospitals to *overcome* the bureaucratic inefficiencies of nonprofit hospitals.

It shouldn't surprise us that for-profit hospitals would be more efficient than nonprofit ones. Most private businesses are more efficient than government-run enterprises (compare Federal Express to the United States Post Office, for example). Like any business person, the owner of a for-profit hospital has to make profits to stay in business. But he makes these profits only by attracting patients, having doctors recommend his hospital, and offering the best quality service at the lowest cost. Reputation is an important asset in any service business. Just as car companies keep improving the quality of their cars to attract buyers, so would hospitals. Fierce competition and the profit motive would force for-profit hospitals to reduce costs and improve the quality of service to their patients.

If for-profit hospitals competed with nonprofit ones on a level playing field, the nonprofits would soon have to shape up or go out of business. But the competition is not on a level playing field. Government tax policies and regulations stack the competition in favor of nonprofit hospitals.

For-profit hospitals have to pay real estate and corporate taxes. Nonprofit hospitals don't because they're tax-exempt organizations. Also, the federal government subsidizes nonprofit-hospital construction and improvements. The Hill-Burton Hospital Construction Act of 1946 provided millions of dollars to build and equip nonprofit hospitals, but gave nothing to proprietary hospitals. Between 1947 and 1966, the Hill-Burton program funded the construction of 1,680 new hospitals and 2,998 additions and alterations to existing hospitals, all nonprofit.[38] In effect, the federal government created our nonprofit-dominated hospital system.

Also, charitable contributions to nonprofit hospitals are tax deductible; contributions to proprietary hospitals are not. These contributions are important. Between 1960 and 1966, almost 34 percent of hospital expansion funds came from charitable contributions.[39] Because tax law deprives proprietary hospitals of huge amounts of capital for expansion and modernization, they can't compete with nonprofit hospitals on an equal footing.

Having to compete under such backbreaking disadvantages, it's a wonder that proprietary hospitals still manage to thrive. It's to their credit and the credit of the free-market system that they do. Their efficiency and good service to patients help them survive in spite of government's efforts to put them at a competitive disadvantage to nonprofit hospitals.

Because nonprofit hospitals predominate in this country, hospital care doesn't fully benefit from the free market. Nonprofit hospitals are not really business enterprises; instead, they're service enterprises, like the Post Office. Since they don't have to make profits to stay in business, they have less incentive to be efficient or to lower costs.

Most nonprofit hospitals are trying to lower costs today, but not to make profits. They have to lower costs because Medicare now pays them a set fee per procedure that often doesn't cover their expenses. If a hospital's expenses exceed the Medicare payment schedule, the hospital loses money.

Nonprofit hospitals rarely compete on price. Instead, they compete by offering patients the newest medical technology. This high-tech contest pushes many hospitals into buying expensive equipment they can't afford and won't use enough to justify the cost.

> 30% of the 777 hospitals equipped to do closed-heart surgery had no such case in the year under study. Of the 548 hospitals that had cases, 87% did fewer that one operation per week. Of all hospitals equipped to do open-heart surgery, 77% did not average even one operation per week, and 41% averaged under one per month.[40]

A for-profit hospital in a free market wouldn't buy expensive equipment it didn't use; that would be economic suicide. The hospital would simply refer patients to larger hospitals that used such equipment more often.

But a nonprofit hospital needs expensive technology to lure patients. Inevitably, once one hospital has the equipment, other hospitals want it. Since most hospitals are nonprofit, duplication of equipment becomes rampant and hospital and health insurance costs increase.

The Health Insurance Mess

There are basically two ways of paying for medical care in this country: the indemnity plan, or fee-for-service system, and the nonindemnity (HMO-type) plan.

Under the fee-for-service system, people buy insurance policies to pay for health care. If a person gets sick, Medicare, or a third-party insurance company pays the bill, minus a small deductible. Nonindemnity plans provide medical care rather than insurance. These plans are often called "prepaid," because the annual premium pays for all medical care a subscriber may use that's covered under the plan. HMOs are prime examples of nonindemnity plans.

In indemnity plans, because an insurance company pays the

doctor's or hospital's bill, both the doctor and patient have little incentive to worry about costs. If a doctor does more procedures, he makes more money. Also, the patient doesn't care about cost because he gets good medical care and the insurance company pays for it. The system invites abuse, has little consideration for cost controls, and sharply increases demand for medical care. As a result, the fee-for-service system increases health care costs.

Under nonindemnity plans, the HMO generally restricts patients to a select group of doctors and hospitals. The patient receives medical treatment for conditions listed in his policy from doctors that the HMO supervises. The HMO controls doctors' fees and screens his procedures. Because HMOs control costs, they often charge patient-customers less for medical care than fee-for-service systems.

Organized medicine fought against prepaid medical plans for many years. Local medical societies often punished doctors who joined HMOs, and the AMA lobbied state governments to ban or restrict such plans.[41] The AMA's House of Delegates adapted a resolution in 1932 stating that prepaid plans were unethical under the following conditions:

1. Where there is solicitation of patients, either directly or indirectly.
2. Where there is competition and underbidding to secure the contract.
3. When the compensation is inadequate to secure good medical service.
4. When there is interference with reasonable competition in a community.
5. When free choice of physicians is prevented.
6. When the contract because of any of its provisions is contrary to sound public policy.[42]

Notice that the provisions tried to restrict free-market competition between HMOs and fee-for-service doctors. The AMA seemed to consider HMOs unethical because they forced doctors to compete in the open market like everyone else.

States also burden prepaid plans with special restrictions if they operate under corporate practice of medicine statutes. Some states forbid HMOs from advertising, but allowed indemnity plans to advertise. Many states also limited HMOs' asset holdings, forced them to maintain large financial reserves, or required them to charge unreasonably low rates.[43]

For over forty years, state regulations shackled the competitive, for-profit HMO industry. In 1972, nine states prohibited HMOs, and another twenty states applied such severe restrictions to them that they couldn't operate. Many states required medical society approval of an HMO's articles of incorporation, medical society sponsorship of the directors of the plan, or medical society control of the plan itself.[44] State restrictions against HMOs therefore strangled competition and deprived consumers of the right to choose lower-cost HMO plans. That inevitably increased health care costs.

In 1973, the federal government finally ended restrictions on HMOs by passing the Health Maintenance Organization Act. This act preempted state laws that restricted HMOs. Once HMOs were free to develop, their numbers exploded. In the early 1970s there were 26 plans with about three million subscribers. By 1987, there were nearly 700 plans with 28 million customers.[45] By June of 1993, HMO plans had 47 million subscribers.[46]

Now that spiraling health care costs are ringing alarm bells with voters, government has seen the light about the cost effectiveness of for-profit HMO plans. Only liberals didn't want to end regulations. Instead, as usual, they wanted to give us more regulations to "cure" 30 years of regulatory poison that caused the health care crisis. In a typical, knee-jerk liberal response, Bill Clinton wanted to solve the health care crisis by turning our health care system into a huge, government-controlled "managed-care" HMO.

He wanted to club us over the head with government health-care commissars imposing their orders on us. He wanted price controls (like Medicare has) to curtail doctors' fees, drug prices, and hospital reimbursements. This system would eventually lead to rationing like they have in Canada and England, where socialized-medicine reigns supreme. President Clinton wanted to turn our health care system over to the same bureaucrats who gave us the federal deficit, the savings and loan scandal, and other models of government competence and efficiency.

The Assault on Commercial Insurance Companies

Fee-for-service payment plans give doctors and patients little incentive to watch costs. But commercial insurance companies have a strong incentive to scrutinize medical bills. After all, their profits depend on this. If they're lax, their payouts will mushroom and they'll be in financial hot water.

This isn't as true for nonprofit Blue Cross and Blue Shield insurance companies. Data suggests that some Blue Cross and Blue Shield plans only reject about .04 percent of doctors' bills because of questionable practices.[47] Why don't the nonprofit Blues act like commercial insurers and screen more?

One reason the Blues may be lax in reviewing medical claims is because these plans are nonprofit and protected by state regulations. If they lose money because of bad management or lax screening policies, they simply go to their state legislature and ask for rate increases on their already overburdened customers. State governments can't let the Blue Cross and Blue Shield plans go under, so they keep granting the rate increases. In effect, state governments subsidize these companies on the backs of their customers.

Also, by law, in most states Blue Cross and Blue Shield plans have to insure everyone. They can't deny insurance because of an existing medical condition. Commercial insurers can deny such coverage. As a result, Blues have higher risks than commercial companies. That makes it more likely that Blues will lose money and have to ask for rate hikes. In effect, healthy Blue Cross and Blue Shield customers pay high premiums to cover the company's losses on sick people it's forced to insure.

Blues are major insurers in all fifty states. In some states, these plans have market shares as high as 80 percent. As a result, the dominance of Blue Cross and Blue Shield plans throughout the country increases health care costs and insurance premiums for millions of Americans.

Federal and state laws also give Blue Cross and Blue Shield plans competitive advantages. These plans are nonprofit. As a result, they were exempt from federal income taxes until 1986, when Congress eliminated this loophole. In many states, Blues don't have to pay real estate taxes. Commercial insurers have to pay full taxes. In many states, Blue Cross and Blue Shield plans are exempt from reserve requirements, while commercial companies are not.

In exchange for these tax benefits, most states require Blue Cross and Blue Shield plans to insure everyone. Commercial insurers, up to now, can set rates based on a customer's medical history. Rates are set lower for healthy people and higher for those with medical problems or higher risks, like smokers or overweight people. This policy has helped commercial insurers keep their rates lower than most Blue Cross and Blue Shield plans.

As a result, commercial insurers take business away from the Blues. For example, New York Blue Cross and Blue Shield has lost about 400,000 customers to commercial insurers in the last five years, increasing its financial losses. To prevent bankruptcy, Blue Cross and Blue Shield, in effect, tried to kill the competition. It lobbied New York State legislators for laws that would force commercial insurers to insure any applicant, regardless of medical history. To create "fair" competition, it wanted commercial insurers to obey the same regulations that are now bankrupting some Blue Cross and Blue Shield plans.

Blue Cross and Blue Shield succeeded in its lobbying efforts. In 1993, New York State passed a law requiring commercial health insurers to insure anyone, regardless of medical history. The insurers said they would leave the state if the law passed, and that's exactly what they did. Many big insurers now refuse to do business in New York State, leaving millions of customers stranded.

New York State regulators strangle commercial insurers in another way. Right now, hospitals charge insurance companies a set fee for each procedure. The Blues reimburse hospitals at cost, but state laws required commercial insurers to pay an additional 13 percent. Under new legislation proposed by state regulators, commercial insurers would have to pay an extra 24 percent. Recently, the U.S. Court of Appeals struck down this surcharge, but only on a technicality.[48] Currently, about twenty-four other states also impose hospital rate surcharges on commercial companies.

"This is an economic device that the State uses to help manage the competition between nonprofit carriers (Blue Cross and Blue Shield) and commercial carriers," said Geoffrey Taylor, spokesman for a conference of Blue Cross and Blue Shield Plans.[49] Translation: state regulations make it impossible to beat commercial insurers in open competition. So government should "manage" the competition by hitting commercial insurers with heavy tax surcharges.

Managed competition is a contradiction in terms. Competition that's "managed" by bureaucrats is not free and it's not competition. *Managed competition is simply a code word for government control and extortion of private insurance companies.* State laws that burden commercial insurers with regulations and tax surcharges inevitably cause health insurance premiums to rise. Regulations and tax surcharges increase insurers' expenses. Insurance companies have to pass these expenses onto their customers. One study showed that where Blue Cross and Blue Shield plans predominate in a state, per day hospital costs rise more than 22 percent compared to states where such plans don't predominate.[50]

Organized medicine's influence over hospitals, medical schools, and licensing laws, and state health insurance regulations have increased health care costs. But organized medicine is not the real villain in this story.

THE REAL CULPRIT

My description of organized medicine's influence over medical practice in this country is not, *in any way*, meant to be a blanket criticism of doctors. Most physicians work hard to get where they are, and they're honest, dedicated professionals who do a great service for their fellow man. We owe them a great debt of gratitude for their humanity, compassion, and heartfelt efforts to alleviate the pain and suffering of others. But organized medicine is a different story. Its controls insulate medical practice from the free market and benefit the medical profession through its licensing and accreditation powers.

I have no objection to doctors trying to make as much money as they can. That's their absolute right, and they deserve every penny they might earn *in a free market*. Like any other profession, they have the right to ask for the highest fees that consumers are willing to pay. But organized medicine doesn't have the right to restrict the free market in health care.

In America, no one is above the law. Likewise, *no group should be above the free market*. Doctors do a great service to their fellow human beings, but so do other professions. Builders create homes that shelter us; clothing manufacturers make clothes that keep us warm; and farmers grow food that keeps us alive. Most people have enough confidence in themselves to compete openly in the free market. They don't ask for special privileges or immunities. The same should apply to doctors.

Unfortunately, other professional groups have acted like the AMA. Teachers' unions have fought against a free market in education. In California and other states, they vigorously opposed school vouchers and other free-enterprise ideas. They claim that they want to keep our public schools intact for the sake of the children. Just as the AMA claims that the profit motive threatens good medical care, so teachers' unions claim that the profit motive would threaten our children's education.

But I believe that their primary concern is to block free-market competition. Can we really blame them? If public school teachers and administrators had to compete in a totally free market, their tenure, pensions, and high union salaries would be threatened. Public schools stay open only *because* they have a monopoly. If there was a free market in education, most public schools would probably close, and many public school teachers and administrators would lose their jobs. Parents would decide who should teach their children, not state and local governments.

If we ended the U.S. Post Office's monopoly on first-class mail delivery and forced it to compete with Federal Express, the Post Office would soon be out of business. The same would happen with government-run public schools. That's why teachers' unions are afraid of the free market.

State governments have also passed laws that give lawyers, architects, and other professional groups the right to set accreditation standards for their professions. Bureaucrats say we need licensing laws to protect the public from the charlatans of these professions. As we'll see later, that isn't true. These laws simply restrict entry into these professions.

The problem, you see, is not greedy doctors, lawyers, or teachers. The problem is human nature. Give most men the chance to have power over their fellow man for their own selfish benefit, and they'll take it. If doctors, lawyers, teachers, plumbers, or the clockmakers of medieval England get the chance to have monopoly powers over their profession, they'll usually take it.

We can end this monopoly power only by *never giving a professional group such power in the first place.* So the real culprit is government. Only government can create regulations that give monopoly powers to special-interest groups. The AMA and other groups can use government for their own purposes only because government has the right to make such regulations in the first place.

Organized medicine has so much power only because it has big brother as an enforcer. Government creates licensing laws that give the AMA its power. Without government, organized medicine would be impotent to cause harm. Forbid government from enacting any regulations in the health care field and the AMA is reduced to a harmless fraternity of doctors. It would have no power to control licensing, hospitals, medical schools, or competition between doctors.

The way to end organized medicine's influence over the medical profession is to forbid government from making any regulations that control health care. This ban on government interference would also end regulations and punitive taxes on commercial insurers. It would force Blue Cross and Blue Shield plans to compete fairly or go out of business. The solution is to get government out of the health care business. I'll discuss this in more detail later.

OTHER REGULATIONS ON THE
HEALTH CARE INDUSTRY

Government imposes thousands of other regulations on the health care industry. Mind-bending rules, restrictions, and regulations make the health care sector one of the economy's most regulated industries. These regulations make it impossible for a free market to develop in the health care industry. They restrict the supply of efficient, competitive, for-profit hospitals. They stifle medical technology and new drug development, and strangle the private health insurance industry.

A festering mountain of regulations adds hundreds of billions of dollars to the cost of doing business for doctors, hospitals, drug companies, and insurance companies. The unconscionable cost of these regulations is then passed on to us, the hapless consumer of government-controlled medical care.

Hospitals

About one-third of America's community hospitals now have their rates, revenues, or budgets regulated at state level.[51] Hospitals also have to comply with thousands of other state, local, and federal regulations dealing with employment policies, waste disposal, fire, safety, and building codes, and many more. For example, a hospital in New York is now governed by about 99 separate regulatory agencies, one in New Jersey by about 119 agencies, and over 500 government regulations apply to nursing homes.[52]

> Scripps Memorial Hospital, a medium-sized (250-bed) acute care facility in San Diego, California. . .must answer to 39 governmental bodies and 7 nongovernmental bodies, and must periodically file 65 different reports, about one report for every four beds. . .Regulatory requirements intrude in a highly visible way on the activities of the medical staff and affect virtually every aspect of medical practice.[53]

It costs hospitals billions of dollars to comply with these regulations. In 1976, the Hospital Association of New York State conducted a comprehensive study of 148 acute care hospitals governed by 164 different regulatory agencies.

> According to the study, 25 percent of hospital costs– $1.1 billion (in 1976 dollars)–were attributable to government regulatory requirements. About 115 million staff-hours per year were needed to meet the regulatory requirements, the equivalent of having more than 56,000 hospital employees work full-time on regulatory matters. Without such regulatory burdens, enough time would have been made available to staff 75 hospitals and thereby provide medi-

cal services for about 600,000 patients.[54]

And this was the cost in 1976!

Medicare Regulations

Government now consumes over 42 percent of health care spending in this country because of Medicare, Medicaid, and similar programs. Bureaucrats run these programs, with the inevitable results.

For example, in 1983 the Medicare program changed the way it paid for medical care from cost-plus to predetermined payments for each procedure. The intent was to control spiraling costs by putting a lid on what Medicare paid doctors for each procedure.

To carry out this new system, Medicare created new and complicated procedures for billing, record keeping, and patient care reviews. And in 1991, Medicare introduced a new doctor reimbursement system called the Resource-Based Relative Value Scale (RBS). This new system is expected to make things even worse.

""The *National Journal* has called RBS "the most sweeping regulatory scheme since the government imposed wage and price controls in the early 1970s." The Washington, D.C.-based Heritage Foundation calls RBS "the largest regulatory expansion in the history of the Medicare program" and "a regulatory nightmare.""[55]

Here are just a few of the thousands of other Medicare regulations:

1. Medicare rules require hospitals to provide 24-hour nursing service by a registered nurse in each department or unit of the facility, including the emergency room.

2. Medicare requires hospitals to use licensed laboratory and radiology technicians and to have a full-time director of food and dietary services.

3. Medicare requires hospitals to meet expensive fire and safety rules, including having emergency power, emergency water supplies, and corridors of minimum width.

4. Medicare requires extensive and burdensome paperwork. . .and does not reimburse for the cost of meeting the requirement.

5. Medicare requires a full-time registered nurse who is responsible solely for the home health service and certified instructors to conduct classroom teaching for home health aides.

6. Medicare and Medicaid have "antikickback" regulations that prevent hospital-physician joint ventures, physician ownership of hospitals, and other arrangements that might induce more physicians to practice in rural areas.[56]

The list goes on and on. These regulations add billions of dollars to health care costs and increase the administrative and psychological burdens on doctors and hospitals.

Insurance Mandates

Most state governments require insurance companies to cover specific diseases or therapies they wouldn't cover if given the choice. In 1974, there were 48 such mandates; by 1991, there were over 700. Examples of insurance mandates include the treatment of alcoholism (49 states), chiropractic (37 states), podiatry (25 states), and drug addiction (25 states). Forcing insurance companies to cover these diseases sharply increases health insurance premiums for everyone else.

According to John Goodman, president of the National Center for Policy Analysis, coverage for heart transplants is mandated in Georgia, liver transplants in Illinois, hair pieces in Minnesota, marriage counseling in California, pastoral counseling in Vermont, and deposits to a sperm bank in Massachusetts. Goodman and economist Gerald Musgrave estimate that as many as *8.54 million people are priced out of the health insurance market by costly mandates. Ending all state mandates could lower insurance costs by 30%* (emphasis added).[57]

States require insurance companies to cover sperm banks, alcoholism, hairpieces, drug addition, marriage counseling, and pastoral counseling. Isn't this incredible? An insurance company has to cover people who drink, take drugs, or need marriage or pastoral counseling? We all pay high premiums because state governments force insurers to cover these conditions.

Here's a prime example of the vicious effects of government regulations. Over eight million Americans can't afford high-priced health insurance because states force insurance companies to cover alcoholics and drug addicts. A serious illness can bankrupt over eight million hardworking people because insurers have to cover drug addiction, marriage counseling, and sperm bank deposits.

Can you imagine what California insurance companies pay out to cover marriage counseling in that state? Can you imagine how this increases health insurance premiums for millions of Californians who don't need counseling? States have no right mandating *anything* to insurance companies, no less for such ridiculous things.

Commercial Insurers Are Not Welfare Agencies

Medicare and Medicaid combined bring in over 37 percent of hospital revenues.[58] Medicare pays predetermined fees for each medical procedure, and these fees are usually much lower than doctors and hospitals get from private insurance companies.

As a result, hospitals shift the cost of treating Medicare patients to privately insured patients. They add surcharges to private patients' bills to cover losses from Medicare, which increases these patients' hospital bills. This forces commercial insurers to pay more and then raise insurance premiums to cover these higher payouts.

Insurance companies claim that 30 percent of employers' increased health insurance payouts for 1989 came from cost shifting by hospitals.[59] In effect, cost shifting is a welfare scheme. It forces employers and privately insured patients to pay high premiums to cover losses from Medicare patients.

New Jersey tried to pass a similar cost-shifting law. The law would have forced about 2.4 million people covered by union and company self-insurance plans to pay a 19 percent surcharge on their hospital bills. The approximately $900 million collected by this surcharge would go into a state fund. The fund would pay hospital bills for people who had little or no insurance—another cost-shifting welfare scheme.

New York State passed a law that requires commercial insurers to insure anyone who applies for coverage. The law forbids the companies from setting rates based on age, gender, or medical condition. Everyone is combined into one big risk pool, as they are in nonprofit Blue Cross and Blue Shield plans. Vermont, Florida, Hawaii, Oregon, and Minnesota have also passed similar legislation.

As a result, these regulations penalize young or healthy people with few medical problems. Healthy peoples' premiums increase to cover insurance company losses on people with serious, pre-existing conditions who they now have to insure. This is another cost-shifting welfare scheme.

Prudential Insurance Company's vice-president of government relations, Phillip J. Harrington, Jr., indicated there would probably be 20 percent to 50 percent rate increases on 70 percent of his small-group customers. That's because of the New York State law that now requires the company to insure everyone. He also said the law might force his company and many other commercial insurers to stop insuring small groups in New York.[60]

In effect, liberals try to solve the health care cost crisis on the backs of private insurance companies and millions of healthy Americans who are forced to pay higher insurance premiums. They're trying to turn commercial insurers into private welfare agencies.

Insurance companies are in business to make profits. *They are not welfare agencies* and should not be forced into that role. Also, healthy, hardworking Americans who are barely able to afford health insurance, are not sacrificial animals. They should not be forced to pay for other peoples' insurance.

Drug Regulations: Dangerous to Our Health

The FDA is responsible for approving drugs in this country, and the approval process has become a bureaucratic nightmare. It can take up to seven years to approve a drug[61] and, "it's been estimated that FDA reviews require an average of 120,000 pages of complex data for each drug. In 1962, research and development costs for new drugs was estimated to be about $4 million. Today that figure is over $50 million."[62] That was the cost in 1979; by 1990, the 1979 cost doubled again.

"Based on a 1990 study at Tufts University, drug companies claim that it costs an average of $231 million to bring a drug to market. But only half of that is budgeted for development."[63] This means the average cost to develop a new drug is now over $100 million.

What's been the effect of this regulatory nightmare? The number of new drugs introduced into the American market has declined each year from an average of 52 in 1960, to 16 in 1977.[64] In 1993, the FDA approved only 25 new drugs.[65]

FDA regulations increase the price of drugs because they force pharmaceutical companies to risk years of research and millions of dollars to get a drug approved. When the FDA finally approves the drug, the company has to pass this cost on to consumers. And many new drugs never make it to market. The huge risks in time and money strangle new drug development. When new drug development slows down, competition between pharmaceutical companies becomes weaker. Weak competition inevitably creates higher drug prices.

Then there's the problem of orphan drugs. The FDA gives pharmaceutical companies a seven-year monopoly on these drugs. Of course, once the monopoly is in place, the company charges high prices, free from competition.

FDA regulations also create huge hidden costs. New drugs not only save lives, they also create new therapies to treat conditions that only expensive operations used to cure.

In 1976, the year before the introduction of the first modern anti-ulcer drug, there were 155,000 ulcer operations. By 1987, the number had dropped to under 19,000. And today, while ulcer drug therapy costs a sizable $1,000 a year, it is far less expensive than surgery which averages $25,000, resulting in an estimated savings of $3 billion a year.[66]

This is the cost savings from just one drug. If you consider that hundreds of new drugs may not be developed because of FDA regulations, the increased health care costs are staggering.

The same applies to medical technology. The FDA has extended its tentacles over medical instruments and procedures. New technology now has to go through an FDA review process. The FDA can take up to two years to approve a new instrument or surgical technique. Meanwhile, delay adds billions of dollars to health care costs and causes untold human suffering to thousands of people.

New drugs to prevent postsurgical infections can reduce hospital stays as much as 10 days. Gene therapy for illnesses like cystic fibrosis and Parkinson's disease can eliminate years of chronic care costs, while also improving patients' quality of life. New cell therapy techniques can reduce the cost of a bone-marrow transplant as much as $50,000. Similarly, the laparoscope, originally developed for use in gynecology, has reduced the bill for gall bladder surgery to $6,400 from $21,000 and turned a six-day hospital stay into an outpatient procedure.[67] Last year, 500,000 Americans underwent laparoscopic gall-bladder surgery. 3 million days of hospital stay costs were eliminated. 2.5 million weeks of insurance reimbursement were eliminated. 100 million hours were added to American productivity. *Gallbladder surgery is just the tip of the iceberg* (emphasis added).[68] (see U.S. Surgical Corporation copyright notice in notes).

This is just one new medical technology. FDA regulations that cause long delays in approving new technology and procedures therefore add billions of dollars to health care costs.

HOW GOVERNMENT EXPLODES HEALTH CARE DEMAND

We now come to the demand side of the health care nightmare. Government explodes health care demand through its tax policies, entitlement programs, and government-supported cost-plus insurance system.

Tax Laws

Tax laws have a big effect on health care spending. Current tax policy allows employers to deduct the full cost of employees' health insurance premiums as an expense. This means that employers pay their employees' premiums with pretax dollars. People who don't work for a company that pays their health insurance are not so lucky. They pay for their own insurance with after-tax dollars.

Whether people pay their insurance premiums with pretax or

after-tax dollars greatly affects health care spending. The average American pays almost 35 percent of his income in taxes (including federal and state income taxes, Social Security, and other taxes).

A worker who pays for insurance with after-tax dollars has to earn one dollar for each 65 cents worth of insurance he buys. The employee covered by a company plan gets a dollar's worth of insurance for every dollar taken from his salary. High tax rates therefore give both employers and employees a strong reason to replace wages with nontaxable health insurance benefits. As a result, current tax laws push Americans into relying on health insurance paid by their employers.

The share of health care spending paid by business increased from 17% in 1965 to 28% in 1987, while the share paid directly by individuals fell from almost 90% in 1930 to just 25% in 1987. In 1985, 90% of the privately insured population obtained its insurance from employers or unions.[69]

Since 1930, Americans have increasingly relied on tax-free, employer-provided insurance to pay their medical bills, rather than on their own money. Worse, employees and unions push their employers to buy group policies with low-deductibles. As a result, the tax laws subsidize and encourage overinsurance with low-deductible policies.

But insurance that covers small medical bills is extremely wasteful. "For one thing, it can cost an insurance company more than $25 to administer and monitor a claim for a $25 physician's fee, thereby effectively doubling the cost of health care. For another, people are far less prudent in purchasing health care if the bills are paid by someone else."[70]

Most people with low-deductible policies have little incentive to be careful health care consumers. They don't comparison shop for the best prices because the insurance company pays the bill. They also overuse medical services for the same reason. Insurance coverage with no or low deductibles makes consumers act as if medical care was free. This attitude sharply increases demand for medical care and increases health care costs.

Employer-paid insurance has important tax benefits. So most workers prefer policies with low deductibles, low coinsurance payments, and that cover a wide range of medical conditions.

Insurance premiums for these policies are much higher than for high-deductible policies designed to cover only catastrophic illness. Because employees push for low-deductible, low-coinsurance plans, health insurance premiums keep escalating.

Medicare and Medicaid: Monsters Out of Control

Like most other entitlement programs, Medicare and Medicaid have become monsters out of control. Congress created these programs to help older people pay for catastrophic illness. As with other entitlement programs, they started small. But human nature, bureaucracy, and government incompetence caused their usual, inevitable results. Just as welfare, food stamps, and farm subsidies grew out of control, so have these programs.

In 1970, government spent about $24.9 billion on health care. In the 1995 fiscal-year budget, Medicare and Medicaid combined will cost about $273 billion.[71] Government now spends about 42 percent of total health care dollars in this country.[72] Like a cancer, once entitlement programs start, it's almost impossible to stop them.

Liberal politicians think of themselves as Santa Clauses with other peoples' money—they keep their jobs by offering ever more goodies to their constituents who keep demanding more. Once one group gets a special benefit like health care, then everyone wants it. Once a person gets $10 in benefits, he then wants $20, then $30, and so on. Soon he wants more to cover follow-up visits to the doctor or for higher drug or hospital costs. The cost escalations never end.

When one group gets entitlements, other groups soon shout, "Unfair!, I'm also a taxpayer. I want it too. Why do they get it and not me?" Our congressmen have no answer to that except capitulation. They have to give in or admit that creating the entitlement program was wrong from the start. So over the years, Medicare and other entitlement programs that started small, grow into monsters.

And once an entitlement program starts, it has to keep up with inflation. If inflation increases health care costs, Medicare payments have to keep pace. If they don't, older people suffer and the whole purpose of Medicare is compromised. That's why

Medicare, Social Security, and other entitlement programs index their benefits to inflation. As a result, total payouts keep escalating and the program spirals out of control.

It's extremely difficult to end entitlement programs once they're entrenched. Millions of people depend on these programs, and they would scream bloody murder if you try to take away their benefits. If you want proof, just campaign for political office in Florida and suggest that we reduce or phase out Social Security. You'd be lucky to get out alive.

Once you start an entitlement program, you can't stop it. When something is free, everyone wants it, and health care is no exception. As a result, Medicare creates unlimited demand for health care by older Americans. If government pays for it, why not?

Think of what happens when you go to a party and the host says, "The food is free, take what you want." What do most people do? Did you ever see a stampede by a herd of buffalo? They gorge; they fill their plates and stuff their mouths; they wrap up some more to take home. Why not? The food's free. It's the same with free medical care. That's why the cost for Medicare and Medicaid has exploded since 1965.

Also, all entitlement programs invite massive fraud, and Medicare and Medicaid are no exception.

> The General Accounting Office, an investigative arm of Congress, released a study that said fraud and abuse in paying for health care were out of control and getting worse. It estimated that fraud would cost $100 billion a year by 1995. . ."The savings and loan crisis, the worst financial scandal in U.S. history, will cost taxpayers $200 billion," said Representative Ted Weiss, Democrat from Manhattan and chairman of the House Human Resources and Intergovernmental Relations Subcommittee. "But that will eventually seem like a penny-ante affair compared to the $100 billion-a-year price tag of health care fraud and abuse."[73]

Medicare bureaucrats have no incentive to check medical bills carefully because *they're not spending their own money*. Patients, physicians, and hospitals who know how to take advantage of the system, milk it for all it's worth. The patient-customer is not alert to the fraud, because what does he care? He pays only a small portion of his Medicare bills.

Like Social Security, Medicare is a huge income transfer pro-gram for retirees.[74] Most people think that Medicare is just an insurance program that we paid for with our Medicare payroll taxes while we were working. Like Social Security, this isn't true. Medicare is a pay-as-you-go-system with no accumulating trust fund. Working peoples' payroll taxes pay for retirees' Medi-care benefits. And most Medicare beneficiaries get back much more in benefits than they paid into the system while working.

A little known fact about Medicare is that its beneficiaries have paid into the program in taxes only a small fraction of the amount they are receiving and can expect to receive in benefits. For a re-tiree who earned the median wage, all Medicare tax payments can be expected to be recovered in one year and five months. . .For example, male beneficiaries who are now age 65 can expect to re-ceive 17 times more in Medicare benefits than they paid in taxes, those who are 70 can expect 31 times more, those who are 75 can expect 63 times more, and those who are 80 can expect 137 times more. . .[75]

Medicare is a huge income transfer program from the young to the old and from poorer working people to mostly better-off retirees. We pay for these subsidies through higher taxes and escalating insurance costs. The Medicare and Medicaid pro-grams have sharply increased demand for medical services and are major culprits in increasing health care costs in this coun-try.

The Cost-Plus Insurance System

In the free market, a producer tries to beat the competition by lowering his costs and prices. Until recently, however, most hospitals used the cost-plus system to determine what they charged. The price for a procedure was based on the hospital's costs plus a surcharge.

The cost-plus system set up perverse financial incentives. Hos-pitals realized that the way to increase revenues was to increase costs. So they added more beds even if the beds stayed empty, or bought expensive medical equipment even if they didn't use the equipment. Anything hospitals did to increase costs increased their revenues. Conversely, anything hospitals did to lower costs decreased their revenues. Under such a system, hospital costs naturally increased.

In the last twenty years, Medicare and Blue Cross and Blue Shield plans have changed the way they reimburse hospitals from a cost-plus to a price-per-procedure system. But under these programs, prices don't operate the way they do in a free market.

The new Medicare system sets allowable charges for each procedure. But many nonprofit hospitals don't set prices based on competition and market forces. Instead, they set prices to manipulate the way they get reimbursed from Medicare or insurance companies. Hospitals set prices to get the most revenues they can out of the price-controlled Medicare system. "Consequently, it is probably fair to say that all traditional Blue Cross reimbursement methods are ultimately cost-plus."[76]

The federal government also adopted the cost-plus system under the original Medicare and Medicaid programs. Eventually, the system spread throughout the health care system and, as a result, health care costs have escalated.

The stage had been set for the health care crisis. Government regulations strangled the free market in the health care industry. At the same time, Medicare, Medicaid, the cost-plus system, and government tax policies exploded health care demand. We had the classic scenario for a price explosion—restricted supply and unlimited demand. And government manufactured the entire crisis.

A FREE ECONOMY: HOW TO SOLVE
THE HEALTH CARE CRISIS

We began this chapter with the questions: Why are health care costs exploding? What's creating our health care crisis? Let's summarize what we've learned up to now.

Three types of problems have created the health care mess. The first includes issues like population changes, medical technology, the lawsuit problem, our standard of living, and the aggressive nature of American medicine. The second and third involve problems caused by government.

We can't easily change the first group of problems. If people have more money, they'll spend more on health care. We demand the best medical care, so we'll always have aggressive medicine with expensive new technology. And more people are living longer, which increases health care costs. Now, if you think about it, what's wrong with people living longer, spending more on health care, or demanding the best treatment? We all want to live long and happy lives.

Also, aggressive medicine, medical technology, a high standard of living, and older people living longer create demand for more and better health care. This is good and natural. But increased demand doesn't have to increase our health care costs. The free market can solve this problem, as it does for thousands of other products with strong demand.

If the economy is free, demand for a product or service *creates* supply that eventually lowers costs. For example, the great demand for computers created a magnet for many other companies to enter the field. That led to fierce competition and a huge increase in the supply of computers, which drastically lowered prices. In effect, demand creates its own supply.

The same applies to a service or profession. If we had a free economy with a great demand for doctors, then free-market medical schools would be swamped with applicants. That would sharply increase the supply of doctors. If there was free competition among doctors and for-profit hospitals, we would have price wars for patients that would lower doctors' and hospitals' fees. In a free market, doctors would be competing with nurses and other paraprofessionals. Also, medical technology would keep people healthier and reduce the need for doctors.

If we eliminated all regulations on the health care industry, doctors, hospitals, and drug companies would not have to spend billions of dollars and millions of man-hours complying with these regulations. If we ended all regulations on health insurance companies, including mandates, price shifting, and community rating laws, health insurance rates would plummet.

In short, a free market in health care would be dynamic and innovative. Fierce competition would lower costs at every level of the health care industry, just as it does for other industries.

The more that consumers want a particular product or service, the more profits entrepreneurs can make. These profits spur others to enter the field, which increases the supply of the product and lowers its price. That's how the powerful economic mechanism of supply and demand lowers the cost and increases the quality of almost everything we buy.

But supply and demand only work in a free market. If there's heavy demand for a product or service, but government strangles the supply, a monkey wrench is thrown into the system. When this happens, supply can't meet the demand anymore. When everyone wants a scarce product, naturally its price increases. That's one of the root causes of our health care crisis. Medicare, tax policies, and the cost-plus system explode the demand for medical care and health insurance, while regulations strangle the supply.

Wherever we turn, we see that the problem is government: the Welfare State wrecks the economy; government chokes us with taxes and regulations; it destroys the life-giving benefits of the free market; it throttles the supply of doctors, new drugs, medical schools, for-profit hospitals, and inexpensive health insurance; it creates long-term inflation in the economy; Medicare and tax policies explode the demand for, and cost of, medical care and health insurance.

The solution is therefore clear: *We need a free economy, where government is out of the way, totally and permanently.* Let's see how a free market would work, what advantages it would bring, and how it would solve the health care crisis.

Health Care And The Free Market

Free-market solutions for the health care industry could have their greatest effect only if the entire economy was free market. If the general economy was free, competitive, and productive, health care and insurance costs would decrease sharply. If the Welfare State ruins the economy, then health care goes down the tubes with the rest of the country. It would be impossible to maintain a free-market health care island in the middle of a welfare-state ocean. To solve the health care crisis, we would have to phase out all welfare-state regulations and entitlement programs.

With this in mind, let's look at ways to solve the health care crisis. Specifically, the steps we need are:

1. Phase out and dismantle Medicare, Medicaid, and all other health care entitlement programs.

2. End organized medicine's power to control any area of medical practice, including licensing for doctors, nurses, and paraprofessionals, and accreditation of schools, hospitals, and other medical facilities.

3. End all government regulations, controls over, and subsidies to hospitals, medical schools, and other medical facilities.

4. End all regulations on the health insurance and pharmaceutical industries. End all subsidies or government support for nonprofit Blue Cross and Blue Shield plans.

5. Abolish the FDA and other regulatory agencies.

6. End employer tax deductions for employee health insurance premiums. At the same time, create new tax policies that turn people into careful medical-care consumers. Also, create medical IRAs and give tax deductions to people who buy high-deductible health insurance policies.

In short, do the exact *opposite* of what liberals and democrats want. Instead of turning health care over to government, we must build a constitutional wall between the health care industry and government. We must permanently forbid government from making any regulations or entitlement programs relating to health care.

Phase Out Medicare and Medicaid

Most Americans don't realize that Medicare is a welfare program for retirees. Likewise, Medicaid is a welfare program for the poor. Those who now receive Medicare benefits paid taxes into the program while they were working. But as we noted earlier, the taxes they paid cover only a small fraction of the benefits they'll receive once they're in the program.

Congress originally created Medicare and Medicaid to provide health care for old or poor people who couldn't afford it. Yet studies show that the elderly as a group have more after-tax income and wealth than the nonelderly.[77] In effect, Medicare takes money from poor and middle-class working families to pay for the medical care of more financially secure older people. Retirees are getting unearned subsidies from young working people. This was not the original intent of the program, yet this is the reality.

If we had a free, healthy, productive, competitive economy, we wouldn't need Medicare. We could phase it out. If we dismantled the Welfare State, we could slash taxes and raise our standard of living. We would have more money for health insurance and tax-free medical IRAs and Medical Savings Accounts. These accounts would replace Medicare, and give us income for insurance and medical bills when we retire.

If we had a completely free market in health care, increasing demand would create increasing supplies. Prices would stabilize or decrease sharply as they've done for computers and hundreds of other products and services. If there were no regulations that restricted the supply of doctors, nurses, hospitals, medical schools, paraprofessionals, inexpensive drugs, and cheap health insurance, the free market would work its magic. Freedom of choice and fierce competition would lower drug prices, doctors' fees, hospital costs, and insurance premiums.

If we abolished the FDA, pharmaceutical companies would develop more lifesaving drugs. Also, no drug company would have a government-created monopoly, and aggressive competition would sharply lower drug prices.

If we ended all regulations on insurance companies, premiums would decline. If we eliminated all state insurance mandates, community-rating regulations, and cost-shifting to private patients, insurance would be affordable to most Americans.

We would not have the government-created nightmare of exploding demand and restricted supply. Instead, the free market would create abundant supply and careful medical consumers. Competing doctors and hospitals would lower their prices. We could phase out Medicare because most of us wouldn't need it anymore. We would have more disposable income to pay for ever-cheaper insurance and medical care.

Government could help in the transition to the free market by creating tax credits for employer or individual contributions to Medical IRAs and Savings accounts.[78] These accounts, similar to regular IRAs, would encourage people to save money for health insurance and medical bills during their working years and after retirement. These accounts could add to, and eventually replace, Medicare benefits while Medicare was being phased out.

Millions of Americans now depend on Medicare, so we would have to phase it out over many years. In the phase-out process, retirees who truly need Medicare would continue to get their benefits. But we should also apply a means test to current recipients. Those who have extensive assets and get more benefits than they paid into the system, would pay a bigger share of their medical bills. That's only fair. Working people could choose to leave the Medicare program while building up their medical IRA accounts. Medicare would then phase out by attrition.

Get the Fox Out of the Chicken Coop

Organized medicine's control over licensing and accreditation of hospitals, medical schools, and other areas of medical practice would end. This might sound like a crazy idea to many people because most of us think a doctor needs a license to be competent. If doctors and hospitals don't have licenses, won't we all be killed in our hospital beds by greedy, unscrupulous charlatans? Let's explore this idea.

Bureaucrats assume that we wouldn't know how to choose a competent physician if doctors didn't need a license to practice. But they're wrong. We would use our common sense and the free market's protective mechanisms to help us find a competent doctor.

In the free market, *everyone* specializes in one skill or profession and knows little about other areas of expertise. Most of us don't know how to fly a plane, build a house, or fix a television. Yet every day of the year we use experts who can do these things.

If we don't have these experts' technical knowledge, are we stupid? Is there no way to make reasonable judgments about which expert to use? If that was true, our economy would have collapsed into chaos long ago. Most of us manage to make reasonable decisions in choosing experts.

If there were no license requirements to practice medicine, you would check out a doctor before using him. It's only common sense, since choosing the wrong doctor would be hazardous to your health. How would you pick a doctor? First, you would look for recommendations from friends or family. Next, you might check his education credentials. Then you might go to other doctors for second opinions and fee rates, just like you do when you get several estimates from building contractors or auto mechanics. You don't need a college education to be a careful consumer, just common sense.

If you don't have time to check out a doctor's credentials and experience, don't worry. The free market has other, more powerful resources you can tap. First, the insurance industry can be a powerful ally. Most doctors have medical liability insurance to protect them from lawsuits. Insurers would check out a doctor before approving him for a policy. The insurance company could tell you if, and how often, the doctor had been sued, or if his insurance had ever been dropped.

You also want to know a doctor's reputation and educational background. Private companies could research this information and publish it. Voters might contribute one dollar in taxes to have their local government set up medical information services as a substitute for license laws. Government, like private companies, might rate doctors on education and competence.

Such a list already exists. The Quality Assurance Division of the Bureau of Health Professions is an agency of the federal Health and Human Services Department. It has a huge data bank of information on about 62,183 doctors and other medical professionals who have been sued or otherwise cited for criminal behavior or medical incompetence.[79]

HMOs and hospitals would also protect you against incompetent doctors. In a free market, HMOs and hospitals would be for-profit enterprises. Hospitals would check the credentials of any doctor they employed, and HMOs would do the same for their participating doctors. They would also fire any doctor they felt was incompetent.

Why? Because for-profit HMOs or hospitals need to make profits. They want their patients to be satisfied customers who will recommend the HMO or hospital to friends and family. A bad doctor can lose customers for the HMO or hospital. Angry patients also file massive lawsuits. Lawsuits can ruin an HMO's or hospital's most valuable asset: its reputation. *Incompetent doctors are not good for business.* By hiring or associating with the best doctors, HMOs and hospitals protect you, make more profits, and have satisfied customers.

The free market would produce competent doctors without licensing. Does that mean no one would ever be hurt by a dishonest or incompetent doctor? Absolutely not. Just as there are dishonest or incompetent plumbers, accountants, or car mechanics, the same applies to doctors. But that's just human nature. There are always bad apples in any profession. You protect yourself by being a careful consumer and using the doctor, HMO, or hospital with the best reputation. Finally, anyone hurt by an incompetent doctor, even after being a careful consumer, could sue him for damages.

HEALTH CARE AS IT COULD BE

If the health care industry was free of licensing, Medicare and Medicaid, and government regulations, we would be in health care heaven. With government out of the way, the free market would work its magic. Let's see how.

Medical Schools

Today, most medical schools are nonprofit. They're supported by tuition, private grants, and government subsidies. In a free market, government subsidies would end. All schools would have to compete on the open market as profit-making enterprises. This would increase competition and end unfair advantages now given to nonprofit schools.

Free enterprise would create hundreds of new schools. No school would have to meet complex and expensive AMA accreditation requirements. Schools would compete for medical students, which would drive down tuition costs, probably shorten training time, and spur innovation in medical education.

Lower tuition costs would lighten the debt load from student loans. New doctors would then have more leeway to lower their fees to attract patients, because their overhead would be less.

More young people could afford medical school. They wouldn't have to study in Mexico or Guatemala. More minority and low-income parents could afford medical school for their children who wanted to become doctors. Medical schools would graduate thousands more doctors than they do today.

These thousands of new doctors would compete with established doctors and with each other because AMA competition restrictions would end. New doctors would compete for your business by offering their services at lower fees. You would see ads in the Yellow Pages and on television by doctors, HMOs, and hospitals that openly advertised their fee schedules and qualifications.

Competition would eventually weed out incompetent doctors. Better doctors would prevail because they would earn the best reputation. You would have more choice and more sources of information to judge which doctor to use. The fierce new competition would lower doctor fees and hospital costs.

Also, current restrictions on nurses, physician assistants, and other paraprofessionals would end. These health care professionals would be allowed to practice medicine. They could handle routine or relatively simply medical procedures, and service poor or rural areas. They would offer low-cost competition for basic medical care.

HMOs

In the past, state laws tried to restrict HMOs. As we saw earlier, the federal government finally stopped state discrimination against HMOs by passing the Health Maintenance Organization Act in 1973. As a result, by June of 1993, HMO enrollments were up to 47 million subscribers.[80]

Studies show that HMOs lower costs by reducing unnecessary medical procedures, controlling doctors' fees, and making their hospital facilities more efficient and innovative. All remaining state or federal regulations on HMOs would end, which would increase competition and lower HMO costs and prices.

Hospitals

Regulations, punitive taxes, and licensing requirements on for-profit hospitals would be eliminated. Subsidies or competitive advantages given to nonprofit hospitals would end. All hospitals would compete on an equal footing.

As a result, there would be an explosion in new hospital construction. Competition would be fierce. Because most hospitals would be for-profit enterprises, they would keep a sharp eye on costs and doctors' fees. They would be efficient and innovative, which would lower hospital costs dramatically. Health insurance premiums would drop sharply as hospital costs went down.

Low-Cost Health Insurance

Government controls strangle commercial insurance companies. Many state governments give nonprofit Blue Cross and Blue Shield plans unfair competitive advantages and subsidize them with rate increases. They create regulations and tax policies that penalize commercial insurers.

Most state governments force mandates on insurance companies, and some states now require insurers to cover anyone, regardless of medical history. Mandates, regulations, and punitive taxes on commercial insurance companies would end. Subsidies for nonprofit Blue Cross and Blue Shield plans would end. Insurance companies would compete with each other on an equal footing, without government interference. This would create fierce competition and lower insurance premiums.

A free market in insurance would force Blue Cross and Blue Shield plans to shape up or go bankrupt. They could no longer depend on state governments to bail them out. They would become efficient, profit-making businesses that kept a tight rein on medical bill payouts.

Blue Cross and Blue Shield plans can adapt to the free market. In fact, that's starting to happen right now. Recently, the national Blue Cross and Blue Shield Association said it would allow its member plans to sell stock to the public and become for-profit enterprises.[81] The Association had to change its sixty-year policy of nonprofit health care service. That's because Blue Cross and Blue Shield plans are now competing with a rapidly changing health care market made up of large, well-financed commercial companies and merging HMOs. If Blue Cross and Blue Shield plans don't lower their costs and become more efficient as for-profit enterprises, they'll go bankrupt.

In a health-care free market, we would have many innovative insurance options because of fierce competition between HMOs, commercial insurers, and for-profit Blue Cross and Blue Shield plans. We could choose health care plans that meet our special needs, lifestyles, and budget constraints. Young, healthy people could choose low-cost plans with high deductibles and coinsurance payments that covered them for catastrophic illness. Older people could choose plans with lower deductibles.

Insurance companies could compete with each other by offering guaranteed renewable policies. They could do this because ending state mandates and other regulations would lower their costs and increase their profits. If insurers issued guaranteed renewable policies, or policies to individuals rather than employee groups, the problem of job-lock would disappear.

HMOs would compete by offering more freedom to choose doctors outside the plan (this is already happening). Hospitals or groups of doctors might create their own prepaid plans. Major corporations could also offer low-cost prepaid plans to their employees. There would be no end to the innovative new insurance options the free market gave us.

The free market would also turn us into careful consumers. We wouldn't treat medical care as if it was a free service paid by our employer or insurance company. We would shop around for competitive prices. Careful consumers would lower health care costs and reduce demand for unnecessary medical care.

Drugs: Low Cost and No More Delays

In a free economy, we would abolish the Food and Drug Administration and end government control over drugs. This would sharply reduce the cost to develop new drugs. Drug companies would not get a monopoly on orphan drugs—they wouldn't need one, because development costs would be much lower. Pharmaceutical companies could quickly market thousands of miraculous new drugs, which could save thousands of lives and relieve the suffering of millions of Americans. The pharmaceutical industry would be fiercely competitive. We could buy less expensive drugs from Asia or Europe because FDA restrictions would be gone. The free market would lower drug prices while increasing the number and quality of drugs available.

Tax Policies

Current tax policy makes health insurance premiums tax deductible for both employers and employees. This encourages workers to demand low-deductible insurance policies. Low-deductible policies lead to wasteful demand for medical care, and cut incentives for people to be careful, cost-conscious consumers. Also, current tax deductions give tax advantages to employees of large companies, but penalize the self-employed or those working for small companies that don't offer health plans.

To remedy these problems, the tax code would change. Employers couldn't deduct employee health insurance premiums anymore. Also, employees would pay taxes on health insurance benefits they got from their employer. Current tax policies encourage linking health insurance to employers, rather than to individuals or groups outside the workplace. Tax law changes would encourage us to buy health insurance as individuals, not as employees, the way we now buy life insurance.

We would also get tax credits for health insurance premiums we pay out-of-pocket. But we would only get tax credits for no-frills, catastrophic-illness policies with high deductibles. These policies would encourage us to pay small medical bills with our own money.

We would have many insurance options. We could stay with our employer's plan or join local or regional health care groups created by insurance companies. Or, we could join a local social, political, religious, or professional association group plan. For example, we could enroll in the insurance plan of our local PTA, church, baseball team league, Democrat or Republican party chapter, or other group we belong to. Once we separate health

197

insurance from employers, job-lock would cease to be a problem.

Current tax policy creates another serious problem. It doesn't give tax credits for medical IRAs or medical savings accounts. Because these accounts are not available, most people turn to their employers for health insurance. With medical IRAs and savings accounts, we could save tax-free money for medical bills, health insurance premiums, and medical care after retirement.

If we followed the above program, we would end the health care crisis and have a free, competitive, low-cost health care system. Most of us would be able to afford health insurance. Competition would lower costs and improve medical care. The free market would kill the health care monster that is now devouring us.

But a free-market health care system is possible only if we reject the moral and political ideas used to justify the Welfare State. We accept the Welfare State because we accept those ideas. Unless we reject the notion that helping others is our moral and political duty, nothing will change and the crisis will escalate.

Liberals in Congress proposed that we turn health care over to government bureaucrats. They wanted to guarantee all Americans the right to health care. But as we saw earlier, a "right" to health care, like any other economic right, is simply a license to steal. It simply means that government would force us to pay for health insurance for over 35 million Americans who now can't afford it. Government would steal more money from hardworking middle-class families to give unearned benefits to others. Worse, government would steal from us for a problem it created.

THE MORAL QUESTION

Dismantling the Welfare State would end the health care crisis and give us a low-cost, efficient health care system. But all the practical arguments in the world won't convince liberals who oppose the free market on *moral* grounds. "Yes," liberals would say, "a free economy would probably give us a better health care system, but. . ."

But! And here's the great *but* that will ruin us. Liberals complain that in a free market some people won't get the health care they need. No matter how good the system, some people are too poor to afford insurance or medical care. Do we leave them to die in the streets? Is our rich society so heartless that it would let this happen?

That's the usual socialist argument used to justify robbing and enslaving some people to give unearned benefits to others. It's the argument that says helping others is a political duty, not a person choice. For sixty years, liberals used this same argument to create every disastrous, welfare-state entitlement program that's now devouring us.

The answer to this argument must be the same: We have a right to our lives. We have a right to keep what we earn. We, and only we, have the right to decide who we help or don't help. *Compassion for others is a personal choice, not a political duty.* Health care, like food, housing, or education, is not a right. Anyone who claims the right to health care is saying he has a right to force others to pay for his health care. Harsh as this may sound, *anyone who claims the right to health care is claiming the right to steal from others.* And theft is still theft if government does it through tax laws and entitlement programs.

No one has a right to your income or effort without your consent. No one has a right to steal just because he has financial problems. If he had that right, mugging would be legal. This principle applies to health care as it does to anything else.

We can understand the real meaning of the "right" to health care if we look at another human need—food. Suppose you're down on your luck and don't have enough money for food. You go to a supermarket, load $200 worth of food into your cart, and bring the food to the counter. The clerk asks you for $200. You tell him you don't have the money but want the food anyhow. You tell him you're hungry and need the food.

The clerk looks at you oddly and calls the manager. You say the same thing to the manager. The manager tells you to pay for the food or get lost. Now you get angry. You tell the manager again that you need the food, that you have a right to the food even if you can't pay for it. You tell the manager it's his moral duty to feed you.

The manager patiently explains the facts of life to you. If he gives you free food, then he has to raise food prices for everyone else to cover the store's cost to buy the food. That's stealing from the other customers. Or, if other customers also demand free food, the store would soon be out of business and no one would have food.

Your stomach is growling and you're getting angry with the manager. You tell him you don't give a damn about his problems or stealing from other customers. You need the food now, and that's all that matters. The manager again tells you to get lost. Now you're really mad. So you pull out a gun and tell the manager, "the food or your life." You then run out of the store with your loot before the police come.

Did you have a right to the food if you couldn't pay for it? Is the store morally responsible for your problem that you don't have money for food? Did the store cause your problem? Did you have a right to steal simply because you needed the food? If you answered no, you now understand why no one has a right to health care. The principle is the same in both cases.

Are we to become sacrificial animals for anyone who claims the right to take our money because they need it? It's very natural to feel sorry for a sick person. But claiming the right to health care is like a mugger claiming the right to your wallet because he's out of work and hungry. In both cases, your sympathy for the person doesn't give him the right to steal from you. It also doesn't give government the right to mug you with taxes.

I don't say this to be mean to people who can't afford health care. On the contrary, I would love to see everyone happy and healthy. I'm going to get old and sick just like everyone else, and someday I may desperately need medical care and not be able to afford it.

But the best way to insure that we can all afford health care in the future is to have a free, prosperous, competitive economy and health care industry that gives us low-cost health insurance. A free market will slash health care costs and make it easy for most of us to afford health insurance.

When we claim the right to health care and other needs, we sanction mass theft, violate property rights, and give government unlimited power over us. We also wreck our economy and free society. Economic rights lead to a cannibal society where everyone is sacrificed to everyone else's needs. Economic rights are the poison that turns a free society into a fascist, socialist, or welfare-state disaster area. When this happens, we all suffer and we all end up in the poorhouse. We end up like the millions of poor souls who waited on breadlines for hours in the freezing winters of communist Russia. Socialism ends only one way—with everyone poor and brutalized. The Welfare State is just a halfway house on the road to socialism.

Does government have the right to wreck our health care for the sake of the few people who can't afford insurance in a free-market system? Isn't it *immoral* for liberals or those few people to ask for such a sacrifice?

There's another important moral issue to consider. Other people don't usually cause our health problems. If someone can't afford insurance or health care, or has the bad luck to contract a serious illness, did the rest of us cause this problem? We can sympathize with other people's illness, but why do our elected representatives have the right to punish us for something we didn't cause?

Liberals answer this question by laying a guilt trip on us. They claim that everyone's health care is our responsibility, that we're shackled to each other's genetic fate. Well, I'm sorry, but our first responsibility is to ourselves and our families. The help we give to others must be done out of love and free choice, not by government compulsion.

This moral issue comes up all the time in a welfare state. A small group of people are having some problem in life. They can't afford health care, decent housing, education for their kids, or other things. To solve the problem, government turns the rest of us into sacrificial animals. Government turns our natural kindness into a fascist or socialist system of compulsion that kills off the wealth and freedom that would keep such problems down to a minimum.

The relatively small number of Americans who couldn't afford health care in a free economy could depend on the support of family and friends, *as they did before we had the Welfare State*. They could also depend on private charity. Remember, our standard of living would be higher and our cost of living would be lower in a free economy. Family, friends, and private charities would have more excess income to help people who couldn't afford health care.

Americans contribute billions of dollars to charity every year, even in times of recession.

75% of the households in the United States donate to charity, according to Independent Sector, a Washington-based group representing the nation's nonprofit institutions. Those households that gave in 1990 donated an average of $978 to such diverse causes as education, the environment, health care, homelessness, the arts, and nuclear disarmament. . .

In 1990, giving totaled $122.6 billion and 9 in 10 dollars came from individuals, according to *Giving USA*, a New York based magazine that monitors charities. Even adjusting for inflation, the 1990 total is nearly three times greater than in 1955.[82]

And 1990 was a recession year! Imagine how charity would increase in a free economy with no income taxes, Social Security taxes, and most other taxes, and a high standard of living. But if the Welfare State wrecks the economy, and we're out of work or scared about losing our jobs, what happens to charity to the poor? *If we're all poor, who is left to help*? How much charity can people give in Russia, where the average family is struggling just to put food on the table? That is the tragic and ironic effect of the Welfare State. By destroying the economy, liberals end up hurting the very people they wanted to help.

Would a free-market health care system be perfect? Of course not. No system that depends on human beings is perfect. But compared to a socialist, welfare-state hell-hole, it's heaven. If you want to see the grim reality of socialist systems, simply look at life and health care in Cuba, India, or China. Would you want to live in these countries if you were sick? If the thought makes you shudder with fear, then you should fear what's happening in America. That's where our increasingly socialized health care system is leading us.

SOCIALIZED HEALTH CARE IN OTHER COUNTRIES

To see what socialized medicine is like, let's look at England. A

March 1992 article in the *New York Times*[83] described a revealing incident. Voters in England were in an uproar over a Labor Party ad that dramatized the case of two little girls with ear infections. One girl whose parents had to use the socialized National Health System, had to wait a year for her ear infection operation. The other child's parents paid a private doctor to do the operation immediately.

The British public wasn't angry with the National Health System for making the first girl wait a year for her operation. Instead, they resented the parents who got a private doctor for their child.

> Britons who use the National Health Service. . .do not choose their own doctors, but are assigned to so-called general practices near their homes. . .Changing doctors for personal reasons is possible, but requires the *consent of the doctor* (emphasis added) and approval of the Health Service, which is not always given.
>
> Robert M. Worcester, head of the British Mori polling organization said in the same article,
>
> The fact is that the 1990's medicine is just too expensive, so judgments have to be made about rationing.[84] There were a total of 925,663 people on waiting lists to get into National Health Service hospitals at the end of February 1992, according to the Health Department, and 826,487 of them had been waiting for less than one year. The rest had been waiting for up to three years, most of them for elective surgery for problems like defective hip or knee joints, cataracts, and hernias.[85]

How would you like being assigned to a doctor by a medical bureaucrat, or have to ask this doctor's *permission* to see another doctor? How would you like waiting up to three years for a cataract or knee operation while you were going blind or riding around in a wheel chair? Yet the British system is the fully realized embodiment of socialized medicine. Do you think you would stand for this?

In Canada, they have National Health Insurance. Doctors in private practice provide health care, like in the United States, but government pays for health care out of general taxes. Many American congressmen praise the Canadian system as a model we should copy.

What's medical care like in Canada? Budget restrictions have led to rationing of care and serious underinvestment in health technology and facilities. The waiting lists for health care in Canada have grown.

> In British Columbia between November 1989 and February 1990, the average wait for coronary artery bypass surgery was 23.7 weeks; for other open heart surgery, 21.4 weeks; for cataract removal, 18.2 weeks; and for hernia repair, 24.6 weeks. In the province of Newfoundland, the wait for a pap smear is up to five months—reduced to two months if the case is urgent.[86]
>
> At some hospitals in Canada, a dog can get a CT scan in 24 hours if its owner is willing to pay $300. But human beings in pain and suffering may have to wait months to get the same service, regardless of how much money they have.[87]
>
> Canada does not allow patients to use private sector treatment to avoid waiting lists. . .Press reports have suggested that individuals with sufficient wealth travel to the United States for medical services. *In every province, the press reports the deaths of patients on waiting lists for coronary surgery* (emphasis added).[88]

How would you like to wait six months for a coronary bypass operation and die before your number came up? How would you like to wait six months for a hernia operation while you were groaning in pain? That's what it's like in the land of National Health Insurance. It's not a bad system for most healthy Canadians with relatively minor ailments. But if you're really sick, the system can kill you.

Does Canada control health care costs better than we do? No, it doesn't. A study by Health Policy International, a Princeton, N.J. nonprofit research organization, showed that in the 1980s health costs rose faster in Canada than in the United States after adjusting for inflation.[89] Medical costs in Canada are exploding. The Canadian federal government used to pay about half the cost of the national health care system. They're now paying only about 30 percent.[90] The provinces now pay almost 70 percent of health care costs and are running up huge deficits that consume about 30 percent of their total budgets.[91]

We know our health care system is in big trouble. We want to fix it but we don't know who to blame. Enter the liberals' propaganda. They say, "See, we tried the free market and look where we are. That's why we need national health insurance, like in Canada."

CONCLUSION

Liberals have duped us into believing that we have a free-market health-care system in this country, instead of what it really is—government controlled. They tell us it's the free market's fault, not the fault of the regulations that destroy the free market. Liberals tell us that we should put our health care system into the hands of power-hungry, incompetent bureaucrats.

But government isn't the solution to the health care crisis—it's the problem. The free market isn't the cause of our health care crisis—it's the solution. The free market would create a vibrant, low-cost, and efficient health care system. Health insurance would be low-priced, competitive, and affordable to the vast majority of Americans. The small number of people who fall through the cracks could depend on friends, family, and charity.

Liberals close their ears to such arguments. They say that a free economy is immoral if just one person is denied medical care who can't afford it. In the name of this one person, the rest of us must be sacrificed. Our answer to liberals must be: *What right do you have to wreck other peoples' lives? Americans are priceless human beings, not sacrificial animals.*

If we want to solve the health care crisis, we have to reject the idea that our own government has the right to force compassion down our throats at the point of a legislative gun. From there the solution is simple—dismantle the Welfare State and all government controls over the health care industry.

CHAPTER 7

WHY DO WE GO ALONG?

One crucial idea underlies the Welfare State: that helping others is a moral and political duty, rather than a personal choice. Since most Americans won't obey such a duty or sacrifice their lives for strangers, force is necessary. The Welfare State forces compassion on us at gunpoint. Every tax that robs us, every regulation that controls us, and every entitlement program that gives away our money, is justified by the idea that helping others is a political duty, not a personal choice.

If this idea is so destructive, why do we accept it? Why do we keep voting for politicians who give us more of the same? Why don't we see the dangers of the course we're on? *Why do we go along*? We can't fight the Welfare State unless we know the answers to these questions.

In earlier chapters, I explained why regulations, entitlement programs, and progressive income taxes are so destructive. But sometimes understanding is not enough. Many of us smoke cigarettes, eat too much, or don't save money for our retirement. We know we should act differently, but something stops us.

Many of us react to complex or stressful problems by falling back on our emotions. Logic often can't compete with strong feelings and unconscious, deeply held beliefs. That's why many people who might agree with my ideas still support the Welfare State. That reaction is very human and understandable.

In our personal lives, we can't change our destructive behavior unless we know and confront the unconscious thoughts and feelings that make us do what we do. It's the same with the Welfare State. We know it's immoral to steal, yet we go along with progressive income taxes that rob us. We know it's wrong to force someone to do something against his will, but we go along with regulations. We know that no one owes us a living, yet we go along with entitlement programs that give unearned subsidies to special interest groups.

We'll stop being our own worst enemies only when we understand and confront the beliefs and feelings that push us to accept the Welfare State.

THE GUILT TRIP

From birth, our parents teach most of us that being selfish is bad and being unselfish is good. If we helped others, we were a good boy or girl. If we had temper tantrums, didn't share our toys, or didn't help around the house, we were punished for being bad.

Since children want their parents' love, we probably felt guilty when they called us bad or selfish. Later, as adults, we internalize our parents' voices. Acting selfish brings on guilt feelings, and helping others makes us feel good and accepted.

So when we grow up, many of us don't say or do things that could brand us as selfish, and we help others whenever we can. We associate with people who think the same way, which reinforces these beliefs. These ideas become part of our unconscious mind-set, and we accept them so completely that it becomes hard to question or analyze them.

Most of us therefore believe that we should help others in need. By questioning this belief, I'm not saying that helping others is bad. On the contrary, it's very human and natural.

Most of us want to help others who are in need, with whatever means we have available. We have a common humanitarian impulse to do this. By helping others, and hoping others help us when we need it, we also feel less alone in the world and a little more secure. Most of us have natural humanitarian feelings. But our compassion makes us open targets for liberals who promote regulations and entitlement programs. Liberals who push these programs don't say we should help others if we can. Instead, they put no limits on what we're supposed to give. Worse, liberals don't ask for our contributions–they *demand* them.

They claim that it's our moral duty to help others, whether we like it or not, or whether we can afford to or not. They claim that it's our moral duty to help other people, even if we hurt ourselves and our families in the process. They lay a guilt trip on us.

Liberals know we have natural humanitarian feelings, and they play on this. They tell us we're mean or selfish if we don't vote for their programs. Liberals replace our parents in our subconscious minds, feeding on our guilt and pushing us to vote for ever more regulations and entitlement programs. We can end this manipulation only when we realize that there's nothing wrong with being selfish.

To be selfish means that we value our lives. Living creatures know that life is their highest value. Everything we do is for one basic reason–to stay alive. Unlike air or rocks, human beings face a constant choice between life and death. If we don't value our lives, we die.

If life is our highest value, then everything we do to support it is good, and anything we do that threatens it is bad. We need to be selfish to stay alive. Therefore, in this sense, selfishness is good. It's the highest virtue possible and the source of our other values.

A plant or animal doesn't value another plant or animal's life higher than its own. Such a course would be suicidal. It also would be suicidal for people. That's why politically enforced compassion is an evil doctrine–it asks us to sacrifice our vital interests. A moral code is supposed to guide our actions and protect our lives, yet altruism demands that we value someone else's life over our own.

Liberals insist that we must sacrifice our vital interests to help the rest of humanity. They ask us to commit voluntary suicide. They say, in effect, that our lives aren't important and that we're cruel and selfish if we don't help others in "need." In doing so, liberals ruin our lives, our country, and our children's future.

Anyone who accepts any part of this doctrine will experience chronic guilt. Our life force pushes us to act for our own benefit, to value our lives. But if we believe these actions are bad, then everything we do, every virtue we practice, brings us shame, guilt, and unhappiness. Altruism turns people into moral schizophrenics. The person who believes in altruism but still acts selfishly will feel dirty, guilty, and unhappy. The person who follows altruism and sacrifices his life to others will wreck his life.

Liberals get many of us to fall for their doctrine by setting up a con game. The con consists of claiming that selfishness means pursuing self-interest at the expense of others. Liberals claim that a selfish person gets what he wants only by hurting others, by stepping on someone else's neck. They think the world is like a big pizza pie—if someone takes two slices instead of his allotted one, if he's selfish, then he steals someone else's piece.

Liberals then say that the moral alternative to being selfish is to renounce self-interest and live for the sake of others. Liberals claim that we have only two moral alternatives to live by. They say that we can be sadists or masochists, and that masochism is the proper moral choice.

To solve this dilemma, liberals tell us to choose self-sacrifice. But the con is that it's a false dilemma. Through trade in a free economy, we pursue our goals with other peoples' cooperation, not at their expense. A trade requires the voluntary agreement of each party, and no one agrees to a trade unless he benefits by it. If a person doesn't like the terms of the trade, he can look for a better deal with someone else. In a trade, each person recognizes and respects each other's rights. When we trade with each other in a free market, we can be selfish without hurting other people. Liberals deny or evade this fact. They have to promote the lie that selfishness requires hurting others, because they need some way to get their hooks into us. They need to make us feel guilty, because people who feel guilty don't oppose the Welfare State.

The Welfare State gives jobs, power, and prestige to liberals. It also gives them a purpose in life that makes them feel important. When they "help" others, they feel good about themselves. Of course they don't care that they help others with *our* money. So liberals' most important goal is to make sure the Welfare State survives. They do this by convincing most Americans to go along with it.

But liberals have a problem. Most people value their lives, as they should. No one in his right mind willingly gives away up to 50 percent of his hard-earned money to strangers. No one wants his money looted (taxed) to give unearned subsidies to entitlement-program moochers.

So liberals need a hook, a way to convince us to go against our common-sense selfishness. That's where the guilt comes in. If they can convince us that selfishness means hurting others, and that we have to help others no matter what the cost, then we won't fight the Welfare State. At all costs, liberals must convince us that helping others is our moral duty.

They must make us feel guilty. If you ever watch Congressional hearings on television, you'll note that liberals and Democrats always use one fatal argument against Republicans. Whenever Republicans want to stop or curtail some entitlement program, Democrats always accuse them of being cruel and indifferent to other peoples' suffering. Most times, the Republicans cave in to the accusation and pass a modified version of the bill they originally opposed.

If we fall for the liberals' intellectual con job, if we accept the idea that selfishness is bad and always hurts others, we'll have swallowed their con. We'll continue being selfish, as our life demands, but we'll feel guilty about it. We'll agree with the liberals and go along with more welfare-state programs. Socialism is winning in America, and politicians of both parties keep voting for more regulations and entitlement programs, because we've fallen for the liberals' con game. Whenever some group is hurting, we cave in to the guilt trip liberals lay on us.

If retired people are hurting because of inflation or higher medical costs, Congress votes to increase Social Security or

Medicare benefits. When farmers are having a bad year, politicians vote for higher farm subsidies. If the unemployment rate for minorities goes up, Congress votes for higher food stamp benefits and new job training programs.

These bills pass because most congressmen are terrified of appearing cruel or callous. Liberals, Democrats, and many Republicans in Congress believe that we, the taxpaying middle-class, are morally responsible for helping any group having a hard time in life.

Since you don't have to hurt others when you're selfish, it's foolish to feel guilty for valuing your life. It's foolish to feel guilty for being selfish. It's also right and natural to feel outraged when government loots up to 50 percent of what you earn.

In a free economy, you earn your money—you don't loot it. If your neighbors have less than you or are suffering for some reason, you can sympathize with them, but you didn't cause their problem. You have no reason to feel guilty, and if you do, then you're assuming a guilt you don't deserve. This attitude toward helping others applies not only to your neighbor, but to anyone who demands help through government-enforced taxes and entitlement programs.

In a free economy, your success doesn't take anything away from anyone else. What you earn or the standard of living you enjoy is what those others never had in the first place. Other peoples' suffering can touch your compassion. But it can't be a claim on your life because you didn't cause that suffering.

Entitlement programs depend for their existence on making you feel guilty for other peoples' want or suffering. They depend on convincing you that you're morally responsible for ending other peoples' problems, no matter what this does to your life. This is the doctrine of liberals who want you to believe that you have no right to your life, but they do. It's the doctrine of people who openly admit that they need you, and want to enslave you to their needs through your guilt and kindness.

Liberals say we can't allow ourselves to be selfish. Pointing an accusing finger at us, they say there are people in this world who genuinely suffer through no fault of their own. There are the old, the sick, and the weak who need our help to survive. Would you be so cruel to create a society where these people aren't helped, where they're left to suffer or die? If government didn't force us to be humane, liberals claim, then nobody would care about these unfortunate people, and they would be left to die in the gutter.

Even if that was true, which it isn't, it still doesn't mean that other peoples' problems are your responsibility if you don't want them to be. This description of the cruel, selfish, capitalist society is another bedtime story foisted on us by liberals.

Most people are reasonably normal and healthy. Like other living species, if this wasn't so, the human race would have died out long ago. In a free economy, most of us lead active and successful lives (however you personally measure success), and we're able to take full responsibility for our lives.

In a free society, people voluntarily help each other in many ways. First, most of us have family and friends who we turn to in time of need. They help us get over the rough spots in our lives and provide a natural support network that can replace government social programs. Most of us can also turn to local charity, religious, and community groups for additional help.

Most of the millions of immigrants who came to this country at the turn of the century, came with little more than the shirts on their backs. When they stepped on shore, they were on their own because there were few social programs at the time. There was no welfare, Medicare, food stamps, Social Security, or unemployment insurance. *So how did they survive?*

First, they found jobs and worked very hard work to support themselves and their families, though many couldn't speak a word of English. Second, a network of friends, neighbors, family, religious groups, and community social organizations helped them adjust to their new lives. Privately sponsored settlement houses helped my immigrant grandparents who settled in the lower-east-side of Manhattan. Today, Korean immigrants open grocery stores in New York City with the help of Korean friends and families who are already here.

Third, immigrants had a powerful reason to succeed. If they didn't work hard, no entitlement program would come to their rescue. They had to depend on their own resources and look to family, friends, and neighbors for help. They survived and prospered because they wanted a good life for themselves and their children. The only way to get a better life was to work for it.

All they asked was that others leave them alone to pursue their dreams. Perhaps we, the grandchildren who now have a good life, forget what our grandfathers and grandmothers accomplished without government handouts and entitlement programs. Perhaps we've lost the sense of what it means to take full responsibility for our lives.

Another way we help each other voluntarily is that each of us, in pursuing our goals, adds to the wealth and well-being of everyone else. Each person's efforts increase the number, quality, and variety of goods and services produced through free trade. Everyone's knowledge and hard work adds to other peoples' efforts, which creates constantly improving living standards for most of us.

If we had a completely free economy, our standard of living would be much higher than it is today. If we ended regulations and entitlement programs, most taxes we now pay to government would be ours to keep. This includes profits made by businesses. Dismantling the Welfare State would create an explosion of savings, investment, and production in the economy. It would be a rising tide that lifted all boats.

Most physical human suffering comes from disease, old age, or the inability to earn a living. In a free economy, the job market would be so dynamic that anyone willing and able to work could find employment. A free economy would increase our standard of living. The more money we have, the better we take care of ourselves and the healthier we get.

If we dismantled the Welfare State and deregulated the health care industry, health care costs would drop sharply and most of us could afford low-cost health insurance. A free market in doctors, hospital care, drug development, and health insurance would reduce costs for everyone.

Of course a free economy can't eliminate disease and old age. But it could reduce most physical suffering to a modest level. What happens to those unfortunate people who are sick or can't take care of themselves through no fault of their own? These people would rely on friends, family, charity, and religious or community organizations, just as they did between 1790 and 1933, *when America had no Welfare State.*

Voluntary charity is a huge resource for people who need help. Americans donate billions of dollars a year to various humanitarian organizations, from the Red Cross to cancer research centers. Millions of Americans give their time freely, without compensation, working for organizations that help others.

In 1990, voluntary contributions to charity totaled $122.6 billion by an estimated 75 percent of all households in America. The average donation in 1990 was $978.[1] This huge outpouring of charity came in a recession year, when people were afraid of losing their jobs.

Imagine what private charity would be in a free, booming, prosperous economy. In a free economy with low taxes, high living standards, and optimism in the air, charity donations would explode. A free economy would create a country where most of us live long, healthy, productive lives.

By contrast, in a welfare or socialist state like the former Soviet Union, where a free economy was banned, you find the most human want and suffering. Welfare and socialist states usually become economic disaster areas. When government confiscates the bulk of its citizens' earnings to pay for entitlement programs, people stop producing. Or they produce only enough to support themselves. When this happens, production plummets, science and technology wither, and most citizens' lives are reduced to misery, hunger, and disease. This is the future our welfare-state liberals offer us.

Compared to socialist or welfare-state hell-holes, a free economy is a glorious thing. But it's not perfect. No system created by human beings can solve all of life's problems. Unfortunately, many unhappy people cause their own misery. People hurt themselves in many ways. If they don't pursue challenging goals, they'll often feel bored or dissatisfied. If they evade facts, don't correct their mistakes, or refuse to take responsibility for their lives, they'll probably fail. If they don't treat other people with respect and friendship, they'll end up lonely and bitter.

No economic system can cure our weaknesses or imperfections. No economic system can stop us from getting sad, sick, or old. All we can ask of an economic system is that it allows us to reach our highest potential. The rest is up to us.

Most suffering comes from life itself, our human weaknesses, or the social and political systems people live under. It's therefore foolish to feel guilty for the suffering of others. This suffering is outside your control and not your fault.

Does this mean we should be blind to other peoples' problems? Of course not. Most of us would like to help other people in distress, within the limits of our ability to help. But our own life and happiness is our first priority. Everyone has limited time and resources. Yet most of us help others when this doesn't cause sacrifice or hardship to our lives.

But any help we give should be voluntary. Remember, no one has a right to what you've earned. No one has the right to your time, effort, or income without your agreement, no matter what the cause, motive, or suffering involved. How much time or charity you give to others should be a personal decision that comes from the heart, not a bureaucrat's orders.

But voluntary humanitarianism is what liberals can't tolerate. They know that you won't help others when this causes real injury to yourself or your family. That's why liberals can't allow you a free choice. That's why they resort to government force to confiscate your profits or salary to support their programs.

ECONOMIC RIGHTS

Many people go along with the Welfare State because they're seduced by the notion of economic rights. Economic rights eventually destroy our political rights. But they do something much worse—they corrupt us.

Liberals invented the notion of economic rights because they like power. What liberals do best is to give away other people's money. But hardworking, middle-class Americans don't want or need handouts—they're independent, self-sufficient people who simply want government to leave them alone. So to keep their power, liberal politicians need a permanent army of dependents who keep voting them into office to protect their handouts. That's one reason why liberals create entitlement programs—millions of Americans on welfare, food stamps, Medicare, or Social Security depend on these programs.

Once people are hooked on benefits, the liberals have them.

It's no coincidence that people who get government subsidy checks vote for Democrats. Liberal Democrats protect their constituents' benefits against "cruel" Republicans who try to slash entitlement programs. People who get subsidies would be crazy to bite the hand that feeds them. Two thousand years ago, Roman emperors did what liberals do today. They gave free grain to the mobs of Rome to gain their eternal loyalty.

For liberals to stay in power, however, they have to keep their army of dependents content. The problem liberals have is that many people who get subsidies soon feel guilty for what they're doing. People don't like to feel like objects of charity or thieves who steal other peoples' money. They want to keep their self-respect while they keep their benefits.

This is an important matter for liberals. If too many entitlement recipients felt guilty enough to leave the dole or give up their benefits, they wouldn't need liberals anymore. Liberals would lose their power base. So it was important to find some way to take away the guilt. That's where economic rights come in. The liberals' solution was to switch the meaning of charity and property rights.

Property rights imply that you own something because you earned it. Earning something gives a person self-respect. If you own something, we say you have a right to it. Loot, on the other hand, is something you get by stealing. It's here that liberals pull the switch. They tell entitlement recipients that they have a *right* to their loot.

When you have a right to something, it usually means you earned that right. If recipients have a right to their benefits, it must mean they earned the benefits, didn't they? If they earned their benefits, then there's no reason to feel guilty anymore. No one feels guilty for demanding what's his by right.

With this trick accomplished, liberals then expanded the notion of economic rights to include everyone. Liberals now claim we have a right to health care, food stamps, decent housing, farm subsidies, rent subsidies, Social Security, aid to dependent children, and so on. Liberals claim that other people should support us if we can't or won't take care of ourselves.

If you believe you have a right to something, you don't feel guilty for taking it. You don't bother thinking about where the money came from. It's a very convenient idea, but it has an inevitable result—everyone soon wants the same rights you claim for yourself. Those who still aren't beneficiaries of the Welfare State soon come to resent the injustice of the system. They resent being taxed and regulated to support other people. They resent being sacrificial animals for everyone else. Hardworking middle-class people go along with the system because they think it's morally right, but they resent it nonetheless.

Soon they think, if everyone else is getting away with murder, why am I being such a fool? I pay taxes. Why don't I get my fair share, too? Why am I any less the public than my neighbor down the street? If they have a right to my life and income, then I should have a right to theirs—it's only fair. I should have economic rights, too. So, out of this outraged sense of injustice, we become corrupted. Like everyone else, we come to accept the insidious notion of economic rights.

Soon we believe that government should support us and pay for our health care in old age (Social Security and Medicare). We believe that our children have a right to a college education, though we can't pay for it. We believe that we have the right to get something for nothing, and that other people owe us a living. We keep demanding more entitlement programs to fill the bottomless well of our new rights.

Liberals create this Alice-in-Wonderland unreality for us. They tell us we're entitled to everything we want in life, regardless of cost and regardless of who pays for it. Liberals tell us that we can have our cake and eat it too. It's worked up to now, hasn't it? But one day the rotten structure will come crashing down around our heads, as it did for the Soviet Union.

THE TYRANNY OF MAJORITY RULE

Many of us go along with the Welfare State because politicians we elect to office create entitlement programs by majority rule. We have a cherished belief about democracy. We believe that we should obey laws that were enacted by majority rule.

Many of us belong to organizations that decide everyday matters by this method. On every issue, members have different opinions. So without such a rule, no decisions could be made. But whenever we join a group, we do so of our own free will. We join because we see some benefit in being a member. But the group has no powers other than what members delegate to it. Also, we have complete freedom to leave the group if its activities or philosophy goes against our interests.

As we saw earlier in Chapter 2, there are no "collective" rights. A group as such has no rights—only individuals have rights. A group therefore has no right to violate the rights of its members, even if a decision is made by majority rule or approved by 100 percent of the members. The individual rights of each member don't depend on the vote or approval of the group.

A government is simply a large group that sets parliamentary rules for a country. America is a social/economic/political group of over 250 million individual members. But it's still a group, and the same principles apply. Government therefore has no right to trespass on the individual rights of its citizens. Any law that does so is immoral and illegal by definition. It doesn't matter in the least whether the law is passed by a majority or by every member of Congress.

Our Founding Fathers understood this. They knew that individual rights defend us against our deadliest enemy—unlimited government. They understood that individual rights protect us from the tyranny of the majority. They wrote that principle into the Constitution and Bill of Rights. These documents recognize the principle that we have inalienable rights that government may not violate, no matter what the circumstances. Our Founding Fathers created the Bill of Rights to protect those rights.

To understand the difference between majority rule and individual rights, imagine this situation. You join a local social group because you like the people who are members. The group uses majority rule to make decisions. After a while, a bad element gains control of the group. They're a wild bunch of guys. They love to do dangerous things for thrills. By threats and persuasion they get a majority of the members on their side. One day, they invite you to go along on one of their escapades.

They go to the top of the Empire State Building and propose that all members bungee-jump off the roof. You notice that the bungee equipment is old and frayed, and you could die if you do this. The group holds a meeting on the roof. The ringleaders convince a majority to vote for their plan and then demand that everyone must jump off the roof.

Do they have a right to force you to jump off the roof, simply because a majority decided the issue? Of course not. You protest that you joined the group of your own free will, and they have no right to force you to jump. As they grab you and throw you off the roof, you scream that they don't have the right to risk your life. Now you understand the difference between majority rule and individual rights.

Entitlement programs violate our property rights. They confiscate what we earn and give our money to total strangers without our consent. Government assumes it has the right to steal, because it does so by majority rule. It does not have that right. As individual citizens, we don't have the right to steal from our neighbors. We therefore can't delegate such a right to government, who is simply our agent.

Liberals claim that entitlement programs and progressive income taxes are fair. They say it's fair to loot the rich, because the majority voted for it. They say it's fair to tax middle-class families to pay for food stamps, farm subsidies, and bank bailouts because the majority voted for it. Liberals claim the right to steal our hard-earned money and strangle us with regulations because the majority voted for it.

There's a quick way to grasp the moral obscenity of regulations, entitlement programs, and progressive income taxes. Just imagine yourself back on top of the Empire State Building where a majority of your group is forcing you to bungee-jump off the roof. That's the real meaning of majority rule when it violates your rights.

Americans have accepted three deadly ideas that make the Welfare State possible: economic rights, majority rule that can violate our rights, and compassion as a political duty. When we reject these ideas, the Welfare State will be swept away.

HUMAN NATURE

We go along with the Welfare State for another important reason: human nature is imperfect. Sometimes we let our emotions get the best of us. We act short-term and forget long-term consequences. We concentrate on what's before our eyes rather than on dangers we can't see. Let's explore some of these human frailties.

The Dependency Syndrome

Regulations and entitlement programs have an insidious effect on us. Over time, they corrupt our minds and spirits. We come to expect that government will support and protect us. A vicious cycle is created—the more government takes over, the less effort we make for ourselves. In the end, we lose our strength and independent spirit. Worse, we don't realize this is happening to us because the change comes gradually over many years, one new regulation and entitlement program at a time.

For example, ask a person on the street how to solve some of our problems. Ask how we should deal with the problem of drugs, crime, unemployment, homeless people, the high price of houses, skyrocketing health care costs, or dangerous public schools. Most of the time, the first and instant response is: government should do something about it. The person will say that government should make new laws or programs to solve the problem. The response is almost instinctive.

It wasn't always this way. Before the Welfare State came along, people relied on their own strength and common-sense, and on friends, neighbors, and family. They didn't run to government every time they had a problem.

The same applies in the business world. Today, some of our biggest corporations have gotten used to the idea of government subsidies and regulation. They accept and even promote government's right to control the economy.

Under government regulation, many industry giants such as AT&T were legalized monopolies. Government stopped competitors from taking away their business, so they could charge high prices. For many years, AT&T was a regulated monopoly with no competition. It didn't have to work hard to stay in business because no competitors were breathing down its neck. It became more competitive and efficient only after deregulation cracked open its protected markets.[2] Only when MCI and Sprint were allowed to compete with AT&T, did our telephone bills start to go down.

To keep their government-backed security blanket, these companies often lobby for more regulations. The more they depend on regulations, the more they lose their vitality and independence. When this happens, they become even more dependent on government to protect them. It becomes a vicious cycle.

Another example of the dependency syndrome is Social Security. Many Americans plan their retirement around the program. They assume their Social Security checks will support them in old age. As a result, many of us don't save enough money for retirement during our working years. Medicare, Social Security, and similar programs lull us into a false sense of security. We think, "government will take care of us, so why worry?" Why bother to put money aside in our own IRA's?

So now we have over 35 million retirees who depend on Social Security and don't want any changes in the system. Retirees are a large, powerful voting block. That's why most reelection-minded politicians won't tamper with the Social Security system.

Entitlement programs have the same problem. Once people get used to subsidies, once they plan their lives around these benefits, they're afraid to give them up. This fear turns many people into financial and psychological dependents and makes it almost impossible to end entitlement programs.

BUT WHO WILL CATCH ME IF I FALL?

Many people agree that too much government is dangerous. It strangles our economy and does more harm than good. People believe that we should control government waste and cut back on regulations and entitlement programs. But many Americans still want a government safety net. They believe if a safety net wasn't there, some people would fall through the cracks. Some people who just can't make it in life would get sick, go hungry, be homeless, and so on. And voluntary contributions might not reach these people.

Everyone wants a safety net because life has many risks. We might get sick, lose our job, or be unlucky in some other way. It's comforting to know that if life knocks us down, government will help us.

Yes, there's risk and suffering in this world. But government can't take away this risk. The Welfare State doesn't give us a safety net. Instead, it does the opposite. By wrecking the economy, the Welfare State aggravates human suffering and puts us at greater risk.

We can have security without government's help. We can depend on the help of friends, family, neighbors, business associates, and community groups we belong to. They have always been there. The free market is also one of our best friends. A free economy is dynamic and productive. It creates job and business opportunities for anyone willing to work. In a free economy, anyone knocked to the ground can usually pick himself up and find employment or new opportunities elsewhere. In a free economy, the defeated person is the one who gives up.

But the free market won't guarantee anything. It won't guarantee that you succeed in a particular job or business. It won't guarantee that you don't get sick or hit by a car. The free market only guarantees you the right and opportunity to live up to your highest potential. It won't guarantee wealth, happiness, or self-esteem to the person who doesn't earn it.

That's why liberals and malcontents hate the free market. The free market usually gives us what we deserve. Many people don't make the effort needed to succeed in life, however they define success. To get anything worthwhile in life requires work, dedication, and perseverance. Unfortunately, many people are too lazy or too afraid to meet this challenge.

A person who fails usually feels bad about himself. To prop up his self-esteem, he often looks for a scapegoat. Instead of blaming himself, he blames the free-market system. It's not his fault, he says, it's the system. What he doesn't like about the free market is that it forces him to take the consequences of his actions and character—to look at himself in the mirror.

But the free market doesn't have to be scary. Most of us take responsibility for our lives right now. We work hard and don't expect handouts from others. If we do get into trouble, most of the time we turn to friends and family for help.

WHATEVER GOVERNMENT DOES, THE FREE MARKET CAN DO BETTER

If we dismantled the Welfare State, we could still have a safety net. A free economy can give us unemployment insurance, inexpensive health insurance, and a nest egg for our retirement. Even better, the free-market would give us more choices, and the choices would be cheaper and more efficient.

Many people go along with the Welfare State because they mistakenly believe that only government can give us a safety net. We depend on government for Medicare, Social Security, and unemployment insurance. Because these programs have been with us for so long, we automatically assume there's no other way to get the security these programs give us.

But the security of these government programs is a false security. Those Americans who thought they could retire on their Social Security benefits are now learning a hard lesson. Many retirees are finding that their meager Social Security checks don't cover increasing living costs.

The irony is that the Welfare State is the main reason that food, rent, taxes, clothing, car insurance, and health insurance prices keep rising. The regulations and entitlement programs of the Welfare State create inflation and wreck the economy. In effect, the Welfare State destroys our security with the very programs it creates to give us that security.

When you lose your job because taxes and regulations wrecked the company you worked for; when your unemployment checks run out and there are no other jobs around; when your Social Security checks can't pay for increasing rent and food costs, you realize that your government safety net is falling apart.

But many people feel more secure because we have Social Security and other government programs. They feel that Social Security is better than nothing, even if the checks don't cover all their bills. The same applies to unemployment insurance. People want the security of government checks if they get laid off. They want Medicare because who else would take care of them when they're old and sick?

These are very human and legitimate fears. If we're old, sick, or out of a job, we want a safety net. If we're in our fifties and lose our job, if we can't afford health insurance, or if we didn't plan for our old age, at least entitlement programs are a last resort to keep us from crashing. It's understandable why so many Americans want to keep these programs.

Most of us have deep fears about the insecurity of life. We're afraid that if we mess up, no one will be there to help us. The child in us wants to be protected if we fall down and hurt ourselves. But these are fears that we can overcome as adults.

Government doesn't have to be our safety net. The free market can protect us. In a free economy, regulations, entitlement programs, and progressive income taxes would end. In a free economy, any insurance we want as a safety net represents a business opportunity. The free market can supply this insurance better and cheaper than government, and you would only pay for your insurance, not everyone else's.

We already pay for our own car, life, fire, and health insurance. A free economy would have few taxes, no regulations, and fierce competition. We could buy our own unemployment and retirement health insurance. We could pay for this insurance with the money we save from taxes we no longer pay. Private companies could provide unemployment insurance. And the best insurance for finding a new job is to have a growing, dynamic economy that offers you many jobs to choose from.

It also would be easier to afford health care in a free economy. We wouldn't need Medicare. If the economy was booming and the Welfare State dismantled, health insurance would be low-cost and affordable. We would have a higher standard of living. We would have thousands of dollars more to spend because our taxes would be slashed. We could use this extra money to pay for current health bills and health insurance. As for Social Security, it's here that the free market would really shine.

SOCIAL INSECURITY

As we noted earlier, retirees want to keep Social Security intact because they don't want their benefits threatened. The rest of us don't want to change Social Security because liberals have brainwashed us into thinking there's no alternative to it. We think it's an insurance program that only government can supply.

This, of course, isn't true. There's no reason why each of us doesn't have the right, the common sense, and the ability to provide for our own retirement. In fact, if we put our Social Security taxes into our own IRA accounts, we would be better off when we retired.

Studies have shown that if we deposited our Social Security taxes into personal IRA accounts that pay an average of 6 percent interest (in CDs), the following would be the result for average working-class families:

> The worker earning an average salary all his life. . .would retire at age sixty-five with a trust fund of $469,662 in constant 1980 dollars. This fund could pay the worker and his spouse $28,180 per year in constant 1980 dollars. Again, the worker and his spouse could enjoy this annual income until both had died, and then still leave the half-million dollar fund to their children. Alternatively, they could purchase an annuity with the fund that would pay $45,743 annually in constant 1980 dollars while both were alive and $30,495 until the survivor died. . .Social Security should pay this worker $15,408 per year in constant 1980 dollars with both spouses alive and $10,272 with only one alive, along with the $1000 per year per spouse in hospital insurance coverage. . .
>
> Thus the private system would pay this worker about *three times what Social Security would pay* (emphasis added), or alternatively, it would pay twice what Social Security would pay while still allowing the average worker to leave a *half-million dollars to his children* (emphasis added). . .
>
> Also, if both spouses worked and earned average salaries, the *private benefits would again double* (emphasis added) while Social Security benefits would remain the same, except that the annual benefit paid while both spouses were alive would increase by one third, to $20,544.[3]

If you had a half-million dollar nest egg, you wouldn't have to depend on bureaucrats for your security. On retiring, you would get two to three times the monthly income that Social Security would have paid you. Also, no bureaucrat could tell you that you can't start collecting until age sixty-five. You could use your retirement money for emergencies. If you wanted to work part-time after retiring, bureaucrats couldn't reduce your Social Security payments by $1 for every $2 you earned over $5,000 in your job (which is the current law).

With Social Security, you don't end up with a half-million dollar nest egg at age 65. You end up with a zero nest egg. All you have are your monthly Social Security checks. And you hope you don't die early, because if you do, it's your tough luck. You lose all the hard-earned money you paid in taxes over forty years (especially if you don't have a surviving spouse who would get survivor's payments). Also, your children won't get the inheritance you could have saved in your personal IRA account.

The free market would give you much better retirement benefits. It also would end other government-created problems that affect your retirement. Your cost of living would be much lower, so you could buy more with your money. Health care costs would decrease. The economy would be booming, so it would be easier to get a part-time job if you still wanted to work.

In short, why do we need Social Security when we can do a lot better for ourselves? Liberals reply with their standard argument. They say, yes, you could do better with your own retirement account, but what about people who don't earn enough money to save for their retirement. What about those people who don't have the foresight to save? Why should those who were "lucky" enough to save their money while they worked, be better off at retirement than poor people?

This, of course, is the standard liberal argument—that we have a moral and political duty to help others, whether we like it or not. Most of us who work hard and save money must be penalized to support those people who wouldn't save or plan for their retirement.

SOMETHING FOR NOTHING

The Social Security program is a prime example of another human weakness that makes us go along with the Welfare State: we like getting something for nothing. If a special interest group gets unearned subsidies from an entitlement program, it wants to keep the program going for as long as possible.

Most people think that Social Security is a pension plan run by the government. That isn't true. Social Security is often a welfare program, because most retirees get much more in benefits than the taxes they paid into the system.

Liberals claim that many Americans don't have the foresight or ability to save enough money for retirement during their working years. These people are often destitute in old age. Government created Social Security to solve this problem. The original intent of the program was to support impoverished old people, but it has grown far beyond this original purpose.

The Social Security system has become a huge income-transfer program. It transfers money from people who earned more in their lifetimes to those who earned less. It tries to equalize benefits for retirees, despite how much taxes each person paid into the system while working.

This is accomplished through certain provisions of the Social Security laws. One of these provisions is that no matter how much taxes you paid into the system over your lifetime, there's a maximum limit on benefits. You lose the extra taxes you paid into the system that you don't get back in benefits. In effect, government confiscates your money but gives you back less than you paid into the system.

Another provision says that no matter how little you put into the system over your lifetime, Social Security will pay you a minimum amount when you retire. In this case, you'll probably get much more money out of the system than you ever paid into it while working.

Also, payments are heavily weighted to favor poorer people. The benefits poor people get is higher compared to the taxes they paid into the system. Those people who made more money during their working years get smaller benefits compared to the taxes they paid into the system.[4] In this way, the system equalizes retirement benefits by transferring money from those who made more during their lifetime to those who made less.

Another major welfare component of the system relates to the benefits for a worker's spouse or children. A married retired worker will get about 50 percent more in benefits than a widow or single person, even if both retirees paid the same taxes into the system. If a worker still has dependent children when he retires, he'll get even more. The married retiree didn't earn these extra benefits with past taxes paid into the system. Instead, the extra benefits are a welfare subsidy. These subsidies are paid by current workers or by people who get fewer benefits back than the taxes they paid into the system.

Also, government doesn't fund Social Security like a private pension plan or personal IRA that collects interest. Contrary to popular belief, there's no Social Security trust fund. Instead, it's a pay-as-you-go system. Social Security taxes come in, and then go directly out again to pay current retirees. The taxes don't stay in a trust fund. Government taxes working Americans and, after deducting administrative costs, the bureaucrats transfer these taxes to retirees. If there are excess funds available, the Treasury borrows this money to pay down the deficit.

Social Security tax rates for 1995 are now 15.3 percent of the first $61,200 of income. That means the maximum Social Security taxes now paid is $9,363. Many Americans now pay more Social Security taxes than income taxes, a percentage that's increasing each year. Also, that's just Social Security taxes. If we project total taxes needed to support the Welfare State in the future, it really gets scary.

> The (Clinton) budget estimates that as health care and Social Security costs continue to rise, young Americans in general will pay significantly more of their lifetime income as federal, state, and local taxes than their parents and grandparents did. . .
>
> "This is really a catastrophe that we're preparing for our kids," said Laurence J. Kotlikoff, a Boston University economics professor who helped the White House's Office of Management and Budget prepare the figures.
>
> In a more speculative calculation, the Administration forecast that the average net tax rate for future generations would eventually reach *82 percent of their lifetime earnings* (emphasis added).[5]

Please note this figure again. Can you imagine paying 82 percent of your paycheck in taxes to support health care, Social Security, and the rest of the Welfare State? Yet this is where we're heading.

So, out of this desire to get something for nothing, Social Security has become a huge welfare system. We're mortgaging the lives and income of future generations to pay for the present generations' retirement benefits.

These are just a few welfare provisions of the Social Security system. They're welfare because millions of retirees gets unearned benefits, while working people pay heavy taxes to support these benefits. A private pension plan wouldn't allow this. In a private pension plan, your retirement savings are your property. A bank can't give away your savings to someone else. A bank or pension plan manager who did this would be jailed.

The welfare provisions of Social Security have turned the system into a monster out of control.

"Social Security has grown into the biggest welfare system in the world. Total expenditures under the program have grown from $10 million in 1938 to $175 billion in 1981. The program's total expenditures in 1981 constituted 25.5 percent of the total federal budget."[6]

In 1994, the program cost over $230 billion a year. And, as with other entitlement programs, the end is nowhere in sight.

Unfortunately, many of us ignore the long-term consequences of an entitlement program if we currently benefit by that program. Retired Social Security beneficiaries are a prime example. Like Scarlett O'Hara in the movie Gone With The Wind, we say, "I'll think about it tomorrow." We see the consequences, but choose to ignore them, especially if we won't be around when the system finally collapses.

OUT OF SIGHT, OUT OF MIND

Many of us don't think about the long-term consequences of regulations and entitlement programs because we don't even know these consequences exist. I call this the out of sight, out of mind effect. As a result, we go along with regulations or entitlement programs because we only see their short-term benefits.

What we don't see, because they're out of sight, are the disastrous long-term consequences.

Social Security is a good example. Every retiree sees a monthly paycheck from the Social Security office. Though the check doesn't amount to much, it does help to cope with living expenses. So the retiree thinks Social Security is a good program.

What he doesn't see and add up are all the Social Security taxes he paid into the system over his lifetime. He doesn't see the monthly checks that would be double or triple what he gets from Social Security, if he had deposited his payroll taxes into an IRA account. He doesn't see the half-million dollar nest egg he could have saved over a lifetime, which he could live off and pass on to his children.

We also don't see the billions of dollars in Social Security taxes that millions of Americans would have deposited in banks, to be recirculated back into the economy. We don't see the explosion in capital, new homes, and new jobs that would have been created, because this money was never saved and reinvested.

Finally, those receiving Social Security don't see the heavy burden of taxes their children and grandchildren will pay to support the system. More Americans are now living past age sixty-five than ever before, while the birth rate is holding steady or declining. By the year 2030, the number of Americans over age sixty-five is expected to double to about sixty-six million people. Because of this, it's estimated that:

> "If recent fertility trends continue, the number of beneficiaries per one hundred workers will increase from thirty-one today to sixty-three in 2025. Indeed, if fertility trends continue, tax rates will have to *double* (emphasis added) by 2025 to maintain benefits at expected levels."[7]

What does this mean for working people today? The original Social Security tax in 1935 had a combined rate of 2 percent on the first $3,000 of income. The maximum tax a worker paid was $60. Today, the combined rate is 15.3 percent on the first $61,200 in income. As we noted earlier, this means that someone earning $61,200 a year now pays about $9,363 in Social Security taxes.[8] If the prediction quoted above happens by the year 2025, maximum taxes will jump to at least $18,726 a year.

Because Social Security is a pay-as-you-go system, the money paid to current retirees has to come from taxes paid by people who still work. A retiree's Social Security payments come directly from his children's paychecks. In effect, harsh as this may sound, retired Americans have a mortgage on their children's lives. And because of the trends we discussed earlier, the burden on future generations will be much worse.

But because most Americans don't see the problem, it doesn't bother them. The average retiree only sees as far as his monthly check. That's why he likes the Social Security system and votes against any politician who tries to tamper with it—out of sight, out of mind.

Another example is the Food and Drug Administration's control over the sale of prescription drugs. Most people think we need FDA regulations to prevent drug companies from making harmful drugs. We believe that profit-seeking drug companies would purposely make drugs that kill us, or at the very least, would be lax in testing new drugs.

When pregnant women took the drug Thalidomide, they had deformed babies. When something like this happens, the public demands protection against unsafe drugs. But at what cost?

The public sees that the FDA takes drugs like Thalidomide off the market. What we don't see is that the approval process for new drugs has become a bureaucratic nightmare. It can take up to seven years for the FDA to approve a drug, and cost a pharmaceutical company over $100 million to do the testing.

What's been the long-term, unseen effect of FDA regulations? The new genetic revolution is creating an explosion in biological discoveries. Yet the number of new drugs introduced on the American market has declined from 52 in 1960 to 23 in 1993.[9] FDA regulations also increase the price of drugs. This increase is inevitable if the FDA forces pharmaceutical companies to risk millions of dollars to get its approval. When a drug finally gets approved, the company has to pass this cost on to consumers.

And think about the new drugs that never made it to market. These drugs could have saved the lives or reduced the suffering of millions of people. FDA regulations make many pharmaceutical companies think twice about developing drugs with limited markets (orphan drugs). As a result, drug companies don't develop new drugs that could help millions of desperately sick people. FDA regulations hurt far more people than they protect. But no one reads about these victims in the newspapers, so they suffer and die in silence—out of sight, out of mind.

Environmental regulations are another example of out of sight, out of mind. People see their air or water become a little cleaner, so they think these regulations are good. But they don't see the disastrous effects of these regulations.

The Environmental Protection Agency forces factories, home builders, oil companies, logging companies, and electric utilities to spend hundreds of millions of dollars to conform to these regulations. Environmental impact statements cause years of delays in building much needed new homes and factories. Environmental regulations increase the price of nearly everything we buy. Each new tightening of car pollution standards increases the price of new cars. The regulations also increase the price of food, lumber, gasoline, electric power, home heating oil, and many other products we use every day. They also add thousands of dollars to the price of new homes.

Thousands of Americans can't afford their dream house or a new car because of these constant price increases. When consumers can't buy, the economy contracts, companies lay off workers, and millions of jobs are lost. These are some of the disastrous effects of environmental regulations that don't register with the public because no one sees them.

CONCLUSION

We've examined some important reasons why Americans go along with the Welfare State. We can stop doing things that hurt us only if we understand why we do them. It's the same for America. We can stop committing economic suicide only when we understand why we go along with the Welfare State. In the next chapter, we'll see how to use our new understanding to end the Welfare State, once and for all.

CHAPTER 8

THE LAST AMENDMENT

America was once the freest and most prosperous nation on Earth, the great hope of millions who came to its shores to find a better life. It was a country where people could work hard, pursue their dreams, and keep what they earned. It was a place where you and your children had a wonderful future to look forward to.

But a tragedy has overtaken us. In the last thirty years the Welfare State has been expanding at an alarming rate, and America has become a quasi-socialist state. Government attacks our property rights and economic liberty. The Welfare State strangles us with regulations. Federal deficits push us toward bankruptcy and threaten our future. Heavy taxes confiscate our profits, salaries, and savings. Here are some alarming facts:

• In 1970, the federal deficit was less than $20 billion. In 1993 it was over $300 billion. The 1995 fiscal-year deficit was reduced to about $170 billion, but only because Congress passed big tax increases in 1993.

- In 1960, spending for entitlements and interest payments represented one-third of the federal budget. In 1994, it was two-thirds.
- In 1970, the total federal debt was less than $500 billion. By 1995, the total debt was over $4.7 *trillion* and could climb to $8 trillion by the year 2000. In the last twelve years alone, the debt increased by over $3.5 trillion.
- In 1970, interest payments on the federal debt were about $20 billion. In 1994, interest payments have soared ten times that figure to over $200 billion.[1]
- In the fiscal-year 1995 budget, spending for entitlement programs has exploded to over $800 billion, of which 80 percent goes to only four programs: Medicare, Medicaid, Social Security, and pensions for retired government employees.[2]
- In 1981, total health care spending in the United States was about $375 billion. In 1994, the cost exploded to over $1 trillion, with no end in sight.[3]
- Regulations now cost us over $400 billion a year.

What do these grim statistics mean? Simply this: the Welfare State is wrecking our economy and threatening our jobs, our future, our children, and our liberty:

- Almost nine million Americans are now unemployed.
- Over 25 million Americans are on food stamps.
- Over 35 million Americans can't afford health insurance.
- Since 1973, the real median income of working Americans below age 35 has *fallen* by 25 percent.[4]
- Total federal liabilities, including what government owes for future Medicare, Social Security, civil service and military pension benefits, exceeds $15 trillion, or about $150,000 for every household in America. That is a debt our children will pay.[5]
- In spite of the hundreds of billions of dollars poured down the bottomless well of entitlement programs, the United States still has the highest poverty rate among industrial nations.[6]
- The Clinton administration made a speculative forecast that if the Welfare State keeps expanding at its current rate, future generations of Americans may eventually have to pay tax rates of 82 percent of their lifetime earnings.[7]

There's great fear in the American workplace. Big corporations like General Motors and AT&T are eliminating tens of thousands of jobs. People are afraid of losing their jobs. The scary part is that new jobs aren't being created to replace all the lost jobs. For example, the Kansas City region created 93,000 new jobs after the recession of the early 1980s. After the recession in the early 1990s, however, the region gained back only about 20,000 new jobs. It's the same story throughout many parts of the country.[8]

Millions of Americans can't afford a home, a new car, college tuition, or health insurance anymore because welfare-state taxes loot our money and regulations inflate prices. Our inner cities are rotting from drugs and poverty. Many blacks and other minorities feel the rage and despair of people who have no hope and see no future for themselves.

The American dream is fading for millions of Americans. Pessimism is in the air. The pessimism doesn't come from a short-term setback, but from a deeper gut-level feeling that something has gone terribly wrong with America, something structural, something dangerous.

In spite of our problems, it's not too late. What's happened to America isn't irreversible. We've made some bad mistakes, but we can correct them if we go back to basics, back to the principles our country was founded on. We can revise the Constitution to cut out the cancer that's eating us alive. We can regain our health if we dismantle the Welfare State.

A RECAP OF THE PROBLEM

Our Founding Fathers wanted to insure freedom and prosperity to future generations of Americans. They knew that unlimited government is the greatest threat to our freedom. To protect us from this enemy, they created a political structure that limited government power and protected our individual rights. They rejected the ancient doctrine of the supremacy of the state, the king, or even the majority. They affirmed our inviolate right to life and liberty in the Constitution and Bill of Rights.

In a free economy, we use law and reason to settle our differences, and we respect each other's rights. But criminals or the government can violate our rights by using force against us. Political rights protect us and make force immoral and illegal in the marketplace. Political rights recognize and protect property rights and affirm that no one can take your property by force.

But liberals have created a whole new category of rights called economic rights. Political rights protect us against force. Economic rights give government and special-interest groups the right to use force to get what they want. Political rights protect our freedom to work for what we want. Economic rights sanction the freedom to loot what we want. Economic rights are unearned subsidies given to some people at the expense of others. Many Americans now believe they have a right to food, housing, health care, education, farm subsidies, and other entitlements. Of course, these alleged rights are simply the right to steal and the exact opposite of a political right.

The Welfare State violates our property rights on a massive scale. Progressive income taxes loot our hard-earned money to pay for food stamps, Medicare, bank bailouts, farm subsidies, Social Security, and other entitlement programs. Massive layers of regulations now strangle the life-giving free market.

The Welfare State, and the philosophy behind it, is the cancer that's killing our country. We can't cure cancer with a band-aid. We won't solve our problems by tinkering with the Welfare State. If we don't make fundamental changes, we'll be defeated by the same economic, political, and psychological forces that got us into this mess in the first place. By understanding these forces, we'll see why we need the "Last Amendment."

HUMAN NATURE

Unfortunately, human beings have a weak side. People can be lazy, dishonest, vindictive, irrational, envious of others, or downright mean. We act this way because we're not robots—our ego and emotions sometimes overrule our common sense. Also, thinking is not automatic. We have to choose to think, and very often we choose not to. Thinking requires constant effort and the possibility of failure. So we often take the easy way out—we think with our emotions and act out of fear, anger, or envy.

Even when we choose to think, we can be wrong. Everyone makes mistakes. When we're wrong, reality eventually slaps us in the face. At this point, we can learn from our mistakes and do better next time. Or we can evade the facts, stamp our feet at reality, and let our ego, fears, or emotions take over. When we do, we often turn into very nasty creatures.

People can be bad in many ways. They rob, kill, or enslave others. They blame others for their mistakes and failures. Sometimes they commit vicious acts in the name of religion or political doctrines. Five thousand years of bloody human history show what people are capable of.

Yet human beings can also be heroes and heroines. We can be productive, courageous, reasonable, and compassionate. We create wondrous things like cars, skyscrapers, philosophy, electricity, and a country that respects individual rights. The fact that America exists proves this better side of human nature.

If we can be heroes or villains, what determines which side of our nature prevails? What determines whether a country is ruled by looters and murderers, as it was throughout much of human history, or by honorable men of good will like the Founding Fathers of America?

WHAT MAKES US HEROES OR VILLAINS?

A country is like a child in many ways. If a bright, aggressive child is raised by a family of robbers and murderers, he'll probably grow up to be a criminal. The parents would channel the child's energy and intelligence into destructive behavior. They would teach him that there's nothing wrong with murder and stealing, and would bring out the worst in the child's nature.

What if the child's parents were honest, productive, and compassionate? They would also teach their values to the child. They would channel the child's character into positive, life-affirming behavior. The parents would ask for and bring out the best in the child.

The same thing happens with adults. They can be good or bad, honest or dishonest, lazy or productive. A lot depends on the "family" (society) they grew up in. Their character is shaped by a country's moral and political principles and by its economic system.

For example, a person living in a communist country is strongly influenced by the system. Since hard work, honesty, and risk taking won't get him very much, he'll become lazy and corrupt. He'll find that the way to get ahead is by stealing, bribery, or joining the Communist party. Inevitably, he'll do what's expected of him, but no more. He'll live by the values that the system forces on him, and the system will bring out the worst in his nature.

The system also strongly influences a person living in a free society. Only this time, the system rewards him for honesty, risk taking, and perseverance. It rewards him when he creates something that other people value. It also withholds rewards from those who are lazy or dishonest. A free economy brings out the best in us.

So, a country's political and economic system strongly influence our behavior. A bad system like the Welfare State brings out the worst in people; it makes them lazy, dependent, and corrupt. Worse, when bad people gain control of a government with unlimited powers, all hell can break loose.

UNLIMITED GOVERNMENT–
OUR DEADLIEST ENEMY

People join groups to gain two great benefits of social cooperation–the ability to trade goods and share knowledge. Large groups of people have a storehouse of knowledge that no one person could ever learn in a lifetime. By sharing, we use each other's knowledge to improve our lives.

When we exchange goods, we create a unique division of labor. Each of us has different talents and abilities. One person is a plumber, another a teacher, and another a furniture maker. In the free market, we trade our products or services with other people. Through this process, we can buy an enormous number of goods and services that we couldn't buy if we were alone on a deserted island.

We can go into K-Mart or a supermarket and buy toys, fresh food, or bathroom rugs–things we could never make ourselves. We have a richer standard of living because the free market harnesses each person's special talents and abilities, making production more efficient.

But to enjoy these great benefits of social cooperation, we have to nourish the good side and control the bad side of human nature. We have to *produce* knowledge and material goods before we can share them, but people won't produce if they're not rewarded for their efforts.

A society that wants to prosper has to consider human nature. It has to make sure that people produce under conditions that make them happy and secure. People feel happy when they are free. They feel secure when the political system protects their right to keep what they earn. If government confiscates what we earn, we get angry and resentful. When this happens, we stop producing and the economy goes to ruin.

To feel secure, we also have the right to protect ourselves from criminals who can kill us or steal our money. But if we didn't have a civilized way to protect ourselves, we would all have to carry guns for self-defense. We would be vulnerable to violence from thieves and murderers or from natural disputes with our neighbors. The bad side of human nature would endanger us all. America would degenerate into anarchy, into the chaos of perpetual violence and gang warfare like it has in Rwanda and Bosnia.

That's why a society can't allow individuals to use force, even in retaliation, unless it's for immediate self-defense. The right to use force must be given to an impartial organization formed for that purpose–to a government. We transfer our right of self-defense to government to prevent anarchy and have an objective way to deal with force. That's the legitimate function of government, and the reason it's necessary.

Government protects us by creating laws and backing up those laws with police and court systems. We give government the exclusive right to use force, but only in retaliation against criminals who hurt people and have to be stopped.

Unfortunately, the people we elect to government have the same human weaknesses as everyone else. Yet they create and administer laws that give them the exclusive right to use force. Government therefore has a potentially fearful power over us. Throughout history, vicious people fought wars to gain control of government because they lusted after that power. Once in control, they used government to loot their country for personal gain.

Before America, most rulers had total and ruthless control over their subjects—they had almost unlimited power to tax, kill, or enslave their own people. The political structure allowed free rein to power-lust and brutality, to the worst in human nature.

Nero crucified thousands of Christians because Rome's political system gave him that power. The Catholic Church burned nonbelievers at the stake in the Inquisition because Spanish kings gave it that power. The kings of Europe taxed their people into poverty to make wars and build palaces. Hitler and Stalin murdered millions of innocent people because they were absolute rulers of their governments. Human history is one long nightmare of murder and mayhem because, until America, people couldn't create a political structure that stopped rulers from abusing government power. They couldn't invent a political structure that controlled the bad side of human nature.

In every age, there have always been Neros and Hitlers. Monsters like these will always wreak havoc on other peoples' lives. In the past sixty years, another kind of ruler has hurt us—the professional liberal who wants to "help" people by creating a welfare state. The liberal's intentions may be good, but like all "benevolent" dictators in the past, he uses force to strangle our liberty and tax us into poverty.

The problem is not that some men are evil or misguided—that's just human nature, which we can't change. The great problem is that government power was never controlled. When government has too much power, it inevitably attracts men like Nero and Hitler. The way to permanently solve this problem is *to strictly limit government powers*. If government can't make laws that violate our property rights or economic liberty, then no dictator, President, or Congress-of-the-moment could impose its will or ideas on us. We could protect our economic and political liberty.

To accomplish this, government's power has to be rigidly controlled and limited. We need a clearly defined code of laws that control government's right to use force. That legal code must have impartial trial procedures, objective rules of evidence, and fair, clearly defined punishments for various crimes. No government action can be arbitrary or outside the law.

But a strict code of laws isn't enough. Every major civilization had a system of laws, and *it was through those laws that despotic governments enslaved their subjects.* It's through the strict rule of law, their law, that communist rulers keep total and ruthless control over their people. The rule of law is necessary to control government power, but it's not enough. Laws have to be restricted so they don't give government the power to violate the individual rights of its citizens.

The proper function of government is to protect your rights. In a society where rights are respected, the only way someone can violate your rights is through threats or force. Therefore, government's legitimate role is to create a police and court system to protect us, a civil court system to settle disputes, and an army to protect us from threats by other countries.

The civil court system is very important. In a free society, we trade with each other through voluntary agreements. In trade, each person depends on the other to live up to his part of the bargain. If one person arbitrarily breaks his agreement, the other person could suffer serious financial damages. If there was no legal way to make someone live up to the terms of a contract, the injured person would have to use force.

People also have honest disputes. Here, one person doesn't purposely injure the other. Instead, each person interprets an agreement differently. If there was no civilized way to settle these disputes, the economy would collapse into violence. The free market's stability depends on a system of laws to settle civil disputes, protect the sanctity of contracts, and make them enforceable in a court of law.

Government's sole legitimate functions are the police, the armed forces, and the civil and criminal court systems. *We can permanently restrict government's power by banning any laws that go beyond these functions.* That's what the Bill of Rights tried to do. It restricts government's power to make laws that are illegitimate. An illegitimate law is one that gives government the power to violate the rights of its citizens.

The income tax, entitlement programs, and government regulations are examples of illegitimate laws. The income tax and entitlement programs confiscate our hard-earned money to give unearned benefits to others. Government literally steals money from its own citizens. Regulations presume that businesses are guilty of crimes before a crime is committed. They punish companies for potential crimes that never happened, and force businesses to spend millions of dollars to comply with the regulations. They violate property rights. All this is done without a crime being committed or any court proceeding to prove it.

Because unscrupulous or power-hungry people can take advantage of government's power, it's crucially important to prevent this possibility. When a potential dictator or socialist liberal can't use government to gain power or create a welfare state, his power-lust or incompetence is rendered harmless.

The "Last Amendment" to the Constitution would forbid Congress from making any laws that violated our property rights or economic liberty. If Congress passed such laws, the Supreme Court would declare the laws unconstitutional. We would stop future dictators or welfare states because we *dismantled the political machinery for doing harm*. A welfare state would be impossible because the Supreme Court would declare regulations, entitlement programs, and income taxes unconstitutional.

The Constitution established the principle that government can only take those actions the law allows it to take. The Bill of Rights forbade government from making laws that violated our political rights. It established the principle that these rights are outside government's control.

But the Constitution didn't put *economic liberty* outside government's control. It gave the federal government the power to coin money, promote the general welfare, and regulate commerce. Our Founding Fathers couldn't foresee how these powers would be abused. They couldn't foresee how today's liberals would use these economic powers to create the Welfare State.

Most of us see how communist governments violate peoples' political rights. The censorship, secret police, one-party system, rigged legal system, and suppression of free speech are painfully obvious. The close connection between political liberty and property rights is also easy to see. In most communist countries the state is the only employer. Until recently, Cubans, Chinese, or Vietnamese had to work for the state because the government owned everything—all the land, factories, and businesses.

Here, the economy and political power are one and the same. The Communist party makes most economic decisions for millions of helpless citizen-slaves. It decides where a person will work, what he can buy, where he can live, how much he'll be paid, and thousands of other economic decisions that Americans make for themselves and take for granted.

A communist government therefore has the power of life or death over every man, woman, and child in the country. It can fire someone from his job and not let him work anywhere else. It can lower a worker's wages or cut off a retiree's pension. It can dictate who goes to college, and who becomes a laborer. The government can take someone out of the factory and force him to work in the fields, as they did in China and Cambodia.

Through this awesome economic power, it can sentence a man and his family to death by slow starvation without bothering with legal proceedings. *Without property rights and economic liberty, political rights are meaningless.* Most people who are forced to choose between food and free speech will choose food. The communist Chinese government has a constitution that supposedly guarantees political rights, but this constitution isn't worth the paper it's written on. Chinese are already slaves through their government's total economic power over them.

In welfare states around the world, including ours, the same connection exists between political rights and economic liberty. But in a welfare state, people still have political rights and a semi-free economy. As a result, we find it harder to believe that government threatens our political rights when it violates our property rights. In a welfare state, it's harder to see the link between political rights and economic liberty.

Yet welfare states have economic powers that are similar to those in communist countries. Welfare states regulate wages, heath care, employment policies, product standards, safety standards, transportation, the environment, and most other areas of our lives. They also confiscate our earnings through taxes.

A welfare state differs from a communist government only by degree; it's just a milder version of the same poison. Both have the same goals—to "help" people, and both use the same means—compulsion. The difference between the two is how much force the government uses, and whether force is imposed by the communist party or by majority rule. To confirm this, try not paying your income taxes or refuse to obey some regulation and see what happens. If you resist the tax collectors, you'll end up dead or in jail. When government withholds income taxes from your paycheck to pay for entitlement programs, it violates your property rights and economic liberty.

It doesn't matter that a communist government owns all property while a welfare state allows private property. What's important is not who owns property, but who *controls* it. When taxes confiscate up to 50 percent of your income, you own only 50 percent of what you earn. When government bureaucrats can control your property, your ownership is meaningless.

We all spend what we earn on ourselves and our families. Who in his right mind would give away his hard-earned money to pay for other peoples' education, food stamps, subsidized rents, farm subsidies, health insurance, savings and loan bailouts, or retirement benefits? No one would, and *that's why force is necessary*.

Every penny that a "democratic" welfare state takes from you by majority rule represents a theft of your most precious possession—time. It represents a theft of part of your life, the part you spent earning that money. Welfare-state liberals assume that you don't own the money you earn, and therefore that you don't own your life. They assume that your duty in life is to work for the benefit of others, not for yourself or your family. If taxes loot 40 percent of your income, it means you're a slave for over four months of every year of your life.

To stop this injustice, once and for all, we have to forbid government from violating our economic liberty. The way to do this is to build a wall between government and the economy with a constitutional amendment, similar to the First Amendment that separates church and state.

BUILD A WALL BETWEEN
GOVERNMENT AND THE ECONOMY

We need to break the link between government and the economy for the same reason that church and state have to be separated. For thousands of years, people have been killing each other over religion. The Crusades in the Middle Ages was a religious war between Moslems and Christians that lasted more than two hundred years. There were vicious religious wars in Europe between Catholics and Protestants after the Reformation. The wars killed hundreds of thousands of people and lasted for more than a hundred years. Thousands more were tortured and burned at the stake for heresy by the Catholic Inquisition.

Today, after more than a hundred years of fighting, Catholics and Protestants still kill each other in Northern Ireland; Jews and Moslems kill each other in the Middle East; Hindus and Moslems are at each other's throats in India; and Christian Serbs slaughter Moslem Croats in Bosnia. All over the world, blood continues to be spilled over religion.

Our Founding Fathers understood what caused religious wars. They knew that people killed each other over religion because religion had always been linked to government. In different societies down through the ages, rulers created official state religions. People in these societies had to worship the approved gods. Egypt had its state religion of pagan gods. In the Middle Ages, the Catholic Church had a religious monopoly enforced by local rulers. The kings of Europe also created Catholic or Protestant state religions, like the Anglican Church of England.

After a ruler created a state religion, he outlawed all other religions and killed or persecuted those who dared to worship a different faith. The Romans murdered thousands of Christians on the cross, and throughout the Middle Ages, the Catholic Church tortured and burned nonbelievers at the stake.

Different faiths become mortal enemies when one religion has the legal right and power to hurt others. But without the police power of the state, no religion can outlaw or persecute another. It's this link between church and state that has been, and still is, the cause of eternal religious strife.

Our Founding Fathers wanted to make religious conflicts impossible in America. By writing these words in the First Amendment to the Constitution, "Congress shall make no law respecting an establishment of religion, or prohibiting the free exercise thereof," they solved the age-old problem of religious warfare.

In America, the first amendment of the Bill of Rights separates church and state. But through the years, many religious groups still tried to use political power to impose their beliefs on others. They tried to ban abortions, use public funds for religious schools, force religious prayer in public schools, ban business activity on Sundays, ban books that teach the theory of evolution, and so on. The Supreme Court stopped them by ruling such religious laws unconstitutional.

Every religious sect in America can now live side by side in peace and mutual respect while, in other parts of the world, people kill each other over religion. Other countries still haven't grasped the principle of the separation of church and state.

That same principle applies on a wider scale to economic conflicts. People have been killing each other for thousands of years over economic power struggles, for the same reasons they did over religion.

Human nature is such that some men are lazy and vicious and will try to loot what others produce. These criminals want wealth and economic power without having to work for it. Then we have another kind of robber—altruist liberals who presume the right to confiscate our money to help people they consider less fortunate. They claim the right to steal our money for their real or alleged compassion.

Almost every society in history had an elite, wealthy group who had economic power over everyone else. This group usually controlled the existing government. The rulers used government power to enrich themselves at the expense of their heavily-taxed subjects.

These societies had two major classes—the haves and the have-nots, the very rich and the very poor. There was no middle class like America has, where most people have a decent standard of living. That's why, throughout history, there has always been constant warfare and class struggle.

Those on the bottom of the ladder want to live like human beings. They feel a deep sense of injustice against the ruling class and government laws that keep them down and tax them into poverty. The aristocrats on top want to keep their privileged positions. They fight attempts by the lower classes to rise or take away their power. The result: five thousand years of bloody human history.

Economic classes became mortal enemies for the same reason religions were enemies when church and state were united. An elite group can have monopoly economic power over others only if government enforces that power. It's the link between government and the economy that causes economic warfare.

When government makes economic laws that favor one group over others, then everyone joins economic special-interest groups for self-defense (similar to joining different religious sects). Everyone tries to protect his livelihood or gain power over others through control of the government. Such a system leads to eternal warfare, as it has throughout history.

The same warfare exists in the Entitlement States of America. But it's not easy to recognize because it doesn't erupt into open, armed, bloody conflicts—so far. The warring factions are special-interest groups who fight each other, not with guns, but with laws. These pressure groups, called lobbies, try to persuade congressmen to make laws that give their group special handouts, subsidies, or protection at everyone else's expense.

The warfare is constant and widespread. Consumers seek price controls, product safety, or environmental regulations that hurt producers by lowering profits. Producers lobby for price supports, protection from competition, or monopoly franchises that hurt consumers. Farmers want price supports for their crops, which increases food prices for consumers. Property owners make zoning laws that try to exclude anyone not in their economic class. Environmentalists lobby for laws to stop logging, offshore drilling, land development, and car pollution. These laws hurt consumers by raising the price of fuel, cars, houses, and hundreds of other products. Big corporations lobby for regulations that protect them from competition, and small businesses lobby for loans and subsidies. The poor ask for welfare programs paid by the middle class. Blacks want affirmative action programs that discriminate against white workers. Married people are taxed less than single people. Single people pay taxes to educate other people's children. Young workers pay heavy Social Security taxes to support retirees. Working people pay retired people's medical bills. The list is endless, and the injustice is endless.

The Welfare State is nothing but *economic warfare*. Government spends most of its time trying to satisfy the conflicting demands of competing economic groups. It's a nonviolent, "civilized" warfare because so far each group accepts compromises to its demands.

Yet the Welfare State is economic warfare nonetheless. Each pressure group believes that it can use legalized force to get what it wants. Each group lobbies for laws that give it special subsidies or privileges at everyone else's expense. In the Welfare State, everyone's individual rights are violated. Each side now believes that the practical way to deal with other groups is to get them before they get you. The Welfare State has turned America into a savage place.

To end the Welfare State we have to build a permanent wall between government and the economy. We must prohibit government from making any laws that violate our freedom to trade or produce. We have to prohibit government from making any economic laws at all. Government should only be allowed to make laws relating to the police, court systems, and armed forces.

When our Founding Fathers separated church and state, religious warfare ended in America. If we separate government from the economy, economic warfare will also stop. No economic group will get unearned benefits at other peoples' expense. The constitutional amendment I propose will dismantle the political machinery that makes the Welfare State possible.

This amendment would prohibit Congress from making laws that gave special handouts, subsidies, or protection to farmers, retirees, consumers, small businesses, big corporations, welfare recipients, unmarried mothers, or anyone else. It would prohibit entitlement programs. If Congress created a new regulation or entitlement program, the Supreme Court would declare it unconstitutional.

The Last Amendment would forbid government from making laws that violated our property rights or economic liberty. I call it the Last Amendment because once it passed, I doubt we would ever need any others. It would permanently redefine the role of government and protect our economic and political liberty far into the future.

When government is barred from the economy, we'll live at peace with each other because we'll respect each other's rights and property. I believe this is the kind of society that our Founding Fathers envisioned for us.

WHY HALF-WAY SOLUTIONS DON'T WORK

Many of us agree that reducing regulations and entitlement programs is a good thing, but would balk at ending them all. Most people would ask, "Couldn't we at least keep some regulations or entitlement programs like Medicare and Social Security? Why does it have to be all or nothing?" The reason is that when two enemies are in a fight to the death, half measures *just don't work*.

The fight between the socialist Welfare State and a free economy is a fight to the death. It's a fight between two opposite moral codes that are mutually exclusive and eternal enemies. Socialism claims that we have no right to our life, that we have to live to help others. It says that the role of government is to force this moral code down our throats. A free economy recognizes that each of us is unique and precious, and that we have an inalienable right to our life and liberty. In a free economy, our happiness is our highest priority, and helping others is a personal choice, not a moral and political duty.

These two moral codes are opposite, irreconcilable, and therefore deadly enemies. Socialist liberals want to turn us into sacrificial animals. But all we want is to be left in peace to pursue our dreams and have a happy, fulfilling life. How can you reconcile these two opposite goals? You can't.

If a criminal broke into your house to rob you and kill your family, should you compromise with him? Should you tell him it's all right to steal and kill, but that he should only rob the bedroom and kill your wife, not your children? Would that be a fair "compromise?" I believe you would say no. Yet we agree to a similar compromise if we accept any part of the Welfare State.

Once we accept the moral code that justifies the Welfare State, then there's no stopping it. Once we believe that helping others is a moral and political duty, then it's only a matter of time until government turns all of us into slaves. When we agree with the socialist moral doctrine, a full-blown welfare state is inevitable.

Our own Welfare State proves this. For over 130 years, America was almost free of government controls, compared to today. But the socialist moral code gradually crept into our national psyche. Around the turn of the century, government started regulating the economy. It passed the Sherman Anti-Trust Act, and created the Interstate Commerce Commission to regulate big business. Over the years, Congress created dozens of other regulatory agencies. Today, government suffocates us with layers of regulations that control every part of our lives. Minor regulation at the turn of the century has turned into a regulatory nightmare that strangles us.

For over 130 years, there were few entitlement programs. Then Congress passed the income tax in 1913. This tax gave government the revenue source to create entitlement programs. Social Security was enacted in the 1930s. As the years passed, government created other entitlement programs. In 1965, the Welfare State started to explode when Congress created Medicare and Medicaid. The result today: A welfare state gone amok.

Human nature turns entitlement programs into out-of-control monsters. Once one special-interest group gets unearned handouts, then everyone wants them. This applies to groups across the economic spectrum. Farmers, corporations, unwed mothers, defense contractors, organized medicine, Medicare recipients, retirees on Social Security, and unemployed people on welfare or food stamps all want their special programs and subsidies.

Once people get unearned benefits, they soon believe they have a right to them. The insidious notion of economic rights is firmly implanted in their minds. As we noted earlier, once people believe they have a right to other people's money, then everyone demands handouts and everyone becomes corrupt.

And once benefits begin, people depend on them. Then it becomes next to impossible to give up the benefits. Beneficiaries cling to their government checks like drowning people to a life raft. A vicious cycle is set up. We get entitlement programs; other people then demand benefits; we soon depend on the benefits; we lose our independence and look to government to support us; as the Welfare State wrecks the economy at an accelerating rate, we need more government handouts for jobs, food stamps, housing, health care, unemployment insurance, and a thousand other needs; government then has to increase the entitlement payments and create new programs. The process finally ends with the economy destroyed and our lives in shambles. That happened in pre-Nazi Germany and the Soviet Union, and it's happening in America today.

To confirm this, just look at our entitlement programs—they're totally out of control. Welfare, Medicare, and Social Security started as small programs costing a few hundred million dollars. Today these programs cost over $800 billion a year, and the federal deficit is going through the roof.

Government always grossly underestimates the ultimate costs of entitlement programs. In 1965, President Johnson said there would be no problem paying for Medicare because the new program would only cost an extra $500 million a year. Today the program costs over *$150 billion* a year.[9]

The Gramm-Rudman law, which tried to control deficits and force Congress to balance the budget, didn't work. The recent attempt to pass a balanced budget amendment failed. Democrats in Congress do not want any restraints on their power to spend our money. They don't want to end the Welfare State. If we dismantled the Welfare State, they would be out of a job.

Liberal congressmen and bureaucrats can't control themselves. They've proven this time and again over the past sixty years. That's why we have an out-of-control welfare state today. When congressmen can use government's power to give out entitlement goodies to stay in office, they use that power. That's human nature and you can't change it. The only way to protect our liberty is to take that power away, permanently.

The Welfare State will ruin us unless we dismantle it, once and for all. That's why halfway measures don't work, and why we need the Last Amendment.

THE LAST AMENDMENT

This amendment would build a wall between government and

the economy. It would prohibit government from making any law that confiscated our money, violated our property rights, or restricted our freedom to trade and produce. The amendment would affirm these general principles and list specific prohibitions. The following are possible provisions, and will give a sense of the amendment's purpose:

Provisions That Protect Our Individual Rights:

1. Every American has the right to exercise his individual rights free from restraint by others or by government, as long as he doesn't harm or violate the rights of another person.

2. Every American has the inalienable right to keep everything he earns, whether salary, profits, or other legitimately gained income or property.

3. Every American has the right to own property and to use or dispose of his property as he sees fit.

4. No one has the right to use force against others, except for self-defense.

5. Government, at any level, has no right to any part of a person's income or property without that person's consent.

6. Every American may start and run a business, service, or profession free from any fees, license requirements, or other interference by government or any private organization.

7. Every American will pay taxes or duties to government only for services rendered. Government will bill anyone it provides a service to who hasn't paid taxes for that service (such as police protection).

8. No American will be forced to pay taxes or duties to government for any benefits, subsidies, insurance, or entitlement programs that give unearned benefits to others.

Provisions That Restrict Government (at all levels):

1. Government is prohibited from owning land or any other property, except as necessary to carry out its strictly defined functions (for example: prisons, court houses, police buildings, and armed forces bases and equipment).

2. Government will make no laws and take no actions that

confiscate or restrict the use of private property owned by any individual or business enterprise, except as necessary to protect individuals from the immediate or threatened use of force.

3. Government will have no right to incur deficits. It will pay for all necessary goods or services at the time of delivery of said goods or services.

4. Government will make no laws that violate a person's right or freedom to engage in any economic activity, except as necessary to prevent that person from using or threatening force against others.

5. Government is prohibited from making any regulations that restrict a person's or business's freedom to enter into or conduct business in any manner he or it chooses, so long as that person or business doesn't threaten or use force against others.

6. Government will have no right to issue or require licenses from any individual or business to start or continue any business, profession, or other enterprise.

7. Government will have no right to levy compulsory taxes or duties. It will obtain all necessary funds through payments made by individual citizens for services rendered.

8. Government is prohibited from creating any subsidy, insurance, or entitlement program that benefits individuals, groups, private citizens, business enterprises, or foreign governments.

9. Government is prohibited from creating or giving financial support to any educational system, institution, or organization.

10. Government may not own or operate any service, business, or enterprise, including roads, utilities, postal service, and transportation systems. All such services will be owned and operated by private companies in the free market.

11. Government services shall be limited to establishing and maintaining police protection, the armed forces, foreign relations, and civil and criminal court systems.

A PROSPEROUS, FREE AMERICA

The above provisions in a constitutional amendment would build a wall between government and the economy. This would end the Welfare State. The amendment would secure our individual rights and economic liberty, and would reduce government to the minimum size needed to perform its proper functions.

All entitlement programs would end. We would phase out food stamps, Medicare, bank bailouts, farm subsidies, welfare programs, Social Security, and unemployment insurance. The Entitlement States of America would be gone.

The amendment would ban all regulations that controlled or restricted trade or production. This includes regulations on drugs, land use, zoning, health care, employment, licensing, product safety, transportation, communications, the environment, and many more.

Victimless crime laws for gambling, drug use, and prostitution would be repealed. Government could not make laws that interfere with agreements between consenting adults. Government could interfere only where one person uses or threatens to use force against another.

Income taxes would end. We would have a voluntary tax system based on the idea that government is only a paid servant. Each person would pay fees to government only for services that he or she personally used. People would pay for police protection, the court system, or the armed forces for the same reason they now buy life or health insurance—for protection.

If the police helped someone who didn't have a police protection policy, the local government could then bill the person for services rendered. The same would apply to the court system or armed services. This would end the problem of people who tried to freeload on the system.

Paying government for police protection or other legitimate services is possible and practical. Recently, an adventurous group of mountain climbers in Colorado went into dangerous country in the dead of winter. Park officials warned them about the dangers, but they went anyway. Naturally they got lost in the mountains and their lives were in danger. Local government rescue teams finally pulled them out. The mountain climbers were then *billed for the cost of the rescue*. We could apply the same principle to police or court system services.

Government-owned or operated services or property would be sold to private individuals or businesses by competitive bids.

These include parks, libraries, public schools, utilities, the Post Office, fire, sanitation, and public transportation systems, and land and structures owned by local, state, and federal governments. We could then choose our postal delivery company, garbage pickup company, or our child's free-market high-school the way we now choose our supermarket or insurance agent. We would have many competitors vying for our business.

In short, the Last Amendment would end the Welfare State. The amendment would permanently break the link between government and the economy *in practice and in principle*. It would take the yoke of government taxes and regulations off our backs, and we could breathe free again.

Obviously, we can't change the system overnight. Government services, regulations, and entitlement programs would have to be phased out over many years, since millions of Americans now depend on them. We would dismantle them gradually, allowing the free market to take over in the process. The exact steps and details of the changeover are important, but are beyond the scope of this book. What's important at this time is to set the goal and outline a specific timetable of actions that will move us toward that goal.

In a free America, we would take full responsibility for our lives, in the deepest sense. Our success, happiness, and self-esteem would depend on our efforts and character. If we wanted something in life, we could only get it the old-fashioned way—by earning it.

In a free America, we would have to respect each other's rights and property. Income taxes would end, so government couldn't loot what you earned. We would end regulations, so no one could tell you what to do with your property or business.

In a free economy, people who were lazy, dishonest, or malicious would suffer the consequences of their actions. Reality would slap them briskly in the face and force them to change their ways. If they didn't change, they would have no power to hurt anyone but themselves.

A free economy would bring out the best in us. It's a system that tells us that what we make of our lives is up to us. No fairy-godmother bureaucrat will give us handouts or control us with regulations. A free economy forces us to earn whatever we want in life. Necessity and our own life force will push us to live up to our highest potential.

But this doesn't mean that we won't work with or ask the help of friends, family, neighbors, business associates, or local religious and community organizations. Far from it. Human beings are social animals. Our survival depends on social cooperation. A free economy forces us to use every resource we have, both within ourselves and in the outside world. It makes us seek the help and cooperation of others because without that help no lasting success is possible for anyone. It's a system that fosters friendship and mutual respect, because it makes us respect each other's value and rights as unique human beings.

I'm not saying that a free economy is a perfect system. No system that depends on human beings could be perfect. It's sad but true that some people will not find success, happiness, or even economic subsistence in a free market. But that's a fault of life and human nature, not an economic system. In a free economy, most of us would have the opportunity to find success and happiness. That's the most we can ask of an economic system that human beings create.

But a free economy would create an explosion of new jobs, energy, and productivity. It would slash your taxes, give you unlimited opportunities, and promise your children a wonderful future. Your spirit, the American spirit, would create a joyful, vibrant new America. And it would end, once and for all, government's right to rob you and regulate you to death.

WHY A FREE ECONOMY WOULD WORK

Most of us are not afraid to take responsibility for our lives. In fact, we prefer to be left alone to do just that. But we've become so used to the welfare-state safety net, that the thought of being totally on our own seems a little scary. We might like a free economy in theory, but we question whether the ideal is practical in everyday life.

It's natural that most of us would question whether a free, self-regulating market can work. For over fifty years, liberals have been feeding us socialist doctrines. For over fifty years, government has increased its stranglehold over our lives. Millions of Americans now depend on entitlement programs and are afraid to give them up.

Most of us aren't theoretical economists, so we judge issues with our common sense, experience, and personal knowledge. We feel that government regulations and entitlement programs seem to work, however badly. But it's hard for us to understand how a free economy would work, because it doesn't exist now and we've never experienced it.

For the past fifty years, the liberal media has taught us to distrust capitalism, the profit motive, and business people. Ask yourself when was the last time you read a book or saw a movie where a businessman was the hero? Most books, movies, newspapers, and television stories portray businessmen as greedy, scheming, or polluting villains, out to get illicit profits by hurting people. A good example was the movie *Wall Street*, where the Wall Street villain's most vicious remark was that "greed is good." With this kind of propaganda for fifty years, it's no wonder most of us think that a free economy couldn't work. Let's see why this isn't so.

In a free economy, competing companies would take over previously government-run monopolies (privatization), except the police and courts. Companies would compete for your business to provide these services, as they do for everything else you buy. Entitlement programs like Medicare and Social Security would also be phased out.

Each of us would be responsible for our insurance, retirement, and other needs. *But we would not have to pay taxes to support the Welfare State any more.* A free economy would slash your taxes to a tiny fraction of what they are today. You would keep what you earned.

There are many reasons a free economy would be practical and a great success. The primary one is human nature: you value your life. To prosper in a free economy, you have to think, learn, and work hard. There is no other way to succeed. The free market would bring out the best in you.

The proof of this is around you and within you. Ask yourself why you work so hard. It's because you want a good life for yourself and your family. You're alive, and you want to succeed and be happy. You know that reality is a hard taskmaster. You accept this and understand that you'll have to work hard to reach the good life. Since other people value their lives as much as you do, everyone will act the same way.

Most people are born mentally and physically normal, and can act and think to support themselves. We also have a driving force that pushes us to realize our highest potential. In a free economy, we can use that potential. Each of us, pursuing our own dreams and ambitions, would reinforce each other's efforts through trade, giving us a strong, productive economy and a rising standard of living.

This isn't just theory. Look around you. We have one of the highest standards of living in the world, *in spite of* welfare-state controls. Imagine what we could accomplish if all controls and taxes were gone and we had a free economy.

In a free economy, you can go as far as your ability and ambition take you. Millions of immigrants came to America with nothing but their dreams. When the first colonists landed on our shores, there was nothing but bare ground and empty wilderness. Yet we achieved a standard of living in two hundred years that people hadn't even dreamed of in the previous ten thousand years, a standard of living that's still the envy of the world.

END GOVERNMENT-RUN MONOPOLIES

The free market, even burdened by government controls, is a powerful, efficient machine that brings you the goods and services you now enjoy but probably take for granted. It gives you jet planes, fresh food, employment, skyscrapers, television, electricity, and the family car. It lets you talk to people on the opposite side of the world as if they were sitting in your living room. It discovers oil in deserts, transports the oil halfway round the world, then puts it into your car's gas tank. The free market makes the good life possible for all of us. If private enterprise can accomplish these miracles, don't you think it could deliver the mail?

Many Americans believe there are essential services that only government can provide. They believe that the Post Office, public schools, national parks, city sanitation and fire protection, and local transportation systems have to be owned and operated by government. That isn't true.

Think about it. United Parcel Service, who delivers mail around the globe, couldn't deliver your local first-class mail? Greyhound Corporation, an efficient company with thousands of buses going to every major city in America, couldn't run the local bus service in your city? Private carters couldn't pick up your garbage? The company that gave us Disney World couldn't run your local city parks? Today there are thousands of private schools, from kindergartens to graduate universities, that enroll millions of students. Free-market companies couldn't operate government-run public schools?

Free enterprise would provide these government-run services, *precisely because these services are essential.* Giving people what they want and need is what the free market is all about. Because millions of parents want to educate their children, you can be sure that thousands of competing, low-cost schools would spring up almost overnight to meet this demand. If mail service is essential, you can be sure that United Parcel, Federal Express, and hundreds of smaller new companies would soon be competing to deliver your mail.

It's no coincidence that governments use force to stop private companies from competing with them. In the past, many companies tried to start first-class mail delivery businesses, but the federal government shut them down for infringing on its monopoly. Government monopolies like the Post Office are much worse than private monopolies. They exclude competition by force and deny consumers freedom of choice. If government stopped operating these services, competent private companies would step in so fast and so efficiently that it would make the bureaucrats' heads spin.

Many cities throughout America already use private contractors to provide garbage pickup, fire protection, and bus transit systems, and this practice is spreading. For example, the disaster that was supposed to have struck California because of the Proposition 13 tax revolt didn't materialize. Many California towns and cities simply turned over formerly government-run services to free-market contractors. The result was improved efficiency and dramatic cost savings.

La Mirada, California is a good example of the benefits of privatization. In 1980, this suburb of Los Angeles with a population of 40,000 people had about 55 city employees and over 60 service contracts with private companies. Some services contracted out were trash collection, car service, data processing, and maintenance for parks and traffic signals.

La Mirada saved money using private contractors and found that service quality also improved. Former City Administrator Gary Sloan said that he and the City Council had much more control over private contractors than they had over municipal agencies. The city could write very strict, but highly flexible contracts with private companies. With municipal unions, the city was constrained by rigid civil service rules.[10]

The Falck Company, a Danish company formed in 1906, supplies half of Denmark with ambulances, fire protection, and other emergency services. Rural/Metro Fire Department, Inc., a company headquartered in Scottsdale, Arizona, supplies fire protection to thousands of customers in many communities throughout the state. The company also supplies ambulance service and security patrol service in many Arizona cities. It has also expanded its private fire-protection and ambulance services to cities in eight other states.

Because of Metro's excellent service, subscribers in the Scottsdale area got low homeowner's fire insurance rates that were one-fourth the national average for cities of 50,000 to 100,000 population. While the national per capita fire loss for the last twelve years averaged about $12 per year, Scottsdale's average during this time was about $4.44 per year. One study observed that if Scottsdale had gotten its fire protection from a traditional municipal fire department, the city would have paid $475,000, instead of the actual $252,000 contract cost—one-half the price.[11]

A 1971 New York City study discovered that private collectors could pick up garbage at $17.50 per ton compared with the city's $49 per ton. The New York City Sanitation Department spent $207 a year to collect garbage twice a week from single family households in an area of Little Neck and Douglaston, Queens.

In Bellerose, a similar neighborhood three miles away over the Nassau County line, a private firm collected residential garbage three times a week for just $72 a year. One study by Columbia University professor Emmanuel Savas found that in cities with a population over 50,000, the average municipal sanitation department cost 68 percent more than private firms to collect garbage.[12]

Today, practically the entire state of New Jersey is converting to private contractors for local services. Like many other states throughout the country, the recession, tight budgets, and lower federal subsidies have reduced New Jersey's revenues. Towns and cities throughout the state are turning to private contractors to supply services at lower costs with more efficiency.

> From one end of the state to the other, in hundreds of municipalities and in dozens of county and state agencies, officials are experimenting with a concept that stands the traditional notion of government on its head—privatization. . .Many legislators and officials have hailed it as a means of improving efficiency and cutting costs.
>
> Private companies have been hired to operate services ranging from street cleaning and trash collection to ambulance services and traffic control. Proposals have been made to privatize everything from N.J. Transit buses to schools.[13]

I could list many more examples, but the results are the same. Free-market companies run schools, hospitals, trash collection, fire protection, and ambulance services more efficiently and at lower cost.[14] A government-run monopoly has no competition. It doesn't have to make profits. It also has to deal with civil-service employees who get overpriced wages and benefits through political pressure and threats of crippling strikes.

The free market can also supply any insurance we now get from government. Social Security didn't exist in this country until the 1930s. Until then, Americans saved for their own retirement. The question to ask about Social Security is: why do we need government to take care of our retirement? As we learned earlier, we can save money in our own IRA accounts and be far better off when we retire. Are we too lazy or stupid to save our own money? No, we're not.

Millions of Americans already have private pension plans through their employers. Millions more set aside billions of dollars a year in IRA retirement accounts. The idea that we need government to provide for our retirement is silly.

The same applies to other insurance needs. Hundreds of huge insurance companies already offer us many different types of insurance, from car insurance to disability and major-medical. These companies could also give us any kind of insurance we now get from government.

For example, if unemployment insurance is an essential need, it represents a business opportunity for insurance companies. Millions of workers would buy it. Or should we assume that there's something absolutely unique about unemployment insurance that these companies couldn't handle? The answer is obviously no.

Social Security was enacted in the 1930s. Medicare was created in 1965. If we couldn't get along without government insurance programs, or most people couldn't handle their own health or retirement needs, *how did Americans manage to survive and prosper for over 130 years before we had these programs?*

For most of our country's history, we had an economy that was almost free, and it was a smashing success. America had strong economic growth and rising living standards up to the 1950s, when there were far fewer regulations or entitlement programs than we have today. A free economy can work in America *because it worked for over 130 years.* In contrast, our economic problems accelerated after the 1960s when the Welfare State started mushrooming out of control.

There are also other countries with free economies that are smashing success stories. Hong Kong and Singapore are prime examples. Hong Kong is one of the economic dynamos of Southeast Asia. It has a vibrant, growing economy that creates a high standard of living for about eight million free Chinese. Yet it's nothing but a small rocky island with few natural resources.

Another example of the free-market's life-giving powers is Chile, in South America. Between 1970 and 1973, President Salvador Allende imposed socialism on Chile. As a result, he wrecked the economy. His regime ran up huge import deficits, strangled the economy with over 3,000 price controls, and nationalized banks, mines, airlines, steel companies, agribusinesses, and electric and telephone companies. Local government "committees" forced farmers at gunpoint to hand over their property to the government for "redistribution."

On September 11, 1973, Allende was overthrown by another dictator, General Augusto Pinochet. Like other South American dictators, Pinochet trampled on the political rights of his people. But he also believed in the free market. He played a crucial role in his country's economic recovery by dismantling socialism in Chile. He reduced tariffs, forcing his country to accept international competition. Pinochet slashed government spending, eliminated all price controls, returned owners' stolen properties, and sold most companies that had been nationalized. In spite of his political repression, he transformed the Chilean economy into a robust free market.

He also revolutionized Chile's social security system. Previously, social security taxes had been invested in worthless government bonds. Pinochet's government gave Chileans the right to invest 10 percent of their pretax salaries among thirteen private pension funds. These funds invest in private enterprises that create jobs, and in the past ten years have grown 13 percent annually.

In 1988, Pinochet stepped down as military dictator, held elections, and transferred power to a democratic government. With democracy and economic freedom in place, Chile experienced "El Boom." The free market produced spectacular results:

> Chile's economy has grown an average of over 5.6 percent annually for the past seven years. In 1992, according to estimates, it recorded the highest growth of all major nations in the Americas. Inflation, once 1,000 percent, has fallen to 13 percent. Unemployment, 20 percent a decade ago, is now just 5 percent. And Chile's bond rating, a strong indicator of investor confidence, recently became the highest of any Latin American nation.[15]

Today, Chile's booming economy is like a rising tide, lifting all boats. Even though four million Chileans—about one in four—still live in poverty, the number of poor is dropping fast. The Hogar de Cristo is Chile's largest private charity and is a barometer of progress. Nine years ago, its soup kitchens in Santiago fed 3,000

263

people. In 1993 it had only 500 customers.[16]

The success of free-market economies around the world proves that a free economy is good for people, that it makes their lives better and more secure. It also proves that government's most important economic role is to *stay out of our way*.

That, of course, is not what liberals think. They believe the free market has deficiencies, that it's not perfect. Not everyone gets enough food, health care, or education. They claim that government has to "manage" the economy to correct these alleged deficiencies. Liberals want to hand over our complex, dynamic, ever-changing free-market economy to the same people who gave us the Welfare State and the savings and loan scandal. They want to put our lives, our freedom, and our children's future into the hands of bureaucrats.

Bureaucrats aren't bad people, and many work hard and are conscientious. They just work for the government, and that's the problem. As we saw earlier, government agencies, by their nature, are wasteful, inefficient, and incompetent because they're monopolies that don't have to make profits to survive. The federal government subsidizes these agencies with taxes if they lose money.

In 1991, the United States Post Office lost about a billion dollars. They've had a string of losses going back to 1972, though the law requires them to break even.[17] If government can't break even on delivering the mail, then we certainly can't trust it to run the $800 billion health care industry, the entire economy, or *any part* of the economy. It can't be trusted to run a lemonade stand.

Free enterprise creates and organizes an economy with a gross national product of over $3.5 trillion. It gives us everything we need with seemingly effortless ease. It directs international trade on a vast scale with the same ease. It's constantly creative and innovative, and continually brings us new and wondrous products to make our lives safer, better, and happier—from pacemakers to Disney World.

It does this because a free economy fosters competition. Each business has to compete for your dollars to survive. It has to beat its competitors by offering you better products at lower prices. It has to continually strive to serve you better, because its profits depend on this. From the freshness of the food you eat to the fuel efficiency of your car, products and services keep getting better and less expensive. The key elements of a free economy—liberty, competition, the profit motive, and private property—inevitably act to encourage this process.

THE MAYTAG MEN

The free market creates electricity, skyscrapers, and thousands of other wonderful products that make our lives better. But we can't get the benefits of the free market unless government leaves us alone. A free economy breaks down when government taxes and regulates us to death.

To this end, we only need one thing from government—*to stay out of our way*. Government should be our traffic cop and arbitrator, insuring that no one injects fear, force, or fraud into the marketplace. Government's only proper job is to protect our lives and property, and make sure we respect each other's rights. Its job should be strictly limited to maintaining a police force, court system, and armed forces. Other than that, we should legally bar government from interfering in our lives.

In the most fundamental sense, we don't need bureaucrats and politicians. We are the creators and producers of America. Liberal politicians "produce" nothing but taxes and regulations. Out of a misguided desire to help or protect us, liberal politicians rob us, regulate us, and interfere with our lives. *We should give them a clear message: if you really want to help, just stay out of our way.*

Our congressmen and Presidents are usually bright, honorable people. But for our safety, we should turn them into Maytag men. Do you remember the Maytag commercial? The Maytag washing-machine repair man sits in his office all day doing nothing because Maytag machines are so well made they never break down. So the Maytag man sits idly in his office forever, because no one ever calls him to repair a machine that doesn't need fixing.

It's the same with the free market. We should turn our elected officials into political Maytag men: we should pay them to sit in their offices and *do nothing*. They should be barred from making any law that interferes with our economic liberty or that superlative machine, the free market. If liberal politicians feel compelled to help others, they should do volunteer work for private charities, instead of messing up our lives.

We're angry with our elected representatives because they don't seem to know what they're doing. We're furious because they keep strangling us with more taxes and regulations to support an exploding Welfare State. But once we dismantle the Welfare State and turn our elected representatives into Maytag men, all our anger and frustration with government would vanish. We get angry at someone who hurts us or who doesn't give us what we expect from them. The same applies to government. Government hurts us with taxes and wrecks the economy with regulations. With the Last Amendment, that would stop. If you had a smooth-running Maytag washing machine, would you be mad at the Maytag repairman for sitting in his office? In the same way, if we don't expect our elected representatives to support us or regulate the economy, then we won't feel contempt or anger with them if they don't.

In a free economy, government would protect our lives and property, and that's it. There would be no more handouts, subsidies, insurance programs, or entitlement programs for anyone. More important, *we would not expect such subsidies*. We would realize that we're responsible for our lives, not government. We would accept the truth that we have no right to rob people to help special-interest groups or ourselves, that the end does not justify the means.

THE MORALITY OF A FREE ECONOMY

There's no doubt that a free economy works, that it gives us freedom of choice and an amazing standard of living. But liberals don't criticize a free economy because it's impractical. Their complaint is that it's *immoral*.

Liberals say, yes, maybe the free market can deliver the mail better. But what if it's unprofitable to deliver mail to a little old lady living alone on a farm, far from a major city? Yes, private companies can operate government-run schools, but what happens to the poor child, slow child, or problem child that a private school may not want? Yes, private contractors could pick up garbage and run the bus service, but then government workers would lose their jobs. It's true that most people could save for their retirement, but what about those people who squander their money or don't have any money to save? What happens to them? That's the classic liberal refrain again. Helping others is our political duty, whether we like it or not; we're responsible for other people's suffering, mistakes, or misfortune.

Liberals say that a free economy is immoral because it doesn't guarantee complete safety and sustenance for everyone. It won't support someone who is lazy, dishonest, incompetent, irrational, or just unlucky. It won't guarantee a job, health insurance, food on the table, or a decent place to live. It won't guarantee we don't have an unusual reaction to a drug we take. It won't guarantee that the air we breathe on city streets will be 100 percent pure. It won't guarantee that we'll never lose our job or go hungry. It won't guarantee us something we didn't earn. This is true. It won't, it can't, and it shouldn't.

No economic system can make such guarantees, especially a welfare state. No economic system can take all the risks and uncertainties out of life. A society that tries eventually winds up destitute. When we try to guarantee everyone's income and safety, we create a fascist or socialist economic system. This system wrecks everyone's life, including and especially the poor people we were first trying to help. It's simple to confirm this. Just look at the widespread misery and destitution in Russia caused by seventy years of communism. Remember, Russia used to be called the Union of Soviet *Socialist* Republics.

Liberals say that a free economy is immoral. In fact, the opposite is true. It's the most moral economic system human beings have ever devised. It's moral because it's based on the principle that we have a right to our life and liberty. It embodies the idea that every human being is an end in himself, not a means to the ends of others.

A free economy is superbly practical because it gives us the freedom to work for our dreams and the right to keep what we earn. It gives us a high standard of living because it gives free rein to the best in us. It's superbly practical *because* it's moral.

We have to defend a free economy on moral grounds, first and foremost. That's why I've examined the moral premises at the root of the Welfare State. We won't dismantle the Welfare State until we understand that helping others is a personal choice, not a moral and political duty. Unless we embrace this idea, we'll continue to believe that a free, self-regulating economy is immoral, and not even consider its practical benefits.

George Bush's presidency is a good example of this principle at work. Mr. Bush was a fine man and a good president. But he was a moderate Republican who believed, like many other Republicans do, that we should keep many welfare-state programs like Medicare and Social Security. As a result, he didn't attack the moral principle at the root of the Welfare State. His actions implied that there's nothing wrong with the Welfare State, except that it's wasteful. He sanctioned the Welfare State and left the principle and the machinery of government control in place.

But what happened when George Bush sought reelection? The recession had gotten worse, and Americans were suffering from the destructive policies of the Welfare State. Liberal Democrats waiting in the wings told Americans that the free market had been tried, and failed. Bill Clinton was elected. He capitalized on George Bush's failure to attack the Welfare State. During the campaign, Clinton accused the Republicans of practicing "trickle-down" economics, his euphemism for a free economy.

Like all liberals, Clinton made Americans think that our economic system is unfair. He attacked the free market because it doesn't guarantee health care and everything else we need. But he attacked a straw man. America doesn't have a free economy; instead, we have a failed, totally regulated Welfare State. Most Americans don't realize that the Welfare State caused our economic problems, not a free economy that doesn't exist.

Millions of Americans out of work or afraid of the future fell for the old siren song of government support. Being desperate, they looked for scapegoats and a quick, easy solution. It's sad and ironic that we elected Bill Clinton. We elected him out of pain and desperation, a pain and desperation that was *caused* by the Welfare State he loves so much.

Americans elected Bill Clinton by default because Republicans didn't give them a clear, strong alternative. Republicans didn't attack the Welfare State or defend a totally free economy. Many Republicans believe that an economy free of all government controls wouldn't work, and that voters would never accept it.

I believe they're mistaken. Americans are smarter and more courageous than our politicians think. There's a groundswell of anger at the Welfare State, and a desperate need for an alternative. The enormous success of Rush Limbaugh is proof of this. Rush Limbaugh is a lightning rod for that anger, and a blessing for this country. The recent Congressional elections that swept Republicans into power show that Americans want government out of their hair and out of their pockets.

Many Republicans believe that Americans would reject a totally free economy because it's untested and too "extreme." But a free economy is neither untested nor extreme. As we noted earlier, America was almost free for over 130 years before anyone ever heard of the Welfare State. Today, most of us are still conservative in the old-fashioned sense of the term. We believe in hard work, respect for each other's rights, and taking responsibility for our lives. That's what a free economy is all about.

As for it being extreme, it is, *compared to today's Welfare State*. But a free economy would not be extreme to our Founding Fathers. To James Madison, Thomas Jefferson, and Benjamin Franklin, uncontrolled government was our deadliest enemy. They created the Constitution and Bill of Rights to protect us from this enemy. Our Founding Fathers would find the Welfare State extreme, not economic liberty and a free economy.

We're at a critical point in our country's history. The Welfare State is out of control. The deficit will eventually bankrupt us. Our standard of living is going backwards and we're heading for economic ruin. The patient is in serious trouble.

The Welfare State is a cancer spreading across the country; to save ourselves, we have to cut it out. If we leave any trace of the tumor, the cancer can come back. So we have to dismantle the Welfare State, once and for all. We need to pass a constitutional amendment that builds a wall between government and the economy, similar to the separation of church and state. We can then breathe free and look forward to the future again.

What You Can Do

The first and most important thing we can do to change things is to reject the moral precepts of the Welfare State. Reread my book. Ask yourself these questions: Why do you let government turn you into a sacrificial animal? Does Congress have the right to rob you to give unearned handouts to others? Is helping others a personal choice, or should liberals force this down your throat? Do other people have "rights" that you have to pay for? Are *you* entitled to a government benefit that others have to pay for? Think about these questions. When Americans reject the moral precepts of the Welfare State, the structure will topple. When you refuse to allow politicians of any party to control your life or your income, things will change. You'll get angry enough to show your elected officials how you feel. You did this in the November 1994 Congressional elections, and our politicians are starting to get the message.

But the battle has only begun. You must demand more fundamental changes. We need to end the Welfare State, not just trim it around the edges. We have to end most regulations, not just consolidate a few minor regulatory agencies. We need to phase out all entitlement programs, not just transfer funding to the states. The Federal budget should be cut in half, not "balanced" at current bloated levels.

The new Republican Congress is doing some good things, but many Republicans still think there's nothing wrong with regulations and entitlement programs, in principle. Instead of dismantling the Welfare State, they only want to cut off the regulations and entitlement programs they don't like. That doesn't solve the problem. As we know, the Welfare State is a cancer, and you can't cure cancer with a band aid. We need a Constitutional amendment that erects a wall between government and the economy.

Fortunately, we now have a choice. There's another national political party that *would* make the changes we need. The Libertarian Party, based in Washington, DC, stands for individual rights, limited government, and ending most taxes, regulations, and entitlements. Find out more about this party. Call their national headquarters (202-543-1988). Get their brochures that describe how they stand on all the important issues. If a majority of Americans voted for Libertarian Party candidates in every election, the Welfare State would be swept away.

Besides voting for the Libertarian Party, you can do other things. You can join and support organizations that lobby to reduce taxes and government power. Politicians are swayed by the voting power of large groups. Join such an organization. Your voice will be heard and your opinions will have more weight when you're a member of one of these groups.

Here's some groups that may interest you.

National Tax-Limitation Committee – (202)547-4196
This Washington, DC-based group has over 800,000 members. It lobbies Congress to limit spending and reduce taxes. It's a fine organization.

National Taxpayers Union – (202)543-1300
This Washington, DC-based organization has over 200,000 members. It's president, James Dale Davidson, has testified before Congressional committees on many occasions on the need to reduce taxes and the deficit. It's a very worthy organization.

Common Cause – (202)833-1200
This Washington, DC-based group has over 250,000 members. It lobbies Congress to be more open and accountable to the public. It has done good work.

Center For The Defense of Free Enterprise – (206)455-5038.
This group has over 75,000 members and is located in Bellevue, Washington. It defends and promotes the free enterprise system. It lobbies to eliminate government controls and reduce taxes. It's an excellent organization.

Citizens For A Sound Economy – (202)783-3870
This Washington, DC-based group has over 250,000 members. It is very active. It lobbies Congress to protect our free-enter-

prise system, and to reduce taxes and regulations. A fine organization that gets things done.

Free The Eagle – (703)257-4782

This group has over 250,000 members and is located in Manassas, Virginia. It actively lobbies Congress to eliminate government taxes and regulations that strangle the economy. It is a dedicated defender of our liberty.

Citizens Against Government Waste – (202)467-5300

This Washington, DC-based group has over 350,000 members. It actively lobbies Congress to reduce government programs, spending, and regulations that waste taxpayer dollars. It also educates the public about the enormous waste from government programs. This group has done excellent work.

Young Republicans – (202)662-1340

If you are young and a Republican, you might want to join this group. It promotes Republican ideals of fiscal responsibility and protection of our individual rights. The group has over 200,000 members. It's based in Washington, DC.

People For The American Way – (202)467-4999

This Washington, DC-based group lobbies Congress to stop the enactment of laws that threaten our civil and religious liberties. Their efforts protect our basic rights.

Liberty Lobby – (202)544-1302

This group, based in Washington, DC, actively lobbies for the protection of our individual rights, and for less government regulations and intrusion in our lives. They do important work.

National Federation of Independent Businesses (NFIB)–

(202)554-9000. If you own a business, this is one organization you should join. This group's headquarters are in Washington, DC. It is a fierce defender of your liberty as a business owner. It actively lobbies Congress to reduce taxes and regulations on small businesses. It has pursuaded Congress to repeal many laws and regulations that hurt small business owners. Again, if you own a business, you should think about joining this group.

The Institute For Justice – (202)457-4240

This Washington, DC-based organization is not a lobby group. Instead, it's composed of dedicated lawyers who file lawsuits against government laws that violate our property rights and other individual rights. Every lawsuit they file seeks to protect your liberty. They deserve your support.

Cato Institute – (202)842-0200

The Cato Institute is headquartered in Washington D.C. It's a leading policy research foundation for libertarian ideas. It publishes books on a wide range of subjects, such as health care, education, regulations, and the environment. It shows the public and elected officials how to use libertarian solutions to solve the problems caused by the Welfare State. The Cato Institute is worthy of your support.

Laissez-Faire Books – (800)326-0996

If you want to learn more about libertarian ideas, this is the source to go to. This unique San Francisco-based bookstore has a wide range of books on history, economics, education, public policy, political theory, and many other subjects. Their books are fascinating and a rich source of information on libertarian ideas. Call them up. Get their catalogue. Start learning more about the issues discussed in my book. Tell your friends about these books. The more people read these books and understand the issues, the sooner we'll see an end to the Welfare State.

The above list of organizations is just a start. If you do a little research at your local library, you can find other groups you may want to join. Get involved and your voice will be heard.

NOTES

INTRODUCTION

1. B. Drummond Ayres, Jr., "Shadow of Pessimism Eclipses a Dream," *The New York Times*, February 8, 1992, p. A1. Copyright © 1992 by The New York Times Company. Reprinted by permission.
2. Ibid., p. A1. Copyright © 1992 by The New York Times Company. Reprinted by permission.
3. Ibid., p. A1. Copyright © 1992 by The New York Times Company. Reprinted by permission.

CHAPTER 1

1. John Kramer, News release: "Volunteer--Or Else!," Institute For Justice, April 19, 1994.
2. Peter G. Peterson, *Facing Up* (New York: Simon & Schuster, 1993), p. 78; David E. Rosenbaum, "The Clinton Difference? Not Much in the Budget," *New York Times*, February 6, 1994. sect. 1, p. 34.
3. Peter J. Ferrara, *Social Security: Averting the Crisis* (Washington, D.C.: Cato Institute, 1982), p. 2; David E. Rosenbaum, "The Clinton Difference? Not Much in the Budget," *The New York*

Times, February 6, 1994, sect. 1, p. 34.

CHAPTER 2

1. Mobil Corporation, "The Rest Of The Year Belongs To You," *The New York Times*, May 20, 1993.
2. Robert D. Hershey Jr., "Higher Rates Sting The Wealthy,"*The New York Times*, February 27, 1994, p. A13.
3. Peter G. Peterson, *Facing Up* (New York: Simon & Schuster, 1993), back Chart (4.9).
4. Ibid., back Chart (4.10).
5. David Wootton, editor, *Political Writings of John Locke*, (New York: Mentor Books, 1993), p. 325.
6. Peter G. Peterson, *Facing Up* (New York: Simon & Schuster, 1993), p. 30.
7. Richard L. Berke, "Democrats Seek Higher Tax For Richer Americans," *The New York Times*, May 7, 1991. p. A20.

CHAPTER 3

1. Dirk Johnson, "A Recovering Alcoholic Sues, Asserting Job Bias," *The New York Times*, August 26, 1994, p. A22.
2. Peter J. Ferrara, *Social Security: Averting the Crisis* (Washington, D.C.: Cato Institute, 1982), p. 38.
3. Robert D. Hershey Jr., "Where Job Hunters Hit the Jackpot," *The New York Times*, June 30, 1994, p. D1.
4. Thomas Sowell, *Markets and Minorities* (New York: Basic Books, 1981), p. 123, Copyright © 1985 by International Center for Economic Policy Studies.
5. Sidney Zion, "Make Them Legal," *The New York Times*, December 15, 1993, p. A27, Copyright © 1993 by The New York Times Company. Reprinted by permission.
6. Ibid., p. A27, Copyright © 1993 by The New York Times Company. Reprinted by permission.
7. Ibid., p. A27, Copyright © 1993 by The New York Times Company. Reprinted by permission.
8. Frank Fortkamp, *The Case Against Government Schools*

(Westlake Village, CA: American Media, 1979) p. 15.
9. Robert J. Poole, Jr., *Cutting Back City Hall* (New York: Universe Books, 1980), p. 185.

CHAPTER 4

1. Robert Hershey, Jr., "White House Sees A Mission To Cut Business Rules," *The New York Times*, March 23, 1992, p. A13.
2. Anthony Ramirez, "Bell Atlantic Faces Regulatory Hoops," *The New York Times*, October 15, 1993, p. D1.
3. Michael Porter, Elizabeth Teisberg and Gregory Brown, "Innovation: Medicine's Best Cost-Cutter," *The New York Times*, Feb. 27, 1994, sect. 3, p. 11, Copyright © 1994 by The New York Times Company. Reprinted by permission.
4. No author listed, "Lumber Prices Are Soaring On Shortages and Owl Feud," *The New York Times*, March 11, 1993, p. D1.
5. Richard W. Stevenson, "California's Stumbling Economy Absorbs Another Blow," *The New York Times*, May 4, 1992, p. D1.
6. Ibid, p. D1, Copyright © 1992 by The New York Times Company. Reprinted by permission.
7. A Compilation, "Do We Really Need Corporate Welfare?", *Readers Digest*, March, 1992, pp. 70-74.
8. Philip J. Hilts, "Seeking Limits to a Drug Monopoly," *The New York Times*, May 14, 1992, pp. D1, D7.
9. Excerpted with permission from "How Government Makes Housing Unaffordable" by Trevor Armbrister, *Reader's Digest*, March 1992. Copyright © 1992 by The Reader's Digest Inc.
10. Ibid., p. 90.
11. Ibid., p. 90. Copyright © 1992 by The Reader's Digest Inc.
12. Terry L. Anderson and Donald R. Leal, *Free Market Environmentalism* (Boulder, CO: Westview Press, 1991), p. 156.
13. The New York Times Almanac, 1991.
14. Martin L. Gross, *Government Racket - Washington Waste From A to Z* (New York: Bantam Paperbacks, 1992), pp. 9,10,69.
15. Robert W. Poole, Jr., *Instead of Regulation* (Lexington, Mass.: Lexington Books, 1982), p. 375.
16. Ibid., p. 379.
17. John C. Goodman and Gerald L. Musgrave, *Patient Power*

(Washington, D.C.: Cato Institute, 1992) p. 132.

18. Josh Feltman, "Disclosure Laws Can Regulate Gently", *The New York Times*, October 3, 1993, sect. 3, p. 9.

CHAPTER 5

1. Dr. Barry Commoner, *The Closing Circle* (New York: ©Bantam Books/Random House, 1971), p. 230.
2. Ibid., p. 11.
3. Cy A. Adler, *Ecological Fantasies* (New York: Dell Publishing Co., 1973), pg. 127, 128.
4. Richard W. Stevenson, "Shetland Oil Tanker Nears Breakup," *The New York Times*, January 8, 1993; and William E. Schmidt "As Oil Calamities Go, Shetland Spill Was a Wimp," *The New York Times*, August 28, 1993.
5. William E. Schmidt, "Shetlands Oil Tanker Breaks Apart," *The New York Times*, January 12, 1993.
6. John H. Cushman Jr., "Most Marine Life in Persian Gulf Thrives Despite Huge Oil Slick," *The New York Times*, May 26, 1992, p. C4.
7. Dixy Lee Ray and Louis Guzzo, *Environmental Overkill* (Washington, DC: © Regnery Gateway, Inc., 1993), p. 54.
8. Ibid., pp. 55-56.
9. Ibid., pp. 56-57.
10. Ibid., pp. 59-60.
11. Cy A. Adler, *Ecological Fantasies* (New York: Dell Publishing Co., 1973), p. 150.
12. Ibid., p. 151.
13. Ibid.., pp. 153,154.
14. Ibid, p. 149.
15. Michael Specter, "Sea-Dumping Ban: Good Politics, But Not Necessarily Good Policy," *The New York Times*, March 22, 1993, p. A1.
16. Report, *The Council on Environmental Quality,* Washington, D.C., 1971.
17. Dixy Lee Ray and Louis Guzzo, *Environmental Overkill* (Washington, DC: © Regnery Gateway, Inc., 1993), p. 74.
18. Jane E. Brody, "Strong Views on Origins of Cancer," *The New York Times*, July 5, 1994, p. C1._Copyright © 1994 by The New

York Times Company. Reprinted by permission.

19. Ibid., p. C1. Copyright © 1994 by The New York Times Company. Reprinted by permission.

20. Cy A. Adler, *Ecological Fantasies* (New York: Dell Publishing Co., 1973), p.183.

21. Ibid., p. 240.

22. No author indicated, "Are We Running Out of Trees?," *Reader's Digest*, November, 1992 issue.

23. From ENVIRONMENTAL OVERKILL by Dixy Lee Ray and Louis Guzzo. Copyright © 1993 by Regnery Gateway, Inc. All Rights Reserved. Reprinted by special permission of Regnery Publishing, Inc., Washington, D.C., p. 39.

24. From ENVIRONMENTAL OVERKILL by Dixy Lee Ray and Louis Guzzo. Copyright © 1993 by Regnery Gateway, Inc. All Rights Reserved. Reprinted by special permission of Regnery Publishing, Inc., Washington, D.C., p. 50.

25. Associated Press, "Ozone Layer Has Thickened, Scientists Say," *The New York Times*, August 27, 1994, p. A1.

26. Dixy Lee Ray and Louis Guzzo, *Environmental Overkill* (Washington, DC: © Regnery Gateway, Inc., 1993), p. 43.

27. From ENVIRONMENTAL OVERKILL by Dixy Lee Ray and Louis Guzzo. Copyright © 1993 by Regnery Gateway, Inc. All Rights Reserved. Reprinted by special permission of Regnery Publishing, Inc., Washington, D.C., op. cit. p. 45.

28. Terry L. Anderson and Donald R. Leal, *Free Market Environentalism* (Boulder, CO: Westview Press, 1991), pg. 160.

29. Ibid., pg. 160.

30. Dixy Lee Ray and Louis Guzzo, *Environmental Overkill* (Washington, DC: © Regnery Gateway, Inc., 1993), p. 18.

31. Dixy Lee Ray and Louis Guzzo, *Environmental Overkill* (Washington, DC: © Regnery Gateway, Inc., 1993), p. 6.

32. Keith Schneider, "New View Calls Environmental Policy Misguided," *The New York Times*, March 20, 1993, p. A1.

33. William K. Stevens, "Scientists Confront Renewed Backlash on Global Warming," *The New York Times*, September 14, 1993. p. A1.

34. Dixy Lee Ray and Louis Guzzo, *Environmental Overkill* (Washington, DC: © Regnery Gateway, Inc., 1993), p. 163.

35. Cy A. Adler, *Ecological Fantasies* (New York: Dell Publishing Co., 1973), pg. 28.

36. Ibid., pp. 29,168.
37. Ibid., pp. 29,30.
38. Ibid., pp. 30-31.
39. William K. Stevens, "What's a Little Pollution? Europe's Forests Keep on Growing," *The New York Times*, April 7, 1992, p. C4.
40. Terry L. Anderson and Donald R. Leal, *Free Market Environmentalism* (Boulder, CO: Westview Press, 1991), pp. 55-56.
41. Associated Press, "Logging Limits Sought Over 7 Million Acres," *The New York Times*, January 9, 1992.
42. Ibid.
43. James C. McKinley, Jr., "E.P.A. Seeks Emissions Agreement for Northeast," *The New York Times*, August 24, 1994, p. B1.
44. James Bennet, "Will Rising Prices of Cars Imperil Detroit's Recovery?," *The New York Times*, August 22, 1994, p. D1.
45. Keith Bradsher, "Coal Miners Plead for Bailout of Ailing Health Plans," *The New York Times*, June 15, 1992, p. A12.
46. William K. Stevens, "Survival of the Big Cats Brings Them Into Conflict With Man," *The New York Times*, August 2, 1994, p. C1.
47. Ibid.
48. Dixy Lee Ray and Louis Guzzo, *Environmental Overkill* (Washington, DC: © Regnery Gateway, Inc., 1993), p. 103.
49. Excerpted with permission from "How Government Makes Housing Unaffordable" by Trevor Armbrister *Reader's Digest* March 1992. Copyright ©1992 by The Reader's Digest Assn., Inc.
50. Dixy Lee Ray and Louis Guzzo, *Environmental Overkill* (Washington, DC: © Regnery Gateway, Inc., 1993), pp. 98-99.
51. Ibid., p. 118.
52. Ibid., p. 99.
53. Ibid., p. 119.
54. Terry L. Anderson and Donald R. Leal, *Free Market Environmentalism* (San Fransisco: Pacific Research Institute For Public Policy, 1991), pg. 84.
55. Ibid., pg. 84.
56. Ibid., pg. 86.
57. Dr. Dixie Lee Ray, interview, *U.S. News and World Report*, Nov. 26, 1973.
58. Sam Howe Verhover, "Hydropower Under Review in Albany

Bill," *The New York Times*, March 17, 1992, p. B1.

59. Dr. Barry Commoner, *The Closing Circle* (New York: ©Bantam Books/Random House, 1971), pp. 37.

60. Ibid., pp. 11,43,191,144.

61. Ibid., pp. 8,11,13.

62. Ibid., p. 37.

63. Dixy Lee Ray and Louis Guzzo, *Environmental Overkill* (Washington, DC: © Regnery Gateway, Inc., 1993), p. 101.

64. Ibid, p. 117.

65. From ENVIRONMENTAL OVERKILL by Dixy Lee Ray and Louis Guzzo. Copyright © 1993 by Regnery Gateway, Inc. All Rights Reserved. Reprinted by special permission of Regnery Publishing, Inc., Washington, D.C., p. 120.

66. Dr. Barry Commoner, *The Closing Circle* (New York: ©Bantam Books/Random House, 1971), p. 253.

67. Bari, Judy, quoted by Walter Williams, columnist with Heritage Features Syndicate, *State Journal-Register*, June 25, 1992, quoted in Dixy Lee Ray and Louis Guzzo, *Environmental Overkill* (Washington, DC: © Regnery Gsteway, Inc., 1993), p. 203.

68. Dixy Lee Ray and Louis Guzzo, *Environmental Overkill* (Washington, DC: © Regnery Gateway, Inc., 1993), pp. 204.

69. Dixy Lee Ray and Louis Guzzo, *Environmental Overkill* (Washington, DC: © Regnery Gateway, Inc., 1993), pp. 204.

70. James Brooke, "On Amazon, Foes Are Reptiles and Environmentalists," *The New York Times*, June 13, 1992. Copyright © 1992 by The New York Times Company. Reprinted by permission.

71. Rowland Evans and Robert Novak, "California: Paradise Lost?", *Reader's Digest*, April, 1992, pp. 55-57.

72. Randy Fitzgerald, "Quiet Savers Of The Land," *Reader's Digest*, May, 1992, p. 129.

73. Ibid., p. 129.

74. Special to the New York Times, "G.E. to Pay Fishermen Over Polluted Striped-Bass Waters," *The New York Times*, August 12, 1992.

75. Robert W. Poole, Jr., *Cutting Back City Hall* (New York: Universe Books, 1980), pg. 53.

76. Ibid., p. 53

CHAPTER 6

1. St. Paul, Minnesota, "Minnesota Adopting Overhaul of Health Care", *The New York Times*, April 19, 1992, sect. 1, p. 15.
2. Robert Pear, "Health-Care Costs Up Sharply Again, Posing New Threat," *The New York Times*, Jan. 4, 1993, p. A1.
3. Steven Greenhouse, "Wider U.S. Deficits Are Now Forecast For The Mid-1990's," *The New York Times*, Mar. 23, 1992, p. A1.
4. Ibid., p. A1.
5. Ibid., p. A1, Copyright © 1992 by The New York Times Company. Reprinted by permission.
6. This information is reprinted with permission of the Henry J. Kaiser Family Foundation of Menlo Park, California. The Kaiser Family Foundation is an independent health care philanthropy and is not associated with Kaiser Permanente or Kaiser Industries.
7. George J. Schieber and Jean-Pierre Poullier, "Overview of International Comparisons of Health Care Expenditures," *Health Care Financing Review, Annual Supplement*, 1989, p. 172, in Joseph L. Bast, Richard C. Rue & Stuart A. Wesbury, *Why We Spend Too Much On Health Care* (Chicago: The Heartland Institute, 1992), pp. 29-30.
8. Joseph L. Bast, Richard C. Rue & Stuart A. Wesbury, Jr., *Why We Spend Too Much On Health Care* (Chicago: The Heartland Institute, 1992), p. 31.
9. Alf Siewers, "Don't Socialize U.S. Medicine, Sullivan Says," *Chicago Sun-Times*, June 24, 1991, in Joseph L. Bast, Richard C. Rue & Stuart A. Wesbury, Jr., *Why We Spend Too Much On Health Care* (Chicago: The Heartland Institute, 1992), p. 37.
10. Timothy Egan, "When Children Can't Afford Parents," *The New York Times*, March 29, 1992, p. B18.
11. Ibid., p. B44.
12. Dale A. Rublee, "Medical Technology in Canada, Germany, and the United States," *Health Affairs*, Fall 1989, p. 180, in Joseph L. Bast, Richard C. Rue & Stuart A. Wesbury, Jr.,*Why We Spend Too Much On Health Care* (Chicago: The Heartland Institute, 1992), p. 45.
13. Ibid., p. 46.
14. Ibid., p. 47.
15. Ibid., p. 39.

16. Ibid., p. 40.
17. Ibid., p. 40.
18. Copyright © by *The Drug Policy Foundation*. All rights reserved. "Will The Next $150 Billion Make You Safer?," in The New York Times, February 27, 1994.
19. Lawrence K. Altman, "Cost of Treating AIDS Patients Is Soaring", *The New York Times*, July 22, 1992. p. B8.
20. Copyright © by *The Drug Policy Foundation*. All rights reserved. "Will The Next $150 Billion Make You Safer?," in The New York Times, February 27, 1994.
21. "Proceedings of the National Medical Convention held in the City of Philadelphia, in May, 1847, *The New York Journal of Medicine 9*, July, 1847, in John C. Goodman, *The Regulation of Medical Care: Is The Price Too High?* (Washington, DC: Cato Institute, 1980), p. 5.
22. Ronald Hamowy, "The Early Development of Medical Licensing Laws In The United States, 1875-1900, "*Journal of Libertarian Studies*" 3, no. 1, (1979), pp. 73-119, in John C. Goodman, *The Regulation of Medical Care: Is The Price Too High?* (Washington, DC: Cato Institute, 1980), p. 6.
23. Teree P. Wasley, *What Has Government Done To Our Health Care?* (Washington, D.C: Cato Institute, 1992), p. 42.
24. John C. Goodman, *The Regulation of Medical Care: Is The Price Too High?* (Washington, D.C.: Cato Institute, 1980), p. 21,22.
25. John C. Goodman and Gerald S. Musgrave, *Patient Power* (Washington, D.C.: Cato Institute, 1992), p. 145.
26. U.S. Bureau of the Census, *Historical Statistics of the U.S., Colonial Times to 1970, Bicentennial Edition, Part 2,* (Washington, D.C., 1975), Series B 275-290, pp. 75-76, in John C. Goodman, *The Regulation of Medical Care: Is The Price Too High?* (Washington, D.C.: Cato Institute, 1980), p 14.
27. Ibid., p. 39.
28. Forgotson, Roemer, Newman, "Licensure of Physicians," *Washington University Law Quarterly* 332, 1967, pp. 250-251, in John C. Goodman, *The Regulation of Medical Care: Is The Price Too High?* (Washington, D.C.: Cato Institute, 1980), p. 40,41.
29. Teree P. Wasley, *What Has Government Done To Our Health Care?* (Washington, D.C: Cato Institute, 1992), p. 41.

30. Linda Aiken and Claire Fagin, "More Nurses, Better Medicine," *The New York Times*, May 11, 1993, p. A23, Copyright © 1993 by The New York Times Company. Reprinted by permission.

31. Adam Clymer, "Finding, Not Paying, Doctors Is Top Rural Health Concern," *The New York Times*, Feb. 22, 1994, p. A1, Copyright © 1994 by The New York Times Company. Reprinted by permission.

32. Anna Quindlen, "The Nurse Paradigm," *The New York Times*, June 1, 1994, p. A21.

33. Martin Gottlieb, "Questions At The Top On Hospital Policy", *The New York Times*, May 17, 1992, sect. 4, p. 18.

34. Ibid, sect. 4, p. 18, Copyright © 1992 by The New York Times Company. Reprinted by permission.

35. Ibid., sect. 4, p. 18, Copyright © 1992 by The New York Times Company. Reprinted by permission.

36. Steinwald and Neuhauser, "The Role of the Proprietary Hospital", *Law and Contemporary Problems*, Autumn 1970, table 1, p. 819, in John C. Goodman, *The Regulation of Medical Care: Is The Price Too High?* (Washington, D.C.: Cato Institute, 1980), p. 53.

37. John C. Goodman, *The Regulation of Medical Care: Is The Price Too High?* (Washington, D.C.: Cato Institute, 1980), p. 54.

38. U.S. Department of Health, Education and Welfare, "*Hill-Burton Program Progress Report, July 1, 1947, June 30, 1966* (Washington, D.C.: U.S. Government Printing Office), p. 32, in John C. Goodman, *The Regulation of Medical are: Is The Price Too High?* (Washington, D.C.: Cato Institute, 1980), p. 59.

39. Dorothy Rice and Barbara Cooper, "National Health Expenditures, 1950-1966," *Social Security Bulletin 31*, April,1968: 3-22, in John C. Goodman, *The Regulation of Medical Care: Is The Price Too High?* (Washington, D.C.: Cato Institute, 1980), p. 59.

40. Herman and Anne Somers, *Medicare and the Hospitals* (Washington, D.C.: The Brookings Institute, 1967), p.198, quoted in John C. Goodman, quoted in *The Regulation of Medical Care: Is The Price Too High?* (Washington, D.C.: Cato Institute, 1980), p. 71.

41. John C. Goodman, *The Regulation of Medical Care: Is The Price Too High?* (Washington, D.C.: Cato Institute, 1980), pp.74-78.

42. Elton Rayack, *Professional Power and American Medicine: The*

Economics of the American Medical Association (Cleveland: World Publishing Co., 1967), chapter 5, in John Goodman, *The Regulation of Medical Care: Is The Price Too High?* (Washington, D.C.: Cato Institute, 1980), p.74.

43. Frank Sloan and Roger Feldman, "*Competition Among Physicians*" in Warren Greenberg, ed., *Competition in the Health Care Sector, Past, Present and Future* (Germantown,Md.: Aspen Systems Corportation, 1978), p.104, in John C. Goodman,*The Regulation of Medical Care: Is The Price Too High?* (Washington, D.C.: Cato Institute, 1980), p.79.

44. Robert T. Holley and Rick J. Carlson, "The Legal Context for the Development of HMOs," *Stanford Law Review 24* (April 1972), p. 657, in John C. Goodman, *The Regulation of Medical Care: Is The Price Too High?* (Washington, D.C.: Cato Institute, 1980), p.113.

45. Teree P. Wasley, *What Has Government Done To Our Health Care?* (Washington, D.C.: Cato Institute, 1992), p. 70.

46. Milt Freudenheim, "HMO's That Offer Choice Are Gaining in Popularity," *The New York Times*, February 7, 1994, p. A1.

47. John C. Goodman, *The Regulation of Medical Care: Is The Price Too High?* (Washington, D.C.: Cato Institute, 1980), p. 81.

48. Joseph F. Sullivan, "Judge Stays Rate Ruling For Hospitals," *The New York Times*, June 5, 1992, p. B1.

49. Sarah Lyall, "Budget Plan Will Raise Costs for Health Coverage, Private Insurers Say," *The New York Times*, March 30, 1992, p. B7, Copyright © 1992 by The New York Times Company. Reprinted by permission.

50. H.E. Frech and Paul Ginsburg, "Competition Among Health Insurers," in Warren Greenberg, ed., *Competition in the Health Care Sector, Past, Present and Future* (Germantown, Md.: Aspen Systems Corporation, 1978), p. 181, in John C. Goodman,*The Regulation of Medical Care: Is The Price Too High?* (Washington, D.C.: Cato Institute, 1980), p. 101.

51. Congressional Budget Office, *Controlling Rising Hospital Costs* (Washington, D.C.: Government Printing Office,1979), p. 55, in John C. Goodman, *The Regulation of Medical Care: Is The Price Too High?* (Washington, D.C.: Cato Institute, 1980), p. 128.

52. Council on Wage and Price Stability, *The Complex Puzzle of*

Rising Health Care Costs: Can The Private Sector Fit It To-gether? (Washington, D.C.: Gov't Printing Office, 1976), p. 14, in John C. Goodman, *The Regulation of Medical Care: Is The Price Too High?* (Washington, D.C.: Cato Institute, 1980), p. 128.

53. John C. Goodman and Gerald L. Musgrave, *Patient Power* (Washington, D.C.: Cato Institute, 1992), p. 290.

54. John C. Goodman and Gerald L. Musgrave, *Patient Power* (Washington, D.C.: Cato Institute, 1992), p. 293.

55. Joseph L. Bast, Richard C. Rue & Stuart A. Wesbury, Jr., *Why We Spend Too Much On Health Care* (Chicago: The Heartland Institute, 1992), p. 63.

56. John C. Goodman and Gerald L. Musgrave, *Patient Power* (Washington, D.C.: Cato Institute, 1992), p. 630.

57. Joseph L. Bast, Richard C. Rue & Stuart A. Wesbury, Jr., *Why We Spend Too Much On Health Care* (Chicago: The Heartland Institute, 1992), p. 63-64.

58. John C. Goodman and Gerald L. Musgrave, *Patient Power* (Washington, D.C.: Cato Institute, 1992), p. 306.

59. Jack Meyer, Sharon Silow-Carroll, and Sean Sullivan, *Critical Choice Confronting the Cost of American Health Care* (Washington, D.C.: National Committee for Quality Health Care, 1990), pg. 30, in Joseph L. Bast, Richard C. Rue & Stuart A. Wesbury, Jr., *Why We Spend Too Much On Health Care* (Chicago: The Heartland Institute, 1992), pg. 53-54.

60. Sarah Lyall, "Albany Will Pass Bill To Overhaul Health Insurance," *The New York Times*, July 2, 1992, p A1.

61. FDA, Center for Drug Evaluation & Research - Executive Secretariat, Consumer Affairs Office, "New Drug Development In The United States," March 1990, p. 3.

62. John C. Goodman, *The Regulation of Medical Care: Is The Price Too High?* (Washington, D.C.: Cato Institute, 1980), p. 130.

63. Erik Eckholm, editor, *Solving America's Health Care Crisis* (New York: Times Books/Random House, Inc., © 1993), p. 104.

64. Ronald Hansen, "The Pharmaceutical Development Process, Estimates of Development Costs and Times and the Effects of Proposed Regulatory Changes," in Robert Chien, ed., *Issues in Pharmaceutical Economics*,(Lexington, Mass: D.C. Heath and Company, 1979), p. 180, in John C. Goodman, *The Regulation*

of Medical Care: Is The Price Too High? (Washington, D.C.: Cato Institute, 1980), pp. 130-131.

65. FDA, Center for Drug Evaluation & Research - Executive Secretariat, Consumer Affairs Office, "New Drug Development In The United States," March 1990, p. 3.

66. Reprinted with permission of the *Pharmaceutical Research and Manufacturers of America* (ad in Reader's Digest, April, 1993, p. 27.)

67. Michael Porter, Elizabeth Teisberg and Gregory Brown "Innovation: Medicine's Best Cost-Controller," *The New York Times*, February 27, 1994, sect. 3, p. 11. Copyright ©1994 by The New York Times Company. Reprinted by permission.

68. Copyright © 1993 *United States Surgical Corporation*. All rights reserved. Reprinted with the permission of United States Surgical Corp.

69. Joseph L. Bast, Richard C. Rue & Stuart A. Wesbury, Jr., *Why We Spend Too Much On Health Care* (Chicago: The Heartland Institute, 1992), pp. 55-56.

70. *Patient Power,* Goodman and Musgrave (Cato Institute Press, 1992), pg. 44.

71. David E. Rosenbaum, "The Clinton Difference? Not Much In The Budget," *The New York Times*, February 6, 1994, sect. 1, p. 34.

72. Joseph L. Bast, Richard C. Rue & Stuart A. Wesbury, Jr., *Why We Spend Too Much On Health Care* (Chicago: The Heartland Institute, 1992), pg. 51.

73. "National Effort Is Urged To Fight Worsening Fraud in Medical Bills", by Warren E. Leary, *The New York Times*, May 8, 1992, p. A13. Copyright © 1992 by The New York Times Company. Reprinted by permission.

74. John C.Goodman and Gerald L. Musgrave, *Patient Power* (Washington, D.C.: Cato Institute, 1992), p. 424.

75. Ibid., pg. 424.

76. Ibid., pg. 166.

77. Ibid., 1992, pg. 425.

78. Joseph L. Bast, Richard C. Rue & Stuart A. Wesbury, Jr., *Why We Spend Too Much On Health Care* (Chicago: The Heartland Institute, 1992), pp. 97-98.

79. Joel Brinkley, "You Bet Your Life. Do You Know the Odds?," *The New York Times*, May 29, 1994, p. E4.

80. Milt Freudenheim, "HMO's That Offer Choice Are Gaining in Popularity," *The New York Times*, February 7, 1994, p. A1.

81. Milt Freudenheim, "Blue Cross Lets Plans Sell Stock," *The New York Times*, June 30, 1994, p. D1.

82. Felicity Barringer, "In the Worst of Times, America Keeps Giving", *The New York Times*, March 15, 1992, sect. 4, p. 6. Copyright ©1992 by The New York Times Company. Reprinted by permission.

83. Craig Whitney, "Health Care Evolves as Issue in Britain's General Election," *The New York Times*, March 28, 1992, sect. 1, p. 1. Copyright ©1992 by The New York Times Company. Reprinted by permission.

84. Ibid., sect. 1, p. 1. Copyright © 1992 by The New York Times Company. Reprinted by permission.

85. Ibid., sect. 1, p. 1. Copyright © 1992 by The New York Times Company. Reprinted by permission.

86. George J. Schieber and Jean-Pierre Poullier, "Overview of International Comparisons of Health Care Expenditures," *Health Care Financing Review, Annual Supplement*, 1989, p. 172, in Joseph L. Bast, Richard C. Rue & Stuart A. Wesbury, Jr., *Why We Spend Too Much On Health Care* (Chicago: The Heartland Institute, 1992), p. 77.

87. Reprinted by permission of the *National Center for Policy Analysis*, 12655 N. Central Expressway, Suite 720, Dallas, Texas 75243, (214)386-6272 from the Backgrounder #129 - What President Clinton Can Learn From Canada About Price Control and Global Budgets.

88. George J. Schieber and Jean-Pierre Poullier, "Overview of International Comparisons of Health Care Expenditures," *Health Care Financing Review, Annual Supplement*, 1989, p. 172, in Joseph L. Bast, Richard C. Rue & Stuart A. Wesbury, Jr., *Why We Spend Too Much On Health Care* (Chicago: The Heartland Institute, 1992), p.77.

89. Editorial Section, "Canada's No Medical Model," *The New York Times*, May 26, 1992. p. A16.

90. Clyde H. Farnsworth, "Now Patients Are Paying Amid Canadian Cutbacks," *New York Times*, March 6, 1993, sect. 1, p. 1.

91. Clyde H. Farnsworth, "Now Patients Are Paying Amid Canadian Cutbacks," *New York Times*, March 6, 1993, sect. 1, p. 1.

CHAPTER 7

1. Felicity Barringer, "In the Worst of Times, America Keeps Giving," *The New York Times*, March 15, 1992, Sect. 4, p. 6.
2. "Selling is No Longer Mickey Mouse at AT&T," *Fortune Magazine*, July, 1978.
3. Peter J. Ferrara, *Social Security: Averting the Crisis* (Washington, D.C.: Cato Institute, 1982), pp. 46-47.
4. Ibid., pp. 14-16.
5. Keith Bradsher, "Large Tax Burden For Young Is Seen," *The New York Times*, February 8, 1994, p. A17. Copyright ©1994 by The New York Times Company. Reprinted by permission.
6. Peter J. Ferrara, *Social Security: Averting the Crisis* (Washington, D.C.: Cato Institute, 1982), p. 2.
7. Ibid., p. 38.
8. Ibid., p. 7.
9. Food and Drug Administration, Center for Drug Evaluation & Research - Executive Secretariat, Consumer Affairs Office, "New Drug Development In The United States," March 1990, p. 3.

CHAPTER 8

1. Peter G. Peterson, *Facing Up* (New York: Simon & Schuster, 1993), back charts (4.2), (4.3), (4.4), (4.6), (4.7).
2. David E. Rosenbaum, "The Clinton Difference? Not Much In The Budget," *The New York Times*, February 5, 1994, sect 1, p. 34. Copyright © 1994 by The New York Times Company. Reprinted by permission.
3. Robert Pear, "$1 Trillion in Health Costs Is Predicted," *The New York Times*, December 29, 1993, p. A12. Copyright © 1993 by The New York Times Company. Reprinted by permission.
4. Peter G. Peterson, *Facing Up* (New York: Simon & Schuster, 1993), p. 57.
5. Ibid., pg. 59.
6. Ibid., pg. 58.
7. Keith Bradsher, "Large Tax Burden For Young Is Seen,"*The New York Times*, February 8, 1994. p. A17. Copyright © 1994 by The New York Times Company. Reprinted by permission.
8. Tamar Lewin, "Low Pay and Closed Doors Confront Young Job

Seekers," *The New York Times*, March 10, 1994, p. A1. Copyright © 1994 by The New York Times Company. Reprinted by permission.

9. Peter G. Peterson, "For Health Insurance, With No Frills," *The New York Times Magazine*, January 16, 1994, sect 6, p. 36.

10. Robert W. Poole, Jr., "Contracting Rescues California," *Dollars& Sense*, November 28,1981.

11. Robert W. Poole, Jr., *Cutting Back City Hall* (NewYork: Universe Books, 1980), p. 66.

12. Ibid., pg. 22.

13. Joseph Deitch, "A Rush To Privatize Government Services," *The New York Times*, May 31, 1992, sect. 13 NJ, p. 1. Copyright © 1992 by The New York Times Company. Reprinted by permission.

14. Robert W. Poole, Jr., *Cutting Back City Hall* (New York: Universe Books, 1980).

15. Malcolm MacPherson, "Back From The Brink," *Reader's Digest*, June, 1993, p. 196. Copyright © 1993 by Malcolm MacPherson.

16. Ibid., p. 199.

17. Barth Healey, "Post Office Tries Battling Deficit with Stamps," *The New York Times*, June 2, 1992, p. A16.

Bibliography

The following books were major resources that I used in writing this book. For a list of newspaper and magazine articles also used as resource material, see the Notes section.

- Adler, Cy A., *Ecological Fantasies* (New York: Dell Publishing Co., 1973).
- Anderson,Terry L., and Leal, Donald R., *Free Market Environmentalism* (Boulder, CO: Westview Press, 1991).
- Bast, Joseph L., Rue, Richard C., and Wesbury, Jr., Stuart A., *Why We Spend Too Much On Health Care* (Chicago: The Heartland Institute, 1992).
- Brant, Irving, *The Bill of Rights: Its Origin And Meaning* (New York: The New American Library/Mentor Book, 1965).
- Commoner, Dr. Barry, *The Closing Circle* (New York: ©Bantam Books/Random House, 1971).
- Duarte, Joseph S., *The Income Tax Is Obsolete* (New Rochelle, NY: Arlington House, 1974).
- Eckholm, Erik, editor, *Solving America's Health Care Crisis* (New York: © Times Books/Random House, Inc., 1993).
- Ferrara,Peter J., *Social Security: Averting the Crisis* (Washington, D.C.: Cato Institute, 1982).
- Fortkamp, Frank, *The Case Against Government Schools* (Westlake Village, CA: American Media, 1979).
- Goodman, John C., *The Regulation of Medical Care: Is The Price Too High?* (Washington, DC: Cato Institute, 1980).
- Goodman, John C. and Musgrave, Gerald L., *Patient Power* (Washington, D.C.: Cato Institute, 1992).
- Gross, Martin L., *Government Racket - Washington Waste From A to Z* (New York: Bantam Paperbacks, 1992).
- Hamowy, Ronald, editor, *Dealing With Drugs* (San Francisco:

Pacific Institute For Public Policy Research, 1987).

• Hayek, Friedrich A., *The Road To Serfdom* (Chicago: University of Chicago Press, 1944, 1972).

• Johnson, Bruce M., editor, *Resolving The Housing Crisis* (San Francisco: Pacific Institute For Public Policy Research, 1982).

• Maddox, John, *The Doomsday Syndrome* (New York: McGraw-Hill, 1972).

• Olasky, Marvin, *The Tragedy Of American Compassion* (Washington, DC: Regnery Gateway, 1992).

• Patterson, Isabel, *The God of the Machine* (Caldwell, Idaho: The Caxton Printers, Ltd., 1964).

• Peterson, Peter G., *Facing Up* (New York: Simon & Schuster, 1993).

• Poole, Robert W. Jr., *Cutting Back City Hall* (New York: Universe Books, 1980).

• Poole, Robert W. Jr., *Instead of Regulation* (Lexington, Mass.: Lexington Books, 1982).

• Ray, Dr. Dixy Lee, and Guzzo, Louis, *Environmental Overkill* (Washington, DC: © Regnery Gateway, 1993).

• Rand, Ayn, *The Anti-Industrial Revolution* (New York: Signet Books, 1970).

• Rand, Ayn, *Capitalism, The Unknown Ideal* (New York: The New American Library, 1966).

• Richman, Sheldon, *Separating School & State* (Fairfax, Virginia: The Future of Freedom Foundation, 1994).

• Smith, Adam, *The Wealth Of Nations* (New York: Penguin Books, 1970).

• Sowell, Thomas, *Markets and Minorities* (New York: Basic Books, 1981).

• Sowell, Thomas, *Race and Economics* (New York: Longman, Inc., 1975).

• Von Mises, Ludwig, *Socialism* (New Haven: Yale University Press, 1951, 1962).

• Wasley, Teree P., *What Has Government Done To Our Health Care?* (Washington, D.C: Cato Institute, 1992).

• Wootton, David, editor, *Political Writings of John Locke* (New York: Mentor Books, 1993).

• Yates, Steven, *Civil Wrongs: What Went Wrong With Affirmative Action* (San Francisco: ICS Press, 1994).

INDEX

You can order copies of *The Welfare State:*
No Mercy For The Middle Class, from:

BookCrafters,
Order Dep't.
615 E. Industrial Drive
Chelsea, Michigan 48118

or, call BookCrafters toll-free at:
(800) 879-4214